Making Content Comprehensible
for English Learners

Making Content Comprehensible for English Learners

The SIOP Model

SECOND EDITION

Jana Echevarria
California State University, Long Beach

MaryEllen Vogt
California State University, Long Beach

Deborah J. Short
Center for Applied Linguistics, Washington, D.C.

PEARSON

Boston ■ New York ■ San Francisco
Mexico City ■ Montreal ■ Toronto ■ London ■ Madrid ■ Munich ■ Paris
Hong Kong ■ Singapore ■ Tokyo ■ Cape Town ■ Sydney

Series editor: Aurora Martínez Ramos
Editorial assistant: Katie Freddoso
Senior marketing manager: Elizabeth Fogarty
Manufacturing buyer: Andrew Turso
Cover designer: Suzanne Harbison
Production coordinator: Pat Torelli Publishing Services
Editorial-production service: Stratford Publishing Services, Inc.
Electronic composition: Stratford Publishing Services, Inc.

For related titles and support materials, visit our online catalog at www.ablongman.com

Library of Congress Cataloging-in-Publication Data

Echevarria, Jana
    Making content comprehensible for English learners : the SIOP model / Jana Echevarria, MaryEllen Vogt, Deborah J. Short.—2nd ed.
        p.   cm.
    Includes bibliographical references and index.
    ISBN 0-205-38641-5
    1. English language—Study and teaching—Foreign speakers   2. Language arts—Correlation with content subjects.   I. Vogt, MaryEllen   II. Short, Deborah.   III. Title

PE1128.A2E24 2004   2003050282
428'.0071—dc21

Printed in the United States of America
10 9   07 06 05

For my husband, Casey Vose, for his generosity, support and love.   *JE*

To my children and grandchildren: Scott, Kevin, Jeff, Karlin, Kyndal, Kameron and True, for their inspiration.   *MEV*

To my mother and grandmother, for their tradition of strength and determination and for their support and encouragement over the years.   *DJS*

Contents

Preface and Acknowledgments   xi

1. Introducing Sheltered Instruction   1

Objectives   1
Background   3
Changes in Instructional Practice   8
The Sheltered Instruction Approach   10
A Model for Sheltered Instruction   13
Sheltered Instruction Observation Protocol   16
Using the SIOP: Getting Started   17
Summary   18
Discussion Questions   18

2. Lesson Preparation   20

Objectives   20
Background   21
Content Objectives   21
Language Objectives   22
Content Concepts   23
Supplementary Materials   24
Adaptation of Content   26
Meaningful Activities   29
Using the SIOP   30
The Lesson   30
    Unit: The Gold Rush (4th Grade)   30
Teaching Scenarios   31
Discussion of Lessons   37
Summary   42
Discussion Questions   42

3.   Building Background   44

Objectives   44

Background   45

Concepts Linked to Students' Background   48

Links Made between Past Learning and New Concepts   48

Key Vocabulary Emphasized   49

Developing Content Language   50

Developing School Language   55

The Lesson   55

  Unit: *Mrs. Frisby and the Rats of NIMH*   55

Teaching Scenarios   56

Discussion of Lessons   62

Summary   63

Discussion Questions   64

4.   Comprehensible Input   65

Objectives   65

Background   66

Appropriate Speech for ELs   67

Explanation of Academic Tasks   68

Use of Techniques   69

The Lesson   69

  Unit: Buoyancy (9th grade)   69

Teaching Scenarios   70

Discussion of Lessons   75

Summary   78

Discussion Questions   78

5.   Strategies   80

Objectives   81

Background   81

Strategies   82

Scaffolding Techniques   86

Questioning   88

The Lesson   89

  Unit: The Rain Forest (7th grade)   89

Teaching Scenarios   89

Discussion of Lessons   94

Summary   96

Discussion Questions   97

6.   Interaction   98

Objectives   98

Background   99

Opportunities for Interaction   102
Grouping Configurations   105
Wait Time   106
Clarify Key Concepts in L1   106
The Lesson   107
   Unit: Addition and Subtraction (1st grade)   107
Teaching Scenarios   107
Discussion of Lessons   113
Summary   114
Discussion Questions   115

7. Practice/Application   116

Objectives   117
Background   117
Hands-On Materials and/or Manipulatives for Practice   117
Application of Content and Language Knowledge   119
Integration of Language Skills   120
The Lesson   121
   Unit: Ecosystems (11th grade)   121
Teaching Scenarios   121
Discussion of Lessons   126
Summary   128
Discussion Questions   128

8. Lesson Delivery   130

Objectives   131
Background   131
Content Objectives   131
Language Objectives   131
Student Engagement   132
Pacing   134
The Lesson   134
   Unit: The Gold Rush (4th grade)   134
Teaching Scenarios   134
Discussion of Lessons   138
Summary   141
Discussion Questions   142

9. Indicators of Review/Assessment   143

Objectives   143
Background   144
Review of Key Vocabulary   145
Review of Key Content Concepts   147

Providing Feedback on Student Output   147
Assessment of Lesson Objectives   148
The Lesson   151
    Unit: Egyptian Mummies (8th grade)   151
Teaching Scenarios   151
Discussion of Lessons   158
Summary   162
Discussion Questions   162

10. **Issues of Reading Development and Special Education for English Learners   163**

Objectives   164
Issues of Reading Development   164
Issues Related to Special Education   170
Special Education Referral, Assessment, and Placement   171
    Site-Based Intervention Teams   172
Students with Special Needs   175
Summary   175
Discussion Questions   176

11. **Scoring and Interpretation of the SIOP   178**

Objectives   178
How to Score the SIOP   180
    Assigning Scores   181
    Not Applicable (NA) Category   181
    Calculating Scores   182
Sample Lesson   183
Using SIOP Scores   186
Reliability and Validity of the SIOP   197
Summary   197
Discussion Questions   198

Appendix A: **The Sheltered Instruction Observation Protocol   199**
    Complete SIOP   200
    Abbreviated SIOP   208

Appendix B: **Lesson Plans   211**

Appendix C: **SIOP Research: The Effects of Sheltered Instruction on the Achievement of Limited English Proficient Students   214**

Glossary   221

References   225

Index   233

Preface and Acknowledgments

Welcome to the second edition of *Making Content Comprehensible for English Learners: The SIOP Model.* Whether you are already familiar with the SIOP model or are just now beginning the SIOP journey with us, we hope that you will find this new edition to be informative, helpful, and most important, beneficial to the English learners and other students with whom you work. In the first edition of the text, we discussed the need for a comprehensive, well-articulated model of instruction for preparing teachers to work with English learners (ELs). From this need, the Sheltered Instruction Observation Protocol (SIOP) was created. Now, several years after the inception of the SIOP and with its widespread use throughout the country, we offer the second edition.

The genesis of this book was eight years ago when we began reviewing the literature and examining district-produced guidelines for English learners to find agreement on a definition of sheltered instruction, or SDAIE (Specially Designed Academic Instruction in English). A preliminary observation protocol was drafted and field-tested with sheltered teachers. Through this process of classroom observation, coaching, discussion, and reflection, the instrument was refined and changed, and eventually it evolved into the Sheltered Instruction Observation Protocol, or as it has come to be known, the SIOP (pronounced sī-ŏp). The SIOP operationalizes sheltered instruction by offering teachers a model for lesson planning and implementation that provides English learners with access to grade-level content standards. A research project through the Center for Research on Education, Diversity, & Excellence (CREDE) enabled us to engage in an intensive refinement process and to use the SIOP model in a sustained professional development effort with teachers on both the east and west coasts.

Since the first edition of this book was published, we have continued to refine the SIOP, and in our work with thousands of teachers and administrators throughout the country, our own understanding of effective sheltered instruction/SDAIE and the needs of English learners has grown substantially. We believe, and our research confirms, that when teachers use the SIOP for their planning and teaching of English learners, high-quality and effective sheltered instruction results, and student achievement is improved.

As the authors of this book, we have approached our teaching, writing, and research from different and complementary fields. Jana Echevarria's research and publications have focused on issues in the education of English learners, and on ELs with special education needs, as well as on professional development for regular and special education teachers. MaryEllen Vogt's research interests focus on reading and language development, the intersection of reading and the content areas, intervention for older readers, and L1 and L2 literacy development in English learners. Deborah Short is a researcher and former sheltered instruction teacher with expertise in second-language development, methods for integrating language and content instruction, materials development, and teacher change.

The strength of our differences is that we approach the issue of educating English learners from different perspectives. In writing the book, we each provided a slightly different lens through which to view and discuss instructional situations. But our varied experiences have led us to the same conclusion: Educators need a resource for planning and implementing high-quality sheltered lessons for English learners, and the SIOP is fulfilling this need.

Overview of the Book

There are several major changes in this edition of the book, although the Sheltered Instruction Observation Protocol remains the same. Some of the enhanced features of this new edition are:

- **Graphic organizers.** Each chapter in the book begins with a graphic organizer to assist you in previewing the chapter's content.
- **Content and language objectives.** Following the graphic organizer, you will find content objectives (what you will learn) and language objectives (how you will use reading, writing, listening, and speaking to demonstrate what you will learn). As you will soon discover, content and language objectives are critically important for English learners and their teachers.
- **Discussion of the eight sections and thirty indicators of the SIOP.** Each chapter begins with discussion of a section of the SIOP and its various indicators. For example, the discussion of lesson planning and preparation is found in the first half of Chapter 2. As you read about each indicator in this section, think about how it would "look" in an actual classroom setting, and how teachers might use this information to plan and prepare effective sheltered lessons.
- **Teaching scenarios.** The second half of each chapter includes teaching scenarios. In these vignettes, three teachers, while teaching the same grade level and content, attempt to include the focal SIOP indicators, but with varying degrees of success. At the end of each teaching scenario,

you will have the opportunity to use that section of the SIOP to rate the effectiveness of the teacher in implementing the particular SIOP indicators. For example, as you read the teaching scenarios in Chapter 2, think about how well the three teachers included this section of the SIOP in their planning and preparation. Note that the illustrated lessons throughout the book range from grade 1 to high school.

- **Discussion of the three teaching scenarios.** Following the description of the three teachers' lessons, you will be able to see how we have rated the teachers in their inclusion of the SIOP indicators, the elements of effective sheltered instruction. We provide detailed explanations of our rationale for the ratings, and encourage you to discuss these with others in order to develop a high degree of inter-rater reliability.

- **Discussion questions.** At the conclusion of each chapter, you will find a variety of discussion questions. These are appropriate for portfolio development in preservice and graduate classes, for professional development workshops, or for your own reflection.

- **The SIOP.** You will find both the full SIOP and an abbreviated version for your use.

- **SIOP lesson plans.** You will find two different lesson plan formats that can be used for planning and preparation, depending on your needs.

- **Discussion of reading development and special education for English learners.** In our work with the SIOP Institutes, we have found educators had a number of questions about English learners who may have reading or learning problems and are struggling academically. In this edition, we have added a chapter that addresses delayed development in reading and learning disabilities.

- In Appendix C, you will find **an overview of the research findings** for the SIOP model.

- **The enlarged sized of the book.** This will enable you to photocopy the SIOP instrument and lesson plan forms for classroom use. Please respect copyright laws by copying the SIOP only for use with this book.

Overview of the Chapters

The first chapter in the book introduces you to the pressing educational needs of English learners and to sheltered instruction. In Chapters 2–9, we explain the SIOP model in detail, drawing from educational theory, research, and practice to describe each category and item on the SIOP. Following the descriptions are the teaching scenarios, drawn from classroom lessons of sheltered instruction teachers, and the SIOP form you may use to rate each teacher's incorporation of the particular indicators. The classroom scenarios reflect a different grade level and content area in each chapter and are linked to core curriculum objectives. All the classrooms include English learners.

In Chapter 10, we discuss the special needs of English learners who have reading problems and learning disabilities. Chapter 11 provides a discussion of scoring and interpreting the SIOP, explaining how the instrument can be used holistically to measure teacher fidelity to the model, and strategically to guide the teacher in future efforts to explore teacher change in one or more targeted categories. A full lesson from one research classroom is described and scored, revealing areas of strength and areas for improvement that can guide the teacher in future efforts.

As you read each scenario in the chapters that follow, reflect on how effectively the teacher is meeting the linguistic and academic needs of English learners, especially as related to the item being described. If you were observing this teacher, how would you evaluate his or her teaching effectiveness along the five-point scale? Is it clear that the teacher is adjusting his or her instruction to meet and move the students' linguistic and cognitive abilities forward, thus earning a "4" for the SIOP indicator? Or, is he or she attempting to modify the instruction, but with marginal success, thus earning a "2"? Or, is it clear that he or she has not modified the teaching practices at all to accommodate the needs of ELs, thus earning "0"? Then, compare your assessment of the teachers' use of sheltered instruction with our evaluations at the conclusion of the teaching scenarios.

In the Appendixes, you will find the Sheltered Instruction Observation Protocol (SIOP), both the comprehensive and the abbreviated versions. You will also find two lesson planning formats to guide your lesson design and implementation and an overview of research on the SIOP model. The book concludes with a Glossary of terms.

Acknowledgments

Many educators throughout the United States have contributed to this book through their work as sheltered teachers, bilingual specialists, curriculum coordinators, school and district administrators, and professional developers. We thank them for their insights and critical analyses of the SIOP. Further, we appreciate the contributions of those who have participated in the SIOP Institutes throughout the country (for more information, see *http://www.siopinstitute.net*). At each of these Institutes, we gain new understanding about our work from those who participate in them.

We thank the following people for their work with the SIOP and their support of our research and development efforts: Chris Montone, who assisted in the development of an earlier version of the SIOP; and Angie Aldrich, Angela Bennett, Barbara Formoso, Randi Gibson, Gerry Hoyos, and Robin Liten-Tejada, whose expert teaching and participation on the SIOP videos brought sheltered instruction/SDAIE to life. We're grateful for the privilege of working closely with a number of teachers who helped us refine and clarify the model: Martin Castillo, Jennifer Cesta, Prarskevi Contos, Carey Crimmel, Greg Croghan, Danielle Guryansky, Vernon Johnson, Juli Kendall, Lew Kerns, Maggie Kerns, Rebekkah Kline, Jennifer Kumnick, Melissa Sutkus, Janic Tichauer, Leonida Vizcarra, and Debbie Nesbitt Yarrell. We also appreciate the assistance of the following colleagues: Beverly Boyson, Gil Cuevas, Lorri Oliver, Marsha Thicksten, and Keith Vogt. Rebecca Dennis, Cathleen McCargo, Kristy Wuth, and Christopher Montone have helped coordinate our research in schools, and Jerome Shaw organized a demonstration project of our model.

We found the comments and suggestions from our reviewers to be of great help and we thank them: Lu Chang, Notre Dame de Namur University; Gerald McCain, Southern Oregon University; Karen L. Newman, Indiana University; and Judith B. O'Laughlin, New Jersey City University. We also appreciate the ongoing support, assistance, and patience of our Allyn & Bacon team, especially that of our editor, Aurora Martínez Ramos.

This work was supported under the Education Research and Development Program, PR/Award No. R306A60001, The Center for Research on Education, Diversity, & Excellence (CREDE), as administered by the former Office of Educational Research and Improvement, now the Institute for Education Studies (IES), National Institute on the Education of At-Risk Students (NIEARS), U.S. Department of Education (USDOE). The contents, findings, and opinions expressed here are those of the authors and do not necessarily represent the positions or policies of IES, NIEARS, or the USDOE.

Finally, we express appreciation to our families, whose support has enabled us to pursue our professional interests.

Making Content Comprehensible for English Learners

1 Introducing Sheltered Instruction

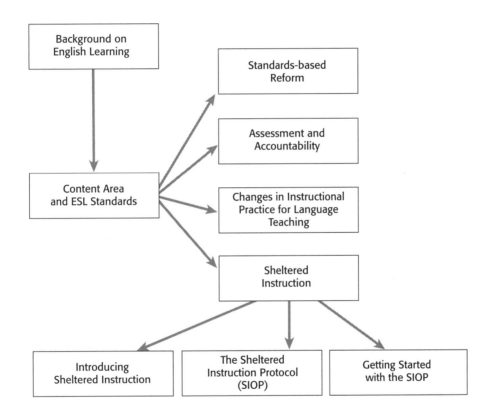

OBJECTIVES

After reading, discussing, and engaging in activities related to this chapter, you will be able to meet the following content and language objectives.

Content Objectives:

Distinguish between sheltered instruction/ SDAIE as a program model and sheltered instruction as a lesson type

Recognize differences and similarities among ESL pull-out, content-based ESL, sheltered instruction, and bilingual education

Explain the development of the SIOP model

Language Objectives:

Discuss the challenges of school reform and its effect on English learners

Develop a lexicon regarding sheltered instruction

Javier put his head in his hands and sighed. He watched Ms. Barnett standing at the board and tried to understand what she was telling him. He looked at the clock; she'd been talking for 12 minutes now. She wrote some numbers on the board and he noticed his classmates getting out their books. Copying their actions, he too opened his social studies book to the page matching the first number on the board. He looked at the words on the page and began to sound them out, one by one, softly under his breath. He knew some words but not others. The sentences didn't make much sense. Why was this class so tough? He could understand the teacher much better in science. Mrs. Ontero let them do things. They would all crowd around a table and watch her as she did an experiment and then he got to work with his friends, Maria, Huynh, and Carlos, trying out the same experiment. He even liked the science book; it had lots of pictures and drawings. Mrs. Ontero always made them look at the pictures first and they talked about what they saw. The words on the pages weren't so strange either. Even the big ones matched the words Mrs. Ontero had them write down in their personal science dictionaries. If he forgot what a word meant in the textbook, he would look it up in his science dictionary. Or he could ask someone at his table. Mrs. Ontero didn't mind if he asked for help. This social studies class just wasn't the same. He had to keep quiet, he had to read, he couldn't use a dictionary, they didn't do things. . . .

Javier is experiencing different teaching styles in his seventh-grade classes. He has been in the United States for 14 months now and gets along with his classmates in English pretty well. They talk about CDs and TV shows, jeans and sneakers, soccer and basketball. But schoolwork is hard. Only science class and PE make sense to him. Social studies, health, math, language arts—they're all confusing. He had a class in English as a second language (ESL) last year, but not now. He wonders why Mrs. Ontero's science class is easier for him to understand than the others.

This book addresses the reasons why the science teacher is more effective than her colleagues in promoting Javier's learning. It introduces a research-based model of sheltered instruction (SI) and demonstrates through classroom vignettes how the model can be implemented well. Sheltered instruction is an approach for teaching content to English learners (ELs) in strategic ways that make the subject matter concepts comprehensible while promoting the students' English language development. It also may be referred to as SDAIE (specially designed academic instruction in English). Sheltering techniques are used increasingly in schools across the United States, particularly as teachers prepare students to meet high academic standards. However, the use of these techniques is inconsistent from class to class, discipline to discipline, school to school, and district to district. The model of sheltered instruction presented here is intended to mitigate this variability and provide guidance as to what constitutes the best practices for SI, grounded in two decades of classroom-based research, the experiences of competent teachers, and findings from the professional literature.

The goal of this book is to prepare teachers to teach content effectively to English learners while developing the students' language ability. The profes-

sional development model evolved from the Sheltered Instruction Observation Protocol (SIOP), seen in Appendix A, an instrument originally used by researchers to measure teacher implementation of sheltered instruction. Through subsequent research conducted by the national Center for Research on Education, Diversity, & Excellence (CREDE), the SIOP model was field tested and the protocol became a training and evaluation instrument that codifies and exemplifies the model. The SIOP may be used as part of a program for preservice and inservice professional development; as a lesson planner for sheltered content lessons; as a training resource for faculty; and as an observation and evaluation measure for site-based administrators, supervisors of student teachers, and researchers who evaluate teachers. The book is intended for teachers of linguistically and culturally diverse students in K–12 settings, university faculty who prepare such teachers, site-based administrators, and others who provide technical assistance or professional development to K–12 schools.

Background

Each year, the United States becomes more ethnically and linguistically diverse, with more than 90 percent of recent immigrants coming from non-English speaking countries. From the 1991–1992 school year through 2001–2002, the number of identified students with limited English proficiency in public schools (K–12) grew 95 percent while total enrollment increased by only 12 percent (National Clearinghouse for English Language Acquisition, 2002). Thus, the proportion of English language learners in the schools is growing even more rapidly than the actual numbers. In 2001–2002, more than 4.7 million school-age children were identified as limited English proficient (LEP, a federal designation)—almost 10 percent of the K–12 public school student population.

The rise in immigrant students conforms to the increase in the immigrant population in the United States. The U.S. Census Bureau (Jamieson, Curry, & Martinez, 2001) determined that in 1999, 20 percent of school-age children had at least one parent who was an immigrant and 5 percent of the students were immigrants themselves. When race or origin is considered, 65 percent of Hispanic students and 88 percent of Asian and Pacific Islander students had at least one immigrant parent. Although not all Hispanic or Asian students are limited English proficient, Hispanic students make up 75 percent of all students in ESL, bilingual, and other English language support programs, according to the *Latinos in Education* report (1999) published by the White House Initiative on Educational Excellence for Hispanic Americans.

According to Ruiz-de-Velasco & Fix (2000), the geographic distribution of immigrants is concentrated in urban areas, primarily in six states that account for three-fourths of all immigrant children: California (35 percent), Texas (11.3 percent), New York (11 percent), Florida (6.7 percent), Illinois (5 percent), and New Jersey (4 percent). However, the number of immigrant children in states that are not among the top six increased by 40 percent (from 1.5 million to 2.1 million) between 1990 and 1995. The researchers found that these states are less likely to deliver language and other services that recent immigrant students need.

While the number of students with limited proficiency in English has grown exponentially across the United States, their level of academic achievement has lagged significantly behind that of their language-majority peers. One congressionally mandated study reported that these students receive lower grades, are judged by their teachers to have lower academic abilities, and score below their classmates on standardized tests of reading and mathematics (Moss & Puma, 1995). Although they have better attendance rates on average than U.S.-born students, their dropout rates are higher and vary by immigrant group (Ruiz-de-Velasco & Fix, 2000; Waggoner, 1999). Hispanics have the highest dropout rate compared with other ethnic and racial groups. In 1998, 30 percent of all Hispanics aged sixteen to twenty-four dropped out of school. For blacks, the rate was 14 percent—less than half the Hispanic rate; and for whites, the rate was 8 percent—almost four times less. Of particular note is that the dropout rate for immigrant Hispanics was 44 percent, double that of native-born Hispanics (21 percent) (*Latinos in Education*, 1999).

These findings reflect growing evidence that most schools are not meeting the challenge of educating linguistically and culturally diverse students well. Ruiz-de-Velasco & Fix (2000) found a serious disparity between the allocation of language resources and the grade-level distribution of immigrant children. A higher percentage of foreign-born immigrants attend secondary schools in comparison to elementary schools, yet spending on language-acquisition programs is concentrated at the elementary level. As a result, a smaller proportion of secondary school English learners (ELs) receive the language support services (e.g., ESL or bilingual education) they need.

The lack of success in educating linguistically and culturally diverse students is problematic because federal and state governments expect *all* students to meet high standards and have adjusted national and state assessments as well as state graduation requirements to reflect new levels of achievement and to accommodate requirements of the No Child Left Behind Act (2001). In order for students whose first language is not English to succeed in school and become productive citizens in our society, they need to receive better educational opportunities in U.S. schools.

All English learners in schools today are not alike. They enter U.S. schools with a wide range of language proficiencies (in English and in their native languages) and of subject matter knowledge. In addition to the limited English proficiency and the approximately 180 native languages among the students, we also find diversity in their educational backgrounds, their expectations of schooling, their socioeconomic status, their age of arrival, and their personal experiences while coming to and living in the United States. All these factors impinge on the type of programs and instructional experiences the students should receive in order to succeed in school.

At one end of the spectrum among immigrant students, we find some ELs who had strong academic backgrounds before they came to the United States and entered our schools. Some of them are above equivalent grade levels in the school's curricula, in math and science for example. They are literate in their native language and may have already begun study of a second language. For these students, much of what they need is English language development so that, as they become more proficient in English, they can transfer the knowledge they learned in their native country's schools to the courses they are taking in the United States. A few subjects, such as U.S. history, may need special attention because these students may not have studied them before.

At the other end, some immigrant students arrive at our schoolhouse doors with very limited formal schooling—perhaps due to war in their native countries or the remote, rural location of their homes. These students are not literate in their native language (i.e., they cannot read or write); and they have not had schooling experiences such as sitting at desks all day, changing teachers per subject, or taking a district- or countrywide tests. They have significant gaps in their educational backgrounds, lack knowledge in specific subject areas, and often need time to become accustomed to school routines and expectations.

We also have students who have grown up in the United States but speak a language other than English at home. At one end of the range of students in this group are those students who are literate in their home language, such as Mandarin, Arabic, or Spanish, and just need to add English to their knowledge base in school. At the other end are those who are not literate in any language. They have mastered neither English nor the home language and may be caught in a state of semiliteracy that is hard to escape.

Given the variability in these students' backgrounds, they often need different pathways for academic success. To meet this challenge, fundamental shifts need to occur in teacher development, program design, curricula and materials, and instructional and assessment practices. This book will address, in particular, strategies for improved teacher development and instructional practice.

Since 1989, when the National Governors Association held an education summit and agreed on the need for national education goals and the National Council of Teachers of Mathematics (1989) subsequently issued their national curriculum standards for mathematics, the United States has been moving toward a new vision of standards-based education. The overall goal has been for all students to achieve high standards. This intention, however, has provoked much debate because not all students have access to appropriate curricula, qualified teachers, or instructional resources (e.g., laboratory or computer equipment). The Goals 2000: Educate America Act passed in 1994, and related legislation encouraged a widespread movement among other professional associations to develop standards for specific content areas such as reading/language arts, science, history, and geography (Tucker & Codding, 1998). The Teachers of English to Speakers of Other Languages (TESOL) association also developed national *ESL Standards for Pre-K–12 Students* (TESOL, 1997) specifically to help English learners gain social and academic English language skills. The overall aim for all associations was to have these national standards used as guidelines for state and local curriculum and assessment design, and for the professional development of teachers.

Standards-based reform has also spurred changes in state testing and graduation requirements. Most states have developed or adopted high-stakes tests based on state standards; all will as a result of the No Child Left Behind Act (NCLB) of 2001, which calls for annual tests of reading and mathematics for all students in Grades 3–8. NCLB deliberately includes English learners in state accountability systems and also requires their English language development to be assessed yearly while they are designated as limited English proficient and in programs receiving Title III funds.

As Coltrane (2002) points out, this act offers benefits and disadvantages to ELs. On the positive side, standards-based reform has increased academic rigor for all students with a push for academic literacy. This is beneficial for ELs, so teachers integrate content and language development in their lessons. The requirement that districts disaggregate their test scores to measure progress of LEP students can also have a favorable impact in the long term. Schools must show that all categories of students, including LEP students, make annual yearly progress according to state benchmarks. If they are not making progress as a group over three years, corrective actions will be taken. Thus, efforts to improve program designs for English learners and teacher professional development are likely outcomes.

Nonetheless, there are negative implications. ELs, especially those at beginning levels, are learning this challenging content in a language they do not speak, read, or write proficiently. The high-stakes tests therefore are more often a test of their English knowledge than their content knowledge or skills (Coltrane, 2002; Menken, 2000). Furthermore, most of the standardized tests that states use have been designed for, and normed on, native English speakers who have spent their educational careers in U.S. schools. Thus, the stakes for English language learners have been raised significantly as states and federal programs have restructured their accountability measures.

Although NCLB calls for highly qualified teachers in every core academic classroom by 2006 (2003 for new Title I teachers), the supply of certified ESL and bilingual teachers is too small for the demand. The National Commission on Teaching and America's Future (1996) and McDonnell and Hill (1993) have reported significant shortages of teachers qualified to teach students with limited English proficiency and of bilingual teachers trained to teach in another language. Moreover, most states do not require *all* teachers with limited English proficient students in their classes to have specialized training for working with them. The majority of teacher preparation colleges do not provide undergraduates with strategies for teaching linguistically and culturally diverse students (Crawford, 1993; Zeichner, 1993). In the 1999–2000 Schools and Staffing Survey (National Center for Education Statistics, 2002), 41.2 percent of the 2,984,781 public school teachers reported teaching LEP students, but only 12.5 percent had had eight or more hours of training in the past three years. Eight hours is not even the minimum that should be required. Given that LEP students are almost 10 percent of the student population now, and their proportion of the total student population increases each year, the status of teacher preparation and development is inadequate for the educational needs of English learners.

To compensate for the shortage of trained ESL, bilingual, or content teachers, principals have hired less-qualified teachers, used substitutes, canceled courses, increased class size, or asked teachers to teach outside their field of preparation. It has not been uncommon to find untrained instructional aides acting as the English language teachers for these students. Thus, many English learners receive much of their instruction from content area teachers or aides who have not had appropriate professional development to address their second language development needs or to make content instruction comprehensible. This situation hinders their academic success.

Some districts try to provide inservice workshops to teachers, but in order to be effective, they must be ongoing, sustained, and targeted to the teachers' classroom and professional knowledge needs. Traditional models of teacher training—one shot or short-term workshops—have been shown to be ineffective (Gonzalez & Darling-Hammond, 1997; NCTAF, 1997). Rather, professional development strategies found to improve teaching are: sustained, intensive development with modeling, coaching, and problem-solving; collaborative endeavors for educators to share knowledge; experiential opportunities that engage teachers in actual teaching, assessment, and observation; and development grounded in research but also drawing from teacher experience and inquiry, connected to the teachers' classes, students, and subjects taught (NCTAF, 1997; Darling-Hammond, 1998; Darling-Hammond & McLaughlin, 1995).

English learners also have difficulty in school when there is a mismatch among program design, instructional goals, and student needs. Historically, schools offered ESL or bilingual education programs to ELs with specially trained teachers, yet kept those teachers and students separate from regular school programs. Depending on school or state policy and resource availability, ELs were schooled in English as a second language or bilingual classes and were not a concern of the regular content classroom teacher until they exited the language support program. In theory, the ELs would make that transition when they were proficient in English and able to perform subject area course work in English-medium classrooms. In practice, however, students exit before they are proficient in academic English, for several reasons: (1) the number of these students increased without a comparable increase in certified teachers, so it became impossible to relegate the education of these students to separate, specialized classes; (2) policies have been enacted where the number of years that students are permitted access to language support services are quite limited, such as in California where students are moved into regular classrooms after one year; and (3) programs failed to recognize that while learning English, ELs must simultaneously learn academic content.

Research has shown that it may take students from four to ten years of study, depending on the background factors described above, before they are proficient in academic English (Cummins, 1981; Thomas & Collier, 2002). In their national research study, Thomas and Collier found that there is a large achievement gap between ELs and native English speakers across most program models. For this gap to be closed with bilingual/ESL content programs, students must gain three to four more NCE (normal curve equivalent) points each year than native English speakers gain. The only way to do that is to have well-implemented, cognitively challenging, not segregated, and sustained programs of five to six years duration. Typical programs of two to three years are ineffective in closing the large achievement gap.

Changes in Instructional Practice

The ESL profession has always been sensitive to student needs and the evolution of ESL methodologies has been a dynamic process over the past five decades. Teachers have realized that students would benefit from new instructional approaches and accordingly have adjusted both pedagogical practice and the content of the curriculum. But ESL and bilingual teachers alone cannot provide the necessary educational opportunities these learners need.

In the first half of the twentieth century, most language teaching relied on the direct method of instruction or a grammar translation approach. Yet by the 1950s, direct method and grammar translation languished and audiolingual methods surfaced. In the 1970s and after, the audiolingual method was displaced by the communicative method for ESL teaching, preparing students to use functional language in meaningful, relevant ways. As districts implemented communicative curricula, students were given opportunities to discuss material of high interest and topicality, which in turn motivated them to learn and participate in class. Students were encouraged to experiment with language and assume greater responsibility for their learning.

The communicative approach has engendered the content-based ESL approach. Viewing the grade-level curricula as relevant, meaningful content for ELs, educators have developed content-based ESL curricula and accompanying instructional strategies to help better prepare the students for their transition to mainstream classes. Content-based ESL classes, in which all the students are ELs, are taught by language educators whose main goal is English language skill development but whose secondary goal is preparing the students for the regular, English-medium classroom (Cantoni-Harvey, 1987; Crandall, 1993; Mohan, 1986; Short, 1994). The content-based language approach transforms an ESL class into a forum for subject area knowledge generation, application, and reinforcement, by addressing key topics found in grade-level curricula. The sophistication of the material presented necessarily varies according to the language proficiency of the students in class, but nonetheless this material is considered relevant and meaningful by the students.

In content-based ESL, content from multiple subject areas is often presented through thematic instruction. For example, in a primary grade classroom, one theme might be "Life on a Farm." While students learn such language-related elements as names of animals, adjectives, the present continuous tense, and question formation, they also solve addition and subtraction problems, read poems and sing songs about farm animals, discuss the food chain, and draw picture stories, thus exploring objectives from mathematics, language arts, music, science, and art. For the high school classroom, a theme such as "urbanization" might be selected, and lessons could include objectives drawn from environmental science, geography, world history, economics, and algebra. Students with less proficiency might take field trips around a local city and create maps, transportation routes and schedules, and plans for new businesses. Advanced students might learn to use reference materials and computers to conduct research on the development of cities and their respective population growth in their native countries. They might study comparative language structures to compare the cities studied or persuasive language to debate advantages and disadvantages to urbanization.

In general, content-based ESL teachers seek to develop the students' English language proficiency by incorporating information from the subject areas that students are likely to study or from courses they may have missed if they are fairly new to the school system. Whatever subject matter is included, for effective content-based ESL instruction to occur, teachers need to provide practice in academic skills and tasks common to mainstream classes (Chamot & O'Malley, 1994; Mohan, 1990; Short, 2002).

Content-based ESL instruction, however, has not been sufficient to help all ELs succeed academically. The growth in numbers of students learning English as an additional language and the shortage of qualified ESL and bilingual teachers has quickly extended the need to teach content to these students outside ESL classrooms. The ESL profession began to develop the sheltered content instruction approach in conjunction with content teachers and this process was accelerated by the educational reform movement. Through sheltered instruction, which is described in more detail in the next section, ELs would participate in a content course with grade-level objectives delivered through modified instruction that made the information comprehensible to the students. The classes may be variously named ESL Pre-Algebra, Sheltered Chemistry, or the like, and a series of courses may constitute a program called Content-ESL, Sheltered Instruction, or SDAIE, yet the goal remains the same: to teach content to students learning English through a developmental language approach.

Content-based ESL and sheltered instruction are favored methods for ELs today, as reflected in the national ESL standards developed by TESOL. Three of the nine standards in the *ESL Standards for Pre-K–12 Students* (TESOL, 1997) fall under Goal 2: To use English to achieve academically in all content areas. Students should be able to use English to (1) interact in the classroom; (2) obtain, process, construct, and provide subject matter information in spoken and written form; and (3) use appropriate learning strategies to construct and apply academic knowledge. It is particularly important, therefore, that more teachers be prepared to teach ELs in appropriate ways so that the students can learn English and the subject matter required for school.

The Sheltered Instruction Approach

This book focuses specifically on sheltered instruction, an approach that can extend the time students have for getting language support services while giving them a jump-start on the content subjects they will need for graduation. The SI approach must *not* be viewed as simply a set of additional or replacement instructional techniques that teachers implement in their classrooms. Indeed, the sheltered approach draws from and complements methods and strategies advocated for both second language and mainstream classrooms.

This fact is beneficial to English learners because the more familiar they are with academic tasks and routine classroom activities, the easier it will be for them to focus on the new content once they are in a regular, English-medium classroom. To really make a difference for these students, sheltered instruction must be part of a broader school-based initiative that takes into account the total schooling they need.

Although not acknowledged or understood by many content area professionals, age-appropriate knowledge of the English language is a prerequisite in the attainment of content standards. We learn primarily through language, and use language to demonstrate our knowledge. As Lemke (1988, p. 81) explained,

> . . . educators have begun to realize that the mastery of academic subjects is the mastery of their specialized patterns of language use, and that language is the dominant medium through which these subjects are taught and students' mastery of them tested.

Without oral and written English language skills, students are hard pressed to learn and demonstrate their knowledge of mathematical reasoning, science skills, social studies concepts, and so forth. Students who lack proficiency in English are at a decided disadvantage.

For English learners to succeed, they must master not only English vocabulary and grammar, but also the way English is used in core content classes. This "school English" or "academic English" includes semantic and syntactic knowledge along with functional language use. Using English, students, for example, must be able to read and understand expository prose such as that found in textbooks and reference materials, write persuasively, argue points of view, and take notes from teacher lectures or Internet sites. They must also articulate their thinking skills in English—make hypotheses and predictions, express analyses, draw conclusions, and so forth. In their content classes, ELs must pull together their emerging knowledge of the English language with the content knowledge they are studying in order to complete the academic tasks associated with the content area. They must, however, also learn *how* to do these tasks—generate the format of an outline, negotiate roles in cooperative learning groups, interpret charts and maps, and such. The combination of these three knowledge bases—knowledge of English, knowledge of the content topic, and knowledge of how the tasks are to be accomplished— constitutes the major components of academic literacy (Short, 2002).

Another consideration for school success is the explicit socialization of students to the often implicit cultural expectations of the classroom such as turn-taking, participation rules, and established routines. As Erickson and Shultz (1991) have discussed, student comfort with the social participation structure of an academic task, for instance, can vary according to culturally learned assumptions about appropriateness in communication and in social relationships, individual personality, and power relations in the classroom social system and in society at large. Therefore, many English learners benefit from being socialized into culturally appropriate classroom behaviors and interactional styles. As Bartolome (1994) states, teachers need to engage in culturally responsive teaching so that their instruction is sensitive to and builds on culturally different ways of learning, behaving, and using language.

The SI classroom that integrates language and content and infuses sociocultural awareness is an excellent place to scaffold instruction for students learning English. According to Vygotsky (1978) and others, students' language learning is promoted through social interaction and contextualized communication, which can be readily generated in all subject areas. Teachers guide students to construct meaning from texts and classroom discourse and to understand complex content concepts by scaffolding instruction.

When scaffolding, teachers pay careful attention to students' capacity for working in English, beginning instruction at the current level of student understanding, and moving students to higher levels of understanding through tailored support. One way they do so is by adjusting their speech (e.g., paraphrase, give examples, provide analogies, elaborate on student responses) to facilitate student comprehension and participation in discussions where otherwise the discourse might be beyond their language proficiency level (Bruner, 1978). Another way to scaffold is by adjusting instructional tasks so that they are incrementally challenging (e.g., preteach vocabulary before a reading assignment, have students write an outline before drafting an essay) and students learn the skills necessary to complete tasks on their own (Vacca, 2000). Through these strategies, teachers can socialize students to the academic language setting. Without such teacher assistance, however, ELs may fail to succeed in content area courses.

Sheltered instruction plays a major role in a variety of educational program designs (Genesee, 1999). It may be part of an ESL program, a late-exit bilingual program, a two-way bilingual immersion program, a newcomer program, or a foreign language immersion program. For students studying content-based ESL or bilingual courses, SI often provides the bridge to the mainstream and the amount of SI provided should increase as students move toward transition out of these programs. Any program in which students are learning content through a non-native language should use the sheltered instruction approach.

In some schools, sheltered instruction is provided to classes composed entirely of English learners. In others, a heterogeneous mix of native and non-native English speakers may be present. Bilingual, ESL, and content teachers may be the instructors for these classes (Sheppard, 1995). Depending on school system regulations, a sheltered pre-algebra course, for example, might be delivered by an ESL teacher or a mathematics teacher. Ideally, all content teachers would be trained in areas such as second language acquisition and ESL methodology although, as mentioned earlier, often that is not the case. At the high school level, sheltered content courses are generally delivered by content teachers so that students may receive the core content, not elective, credit required for graduation.

Research has shown, however, that a great deal of variability exists in the design of SI courses and the delivery of SI lessons, even among trained teachers (August & Hakuta, 1997; Berman et al., 1995; Kauffman et al., 1994; Sheppard, 1995) and within the same schools. Some schools, for instance, offer only sheltered instruction courses in one subject area, such as social studies, but not in other areas ELs must study. It is our experience as well, after two decades of observing SI teachers in class, that one SI classroom does not look like the next in terms of the teacher's instructional language; the tasks the students have to accomplish; the degree of interaction that occurs between teacher and student, student and student, and student and text; the amount of class time devoted to language development issues versus assessing content knowledge; the learning strategies taught to and used by the students; the availability of appropriate materials; and more.

This lack of consistency across SI classes is somewhat predictable. Sheltered curricula for all content areas are few in number and vary widely from school district to school district. Commercial publishers offer a relatively small amount of instructional and pedagogical resources aimed for the SI course. Moreover, much of the literature on SI to date has focused on identifying a wide variety of instructional strategies and techniques that teachers might use to make content comprehensible. Teachers have been encouraged to pick and choose those techniques they enjoy or believe work best with their students and very few teachers are specially prepared to be SI teachers through undergraduate or graduate work. Even those programs that include SI topics on the syllabi of an ESL or bilingual methods course, for example, lack a model for teachers to follow. As a result, teachers do not have sufficient preparation at colleges and universities to implement sheltered instruction effectively. School districts, through inservice workshops may try to address SI techniques on occasion, but there are few systematic and sustained forms of professional development available for SI teachers.

A Model for Sheltered Instruction

The development of an SI model is one key to improving the academic success of English learners: Preservice teachers need it to develop a strong foundation in sheltered instruction; practicing teachers need it to strengthen their lesson planning and delivery and to provide students with more consistent instruction; site-based supervisors need it to train and evaluate teachers. The model described in this book is the product of several research studies conducted by the authors over the past decade. It is grounded in the professional literature and in the experiences and best practice of the researchers and participating teachers who worked collaboratively on developing the observation instrument that codifies it. The theoretical underpinning of the model is that language acquisition is enhanced through meaningful use and interaction. Through the study of content, students interact in English with meaningful material that is relevant to their schooling. Because language processes, such as listening, speaking, reading, and writing, develop interdependently, SI lessons incorporate activities that integrate those skills.

In effective SI courses, language and content objectives are systematically woven into the curriculum of one particular subject area, such as fourth-grade language arts, U.S. history, algebra, or life science. Teachers generally present the regular, grade-level subject curriculum to the students through modified instruction in English, although some special curricula may be designed for students with significant gaps in their educational backgrounds or very low literacy skills. Teachers must develop the students' academic language proficiency consistently and regularly as part of the lessons and units they plan and deliver (Echevarria & Graves, 2003; Short, 1994). The SIOP model we have developed shares many strategies found in high-quality, nonsheltered teaching for native English speakers, but it is characterized by careful attention to the English learners' distinctive second language development needs.

Accomplished SI teachers modulate the level of English used with and among students and make the content comprehensible through techniques such as the use of visual aids, modeling, demonstrations, graphic organizers, vocabulary previews, predictions, adapted texts, cooperative learning, peer tutoring, multicultural content, and native language support. They also make specific connections between the content being taught and students' experiences and prior knowledge and focus on expanding the students' vocabulary base. Besides increasing students' declarative knowledge (i.e., factual information), teachers highlight and model procedural knowledge (e.g., how to accomplish an academic task like organizing a science laboratory report or conducting research on the Internet) along with study skills and learning strategies (e.g., note-taking and self-monitoring comprehension when reading).

In effective SI lessons, there is a high level of student engagement and interaction with the teacher, with other students, and with text, which leads to elaborated discourse and critical thinking. Students are explicitly taught functional language skills as well, such as how to negotiate meaning, confirm information, argue, persuade, and disagree. Teachers introduce them to the classroom discourse community and demonstrate skills like taking turns in a conversation and interrupting politely to ask for clarification. Through instructional conversations and meaningful activities, students practice and apply their new language and content knowledge.

SI teachers also consider their students' affective needs and learning styles. They strive to create a nonthreatening environment where students feel comfortable taking risks with language. They plan activities that tap into the auditory, visual, and kinesthetic preferences of the students. Many effective SI teachers consider the multiple intelligences of their students as well, and provide a variety of assignments that might appeal to the logical/mathematical child, the musical child, the artist, and those with other intelligences (Gardner, 1993).

Depending on the students' proficiency levels, SI teachers offer multiple pathways for students to demonstrate their understanding of the content. For example, teachers may plan pictorial, hands-on, or performance-based assessments for individual students, group tasks or projects, informal class discussions, oral reports, written assignments, portfolios, and more common measures such as paper and pencil tests and quizzes to check student comprehension and language growth. This is very important because teachers can receive a more accurate picture of most English learners' content knowledge and skills through an assortment of assessment measures than through one standardized test (TESOL, 2000).

Sheltered instruction is also distinguished by use of supplementary materials that support the academic text. These may include related reading texts (e.g., trade books), graphs and other illustrations, models and other realia, audiovisual and computer-based resources, adapted text, and the like. The purpose of these materials is to enhance student understanding of key topics, issues, and details in the content concepts being taught through alternate means than teacher lecture or dense textbook prose. Supplementary materials can also aid teachers in providing information to students with mixed proficiency levels of English. Some students in a mixed class may be able to use the textbook while others may need an adapted text.

The Sheltered Instruction Observation Protocol (SIOP) model has been designed for flexibility and tested in a wide range of classroom situations: those with all ELs and those with a mix of native and non-native English speakers; those with students who have strong academic backgrounds and those with students who have had limited formal schooling; those with students who are recent arrivals and those who have been in U.S. schools for several years; those with students at beginning levels of English proficiency and those with students at advanced levels. In a preliminary study of student expository writing (using pre- and post-measures), students who participated in classes taught by teachers trained in the SIOP model significantly improved their writing skills more than students in classes with non-SI-trained teachers.

It is important to recognize that the SIOP model does not require teachers to throw away their favored techniques, or add copious new elements to a lesson. Rather, this model of sheltered instruction brings together *what* to teach by providing an approach for *how* to teach it. As Figure 1.1 shows, the model offers a framework for selecting and organizing techniques and strategies and

FIGURE 1.1 What Students Need to Learn: Language and Content

PLANNING SHEET		
ESL Standards *(What to Teach)*	*How to Teach What Students Need* *SIOP*	*Content Area Standards* *(What to Teach)*
Listening in English	Preparation	Standard
Speaking in English	Building Background	Benchmark
Reading in English	Comprehensible Input	Performance Task
Writing in English	Strategies	Scoring Guide
	Interaction	
	Practice/Application	
	Lesson Delivery	
	Review/Assessment	

Adapted from Juli Kendall (1998).

facilitates the integration of district- or state-level standards for ESL and for specific content areas.

Sheltered Instruction Observation Protocol (SIOP)

The first version of the Sheltered Instruction Observation Protocol was drafted in the early 1990s in order to exemplify the model of sheltered instruction we were developing. The preliminary instrument was field-tested with sheltered teachers and refined according to teacher feedback and observations in the classrooms. This early draft, like subsequent ones, pulled together findings and recommendations from the research literature with our professional experiences and those of our collaborating teachers on effective classroom-based practices from the areas of ESL, bilingual education, reading, language and literacy acquisition, discourse studies, special education, and classroom management.

In 1996, the National Center for Research on Education, Diversity & Excellence (CREDE) was funded by the Office of Educational Research and Improvement, U.S. Department of Education, and included a study on sheltered instruction in its research program. The goals of the research project were to (1) develop an explicit model of sheltered instruction; (2) use that model to train teachers in effective sheltered strategies; and (3) conduct field experiments and collect data to evaluate teacher change and the effects of sheltered instruction on LEP students' English language development and content knowledge. (See Appendix C for a discussion of the research study and its findings.) The project built on preliminary versions of the SIOP as a small cohort of teachers worked with the researchers to refine the SIOP further: distinguishing between effective strategies for beginners, intermediate, and advanced English learners; determining "critical" versus "unique" sheltered teaching strategies; and making the SIOP more user-friendly.

Over the course of the next three years, and with an expanded team of teachers from districts on both the East and West Coasts, the SIOP continued to be refined, strengthened, and used for professional development with research project teachers (Short & Echevarria, 1999). A sub-study conducted in 1997 confirmed the SIOP to be a valid and reliable measure of the SI model (Guarino et al., 2001). The SIOP is used both as an observation instrument for researchers, administrators, and teachers to match the implementation of lesson delivery to the model of instruction and, as will be explained in more detail in the chapters that follow, as a tool for planning and delivering lessons.

From 1999 to 2002, the researchers field-tested and refined the SIOP model's professional development program, which incorporates key features of effective teacher development as recommended by Darling-Hammond (1998). The program includes professional development institutes (see *http://www.siopinstitute.net*), videotapes of exemplary SIOP teachers (Hudec & Short, 2002a, 2002b), a facilitator's guide (Short, Hudec, & Echevarria, 2002), and other training materials.

Specifically, the Sheltered Instruction Observation Protocol provides concrete examples of the features of sheltered instruction that can enhance and expand teachers' instructional practice. The protocol is composed of thirty items grouped into eight main components: Preparation, Building Background, Comprehensible Input, Strategies, Interaction, Practice/Application, Lesson Delivery, and Review/Assessment. These components emphasize the instructional practices that are critical for second language learners as well as high-quality practices that benefit all students.

The six features under Preparation examine the lesson planning process, including the language and content objectives, the use of supplementary materials, and the meaningfulness of the activities. Building Background focuses on making connections with students' background experiences and prior learning and developing their academic vocabulary. Comprehensible Input considers adjusting teacher speech, modeling academic tasks, and using multimodal techniques to enhance comprehension. The Strategies component emphasizes teaching learning strategies to students, scaffolding instruction, and promoting higher order thinking skills. The features of Interaction remind teachers to encourage elaborated speech and to group students appropriately for language and content development. Practice/Application provides activities to extend language and content learning while Lesson Delivery ensures teachers present a lesson that meets the planned objectives. As part of the Review/Assessment component, four items consider whether the teacher reviewed the key language and content concepts, assessed student learning, and provided feedback to students on their output.

Using the SIOP: Getting Started

As you begin using the SIOP as a guide to teaching high-quality sheltered instruction, you may want to assess your areas of strength and areas that you want to begin improving. There are some elements of sheltered instruction that are particularly critical to include when teaching English learners, while other aspects of the model may be implemented as experience in SI/SDAIE is gained. Therefore, you may wish to begin using the SIOP by focusing on one set of indicators at a time. For example, comprehensible input (see Chapter 4) is critical for ELs. If you are unfamiliar with comprehensible input techniques, you may want to practice implementing them as a first step. Another important element of sheltered instruction that increases its effectiveness is setting language and content objectives (see Chapter 2) and the way those objectives influence sheltered lessons (see Chapters 8 and 9). Accordingly, those new to SI may want to start with writing and teaching to language and content objectives early in the process of using SI. As proficiency in SI is attained, other elements of the model should be added to one's teaching repertoire.

It is important for coaches, administrators, and university field-experience supervisors to understand that learning to implement the SIOP model is a process and not all elements will be observed to a high degree in the beginning stages. We encourage supervisors to use a collaborative approach with teachers who are implementing sheltered instruction, including conferencing about observations, setting goals for implementing other features of the model, reflecting on progress in using SI, and so forth. The protocol is an excellent tool for targeted and productive discussions between a teacher and a supervisor and also for teacher self-monitoring and self-reflection.

Summary

Students who are learning English as an additional language are the fastest-growing segment of the school-age population in the United States and almost all candidates in teacher education programs will have linguistically and culturally diverse students in their classes during their teaching careers. However, most of these future teachers—as well as most practicing teachers—are not prepared to instruct these learners. Given school reform efforts and increased state accountability measures, this lack of teacher preparation puts ELs at risk of educational failure.

This book describes and illustrates a research-based, professional development model of sheltered instruction, an effective approach for teaching both language and content to ELs, that can increase English learners' chances of success in school. The model has already been used in a long-term, collaborative, professional development program to train and coach middle school teachers in implementing effective SI in their classes in urban, suburban, and rural districts around the United States. The model is operationalized in the Sheltered Instruction Observation Protocol (SIOP).

The SIOP model does not mandate cookie-cutter instruction, but it provides a framework for well-prepared and well-delivered sheltered lessons for any subject area. As SI teachers design their lessons, they have room for creativity and the art of teaching. Nonetheless, critical instructional features must be attended to in order for teachers to respond appropriately to the unique academic and language development needs of these students. As you read through this book, you will have the opportunity to explore ways to enhance, expand, and improve your own instructional practice through use of the SIOP model.

Discussion Questions

1. How would you characterize the type(s) of instruction offered to English learners in your school or schools you know: traditional ESL, content-based ESL, sheltered content, bilingual content, traditional content? Provide evidence of your characterization in terms of curricula and instruction. Are the ELs successful when they enter regular, mainstream content classes? Explain.

2. Many sheltered teachers, whether they had special training in a subject area or in second language acquisition, fail to take advantage of the language learning opportunities for students in sheltered content classes. Why do you think this is so? Offer two concrete suggestions for these teachers to enhance their students' language development.

3. Would sheltered classes look different if they were part of a bilingual program rather than an ESL program? Explain your response.

4. What do you think are some necessary conditions for offering sheltered classes to English learners in your school, or one with which you are familiar?

2 Lesson Preparation

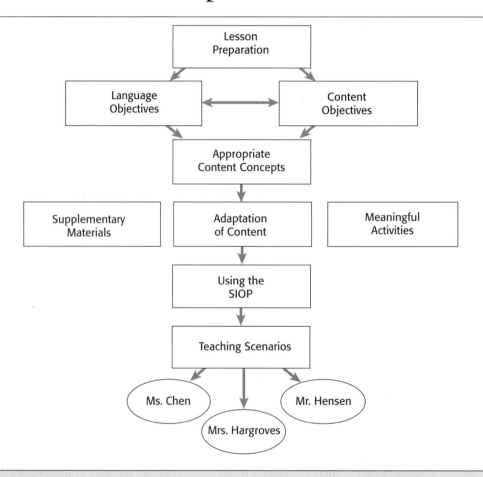

OBJECTIVES

After reading, discussing, and engaging in activities related to this chapter, you will be able to meet the following content and language objectives.

Content Objectives:

Identify content objectives for ELs that are aligned to state, local, or national standards

Incorporate supplemental materials suitable for ELs in a lesson plan

Select from a variety of strategies for adapting content to the students' proficiency and cognitive levels

Language Objectives:

Identify sources for language objectives

Explain the importance of meaningful academic activities for ELs

Discuss advantages for writing both language and content objectives for a lesson and sharing the objectives with students

In this and subsequent chapters, we offer an explanation of each category and indicator on the SIOP (Sheltered Instruction Observation Protocol). This chapter begins with the explanation, and then follows with a description of a lesson taught by three different teachers. The lessons throughout the book are on varied topics and at different grade levels. After the lesson description, you will find teaching scenarios by the three teachers. As you read these, think about the SIOP indicators that have been previously described, and prepare to rate the lessons according to them. Reflect on how effectively the teacher is meeting the needs of English learners (ELs), especially in relation to the indicator that is described. At the conclusion of the teaching scenarios, we offer our assessment of the teacher's attempts to shelter content instruction and we invite you to compare your appraisal to ours.

This chapter introduces the first section of the SIOP: Preparation. Within this section are subsections 1–6: Content Objectives, Language Objectives, Content Concepts, Supplementary Materials, Adaptation of Content, and Meaningful Activities.

Background

As we all know, lesson planning is critical to both a student's and a teacher's success. For maximum learning to occur, planning must produce lessons that enable students to make connections between their own knowledge and experiences, and the new information being taught (Rummelhart, 1995). With careful planning, we make learning meaningful and relevant by including appropriate motivating materials and activities that foster real-life application of concepts studied.

Traditionally, to meet the needs of students who struggled with grade-level reading materials, texts were rewritten according to readability formulae (Gray & Leary, 1935; Ruddell, 2001). The adapted texts included controlled vocabulary and a limited number of concepts, resulting in the omission of critical pieces of information. We have learned that if students' exposure to content concepts is limited by vocabulary-controlled materials, the amount of information they learn over time is considerably less than that of their peers who use grade-level texts. The result is that the "rich get richer and the poor get poorer" (Stanovich, 1986). That is, instead of closing the gap between native English speakers and ELs, the learning gap is increased and eventually it becomes nearly impossible to close. Therefore, it is imperative that we plan lessons that are not negatively biased for students acquiring English and that include age-appropriate content and materials.

Content Objectives

In effective instruction, concrete content objectives that identify what students should know and be able to do must guide teaching and learning. Optimally, these objectives support school-district and state-content standards and learning outcomes. Frequently, in texts and teachers' guides, content objectives and standards are complex and comprehensive, and teachers may or may not present them to students. For English learners, however, content objectives for each lesson need to be stated simply, orally and in writing, and they need to be tied to specific grade-level content standards (Echevarria & Graves, 2002). An effective lesson plan focuses on products and learning directly related to these objectives. In some cases, students with major gaps in their educational backgrounds may be in special classes, which pull objectives from earlier grades in order to provide the foundational knowledge the students need to perform on-grade-level work successfully. Also, it may be necessary to limit content objectives to only one or two per lesson to reduce the complexity of the learning task.

Most of us learned about the importance of writing and teaching to content objectives early in our professional preparation. However, with all of the other things we must remember to include in each lesson, it is often easy to overlook sharing the objectives, orally and in writing, with students. One of the sheltered teachers who has been using the SIOP shared her growing awareness of the importance of clearly stated content objectives for ELs:

> The objectives are still going on in my class. They're on the board everyday and the students are getting used to seeing them, reading them out loud, and evaluating whether or not we achieved them at the end of each class. I still have questions about the wording and what's a good objective . . . but that will come with time and more discussion and study. I just wanted to say that defining the objectives each day definitely brings more focus to my planning and thinking, and it helps bring order to my classroom procedures. So far, it has not been too burdensome and the habit is definitely forming.

For examples of content objectives, see the sample lesson plans at *http://www. siopinstitute.net.*

Language Objectives

While carefully planning and delivering content objectives, sheltered instruction teachers should also incorporate in their lesson plans techniques that support students' language development (Short, 1999). As with content objectives, language objectives should be stated clearly and simply, and students should be informed of them, both orally and in writing.

A wide variety of language objectives can be planned according to the goals and activities in the lesson. In some cases, language objectives may focus on developing students' vocabulary. Other lessons may lend themselves to reading comprehension skills practice or the writing process, helping students to brainstorm, outline, draft, revise, edit, and complete a text. Students also benefit from objectives that highlight functional language use such as how to request information, justify opinions, negotiate meaning, provide detailed explanations, and so forth. Higher-order thinking skills, such as articulating predictions or hypotheses, stating conclusions, summarizing information, and making comparisons, can be tied to language objectives, too. Sometimes specific grammar points can be taught as well; for example, learning about capitalization when studying famous historical events and persons, or teaching language structure to help ELs develop new vocabulary.

To illustrate, in a science lesson on photosynthesis, you might introduce the meaning of the morpheme "photo" along with other words that carry the meaning of "light" such as "photography," "photogenic," and "photo-finish." It is important to draw students' attention to opportunities for identifying English words through analogy, recognizing similarities in English structure. English language development is nurtured in classrooms where language structure is taught in order to help ELs develop new vocabulary.

Remember, as you teach and assess these language objectives in your lessons, you can plan for multilevel responses from the students according to their proficiency in English. For example, you might use group response techniques (e.g., thumbs-up/thumbs-down) for students who are in the early stages of English language development. For students who are more proficient English speakers, incorporate activities that involve partner work and small group assignments so that ELs can practice their English in a less-threatening setting. When possible, accept approximations and multiple word responses rather than complete sentences because this supports English development. However, it is also appropriate to require ELs, depending on their level of proficiency, to give answers in one or two complete sentences. This develops language skills because it requires students to move beyond what may be their comfort zone in using English.

Content Concepts

While planning, carefully consider the content concepts you wish to teach and use district curriculum guidelines and grade-level content standards to guide you. In sheltered classrooms, this entails ensuring that although materials may be adapted to meet the needs of English learners, the content is not diminished. When planning lessons around content concepts, consider the following: (1) the students' first language (L1) literacy, (2) their second language (L2) proficiency, (3) their reading ability, (4) the cultural and age appropriateness of the L2 materials, and (5) the difficulty level of the material to be read (Gunderson, 1991, p. 21).

Additionally, reflect on the amount of background experience needed to learn and apply the content concepts, and include ways to activate students' prior knowledge related to them. For example, fourth-grade students typically learn about magnetism, yet some ELs may not have the requisite background knowledge to understand this concept. Rather than defuse the content, use what prior knowledge students do have and then include explicit background information that builds a foundation for their understanding of magnetism.

Providing adequate background requires teachers to perform a *task analysis*—a process in which you carefully analyze the requisite knowledge a student must possess in order to understand what is being taught. The purpose is to lessen the gap between what a student knows and what he or she must learn. This can be accomplished by modifying the lesson to include substantial background building, or through a small group mini-lesson that precedes the regular whole class lesson (Vogt, 2000). This mini-lesson provides a "jump-start" by reviewing key background concepts, introducing vocabulary, leading a picture or text "walk" through the reading material, engaging in simulations or role-plays, or hands-on experiential activities. The jump-start mini-lesson develops context and access for children who may lack appropriate background knowledge or experience with the grade-level content concepts. In heterogeneous classes in which ELs study with native English speakers, peer tutors can be used to teach some of the requisite background information as well.

You are the one to decide when to modify content concepts by providing extensive background building for the whole class, or by teaching a brief jump-start lesson to a small group. If you have a large number of English learners who are in the early stages of language development, you may need to include extensive background building. If you have a small group of ELs who have intermediate language proficiency, the jump-start mini-lesson may provide sufficient scaffolding and access to the content concepts.

Remember that it is usually inappropriate to teach students curriculum intended for younger children simply because of their limited English proficiency. It is your responsibility to determine students' background knowledge and provide the necessary scaffolding to enable everyone to meet the grade-level standards.

Supplementary Materials

Information that is embedded in context allows English learners to understand and complete more cognitively demanding tasks. Effective sheltered instruction involves the use of many supplementary materials that support the core curriculum and contextualize learning. This is especially important for students who do not have grade-level academic backgrounds and/or who have language and learning difficulties. Since lectures and pencil-and-paper activities centered around a text are often difficult for these students, remember to plan for supplementary materials that will enhance meaning and clarify confusing concepts, making lessons more relevant.

A variety of supplementary materials also supports different learning styles and multiple ways of knowing (multiple intelligences) because information and concepts are presented in a multifaceted manner. Students can see, hear, feel, perform, create, and participate in order to make connections and construct personal, relevant meanings. Supplementary materials provide a real-life context and enable students to bridge prior experiences with new learning.

Examples of supplementary materials that can be used to create context and support content concepts include the following:

- **Hands-on manipulatives:** These can include anything from Cuisinaire rods for math to microscopes for science to globes for social studies.
- **Realia:** These are real-life objects that enable students to make connections to their own lives. Examples include bank deposit slips and check registers for a unit on banking, or nutrition labels on food products for a health unit.
- **Pictures:** Photographs and illustrations depict nearly any object, process, or topic, and magazines, commercial photos, and hand drawings can provide visual support for a wide variety of content and vocabulary concepts.
- **Visuals:** These can include overhead transparencies, models, graphs, charts, timelines, maps, props, and bulletin board displays. Students with diverse abilities often have difficulty processing an inordinate amount of auditory information and are advantaged with visual clues.
- **Multimedia:** A wide variety of multimedia materials is available to enhance teaching and learning. These range from simple tape recordings to videos, DVDs, interactive CD-ROMs, and an increasing number of resources available on the World Wide Web. For some students and tasks, media in the students' native language may be a valuable source of information. It is important to preview websites for appropriateness and readability, especially when using them with beginning and intermediate level students.
- **Demonstrations:** Students' learning is enhanced when teachers or other individuals provide scaffolding for less-experienced students. You can scaffold ELs by carefully planning demonstrations that model how to follow steps or directions needed to complete tasks, and that include supplementary materials. Teachers can also demonstrate and/or model language, like how to give an oral presentation. Students can then practice these steps in groups or alone, with you or other experienced individuals nearby to assist as needed.
- **Related literature:** A wide variety of fiction and nonfiction can be included to support content teaching. The literature enables readers to create what Rosenblatt (1991) refers to as an "aesthetic response." This type of literature response is characterized by personal feelings about what is read. Aesthetic responses to literature promote more reading of literature, and hopefully, a deeper understanding of the concepts that are depicted—what Rosenblatt refers to as a *transactional experience.* Many content teachers create class libraries with trade books on key topics. Students can read these as supplements to the textbook. They offer a more relaxing way to look at a topic in more depth.
- **Adapted text:** A type of supplementary reading material that can be very effective for English learners, as well as struggling readers, is adapted text. Without significantly diminishing the content concepts, a piece of

text (usually from a grade-level textbook) is adapted to reduce the readability demands. Complicated, lengthy sentences with specialized terminology are rewritten in abbreviated form with definitions given for difficult vocabulary, if possible, in context. Please note that we are not advocating "dumbing down" the textbook, an approach that in the past yielded easy-to-read materials with virtually no content concepts left intact. Rather, we suggest that the major concepts be retained and just the readability level of the text be reduced.

Adaptation of Content

In many schools, teachers are required to teach from textbooks that are too difficult for English learners to read. We have previously mentioned the problem of "watering down" text to the point where all students can read it; content concepts are frequently lost when the text is adapted in this way. We also know ELs cannot be expected to learn all content information through listening to lectures.

Therefore, we must find ways to make the text and other resource materials accessible for all students, adapting them so that the content concepts are left intact (Short, 1991). Several ways of doing this have been recommended for students who have reading difficulties (Readance, Bean, & Baldwin, 2001; Ruddell, 2001; Vacca & Vacca, 2001; Vogt, 1992), and they work equally well for English language learners. These approaches can be used throughout a lesson, as a prereading instructional strategy, as an aid during reading, and as a postreading method for organizing newly learned information.

Suggestions for adapting content to make it more accessible include the following:

- **Graphic organizers:** These are schematic diagrams that provide conceptual clarity for information that is difficult to grasp. They help students identify key content concepts and make relationships among them (McLaughlin and Allen, 2002a). Graphic organizers also provide students with visual clues they can use to supplement written or spoken words that may be hard to understand. When used prior to reading, students can use the organizers as a guide and as a supplement to build background for difficult or dense text. When used concurrently with reading, they focus students' attention and help them make connections (e.g., Venn diagram), take notes, and understand the text structure (e.g., a timeline informs students the text will be organized chronologically). When used after reading, graphic organizers can be used to record personal understandings and responses (Buehl, 2001). Graphic organizers include story or text structure charts, Venn diagrams, story or text maps, timelines, discussion webs, word webs, clusters, thinking maps, and so forth.
- **Outlines:** Teacher-prepared outlines equip students with a form for notetaking while reading dense portions of text, thus providing scaffolded

support. These are especially helpful if major concepts, such as the Roman numeral level of the outline, are already filled in. The students can then add other information to the outline as they read. For some students, an outline that is entirely completed may be helpful to use as a guide to reading and understanding the text.

- **Leveled study guides:** These are study guides designed specifically for diverse students' needs. All students are expected to master the key concepts in the text; however, depending on students' language and literacy development, the leveled study guides are written differently. For some students who can easily read the text material, the study guides extend and enrich the subject material and they include challenging questions or tasks. For other students, leveled study guides lead them through the material with definitions and "hints" for unlocking the meaning, and they include less challenging questions and tasks. For some ELs and struggling readers, the study guides may include brief summaries of the text along with more manageable questions and tasks. Questions, tasks, and statements on the leveled study guides can be marked with asterisks as follows (from most manageable to most challenging):

   * All students are to respond to these questions/statements/tasks

   ** Group 1 students are required to complete these questions/statements/tasks

   *** Group 2 students are required to complete these questions/statements/tasks

   Of course, the option to try the more challenging questions or statements should be open to all students.

- **Highlighted text:** A few literature anthologies or content textbooks may be reserved for students acquiring English and/or for those with delayed literacy development. Overriding ideas, key concepts, important vocabulary, and summary statements are highlighted (by the teacher or other knowledgeable person) prior to the students using the books. Students are encouraged to first read only the highlighted sections. As confidence and reading ability improve, more of the unmarked text is attempted. The purpose of highlighted text is to reduce the reading demands of the text, while still maintaining key concepts and information.

- **Taped text:** Key portions (such as the highlighted text just mentioned), or the entire text is recorded and students are encouraged to listen to the tape while they follow along in the book. For some students, multiple exposures to the taped text may result in a more thorough understanding. Ideally, tapes should be available for both home and school learning center use.

- **Adapted text:** As mentioned earlier in this chapter, text adaptation involves rewriting selected sections of text that contain key concepts and information. Although time consuming, rewriting text is an effective modification of curricular materials because information is organized in small sequential steps, avoiding long, dense passages. Short, simpler sentences are rewritten from long, complex ones. An example of a complex sentence from a science text follows: "Electrons have negative electric charges and orbit around the core, nucleus, of an atom." A simple adaptation of this sentence is, "Electrons have negative charges. They orbit around the core. The core of the atom is called the nucleus."

Ideally, rewritten paragraphs should include a topic sentence with several supporting details. Maintaining a consistent format promotes easier reading for information-seeking purposes. All sentences included in the rewritten text should be direct and relevant to the subject. In the following example, a paragraph of original text is taken from an anthology theme in a reading series (Cooper, Pikulski, Au, Calderon, Comas, Lipson, Mims, Page, Valencia, & Vogt, 1999). This passage was excerpted from a piece of nonfiction literature, *Into the Mummy's Tomb*, written by Nicholas Reeves.

Original text: "Tutankhamen's mummy bore a magnificent mask of burnished gold, which covered its face and shoulders. Its headcloth was inlaid with blue glass. The vulture and cobra on its forehead, ready to spit fire at the pharaoh's enemies, were of solid gold" (p. 237).

We have rewritten the original text as follows:

Adapted text: "King Tutankhamen's mummy wore a grand mask, made of very shiny gold. It covered the face and shoulders of the body. The part of the mask over the forehead looked like a gold headcloth. Blue glass was set into the headcloth. Shapes of a vulture (a type of bird) and a cobra (a type of snake) were above the eyes on the mask. They were solid gold. The artist made them look like they could attack the pharaoh's (King Tut's) enemies."

Obviously, adapting text like this takes time and is not easy to do. Note here that the adapted version is slightly longer than the original, which often happens when definitions are included. If you have a large number of ELs in your classroom, adapted text can be very beneficial, and it is worth the time and effort to provide students with more accessible material. Be sure to have a colleague read the adapted text to make sure it clarifies rather than confuses the content.

- **Jigsaw text reading:** Originally designed as a cooperative learning activity for all students, Jigsaw works well with English learners when there is a difficult-to-read text. One or two members from each cooperative learning group come together to form a new group of "experts." Assign each new "expert" group one section of the text to be read. This group either reads the text orally taking turns, or in partners they read to each other, or they can read the text silently. Following the reading, each "expert" group reviews and discusses what was read, determining the essential information and key vocabulary. You need to check carefully with each "expert" group to make sure all members understand the material they have read.

After you feel sure that the "experts" know their assigned information, they return to their original groups and teach fellow group members what they learned. This process scaffolds the learning of ELs because in both groups they are working with others to understand the text. Some classmates may have more background information on the topic. Text can be read with other students, reducing the demands of lengthy sections. Depending on English proficiency, ELs may join an "expert" group individually or with a partner. It is important that you select the "expert" groups rather than letting the students choose their own group members.

■ **Marginal notes:** As with highlighted text, you may wish to reserve a few textbooks for English learners and struggling readers. Print marginal notes directly in the margin of the textbook pages or duplicate notes on a handout that students can put alongside a page they are reading. The marginal notes, or handout, should include hints for understanding the content, key concepts, and/or key vocabulary and definitions. The notes, whether in the textbook's margin or on a handout, are similar to the ones often found in teachers' guides.

Most marginal notes either deal specifically with content (e.g., "Cell division includes two phases: mitosis and meiosis"), or with hints for reading a passage (e.g., "This paragraph explains why General George Armstrong Custer believed he could win the Battle of Little Big Horn. As you read it, think about whether his reasons make sense."). Marginal notes reduce ambiguity as well as the reading difficulty of the text, making it more accessible and less intimidating.

You may be thinking that marginal notes create an unnecessary burden for the teacher. Please note that once you have completed a set for one textbook, whether in the margins or on handouts, teaching assistants (parent volunteers, other adults, or capable students) can copy them in other student texts. Obviously, this type of scaffolding only works when you have extra textbooks you can write in or when you can assign specific books to particular students.

■ **Native language texts:** If some students are literate in their first language, texts written in that language may be used to supplement a textbook or clarify key concepts. Similarly, native language websites might be consulted.

Meaningful Activities

To the extent possible, lesson activities should be planned to promote language development in all skills while ELs are mastering content objectives. Students are more successful when they are able to make connections between what they know and what they are learning by relating classroom experiences to their own lives. These meaningful experiences are often described as "authentic," because they represent a reality for students. That is, classroom experiences mirror that which actually occurs in the learner's world. Authentic, meaningful experiences are especially important for ELs because they are learning to attach labels and terms to things already familiar to them. Their learning becomes situated rather than abstract when they are provided with the opportunity to actually experience what they are learning about.

Too often, however, English learners are relegated to activities that are not meaningful and are unrelated to the content and activities pursued by the other English-proficient students in their classes. It is essential that content standards that apply to students with English proficiency also apply to ELs, and that the planned activities reflect and support these standards.

For example, a class of middle school students is studying insects, butterflies in particular. While the rest of the class learns the scientific names and habitats of varied kinds of butterflies, the teacher has the ELs color and cut out pictures of butterflies to make a butterfly mobile. This activity is neither authentic nor is it meaningful for these adolescent students. And, in this example, the teacher obviously has not provided meaningful activities that support the grade-level science content standards.

Using the SIOP

As you learn to use the SIOP, both for your own teaching and for coaching other teachers, it is important that you rate each indicator as reliably as possible. That is, you need to develop consistency in your rating by having a clear understanding of each indicator and how it "looks" during a sheltered lesson. Therefore, it is very important that you discuss with other teachers and/or supervisors how you determined your ratings on the various SIOP indicators for the teachers depicted in this book. Some schools have group meetings to discuss the ratings, while other teachers work with a partner to establish reliability. You will probably notice that some ratings for the indicators will seem quite obvious to you (usually those that fall on 0, 1, or 5 on the scale) while others will be more challenging. As we learned to use the SIOP, in many classroom settings and with many teachers, we developed consistency in our ratings. With practice and discussion about the ratings you give, you will do the same.

The Lesson

The lesson described below is intended to teach fourth-grade children about the Gold Rush, in particular, about the trails taken by the pioneers.

Unit: The Gold Rush (4th Grade)

The classrooms described in the teaching scenarios in this chapter are all in a suburban elementary school with heterogeneously mixed students. English learners represent approximately 30 percent of the student population and the children speak a variety of languages. In the fourth-grade classrooms of teachers Ms. Chen, Mrs. Hargroves, and Mr. Hensen the majority of the ELs are at the intermediate stage of English fluency.

As part of the fourth-grade social studies curriculum, Ms. Chen, Mrs. Hargroves, and Mr. Hensen have planned a unit on the California Gold Rush. The school district requires the use of the adopted social studies series although teachers are encouraged to supplement the text with primary source materials, literature, and realia. The content topics for the Gold Rush unit include: westward expansion; routes and trails to the West; the people who sought their fortunes; hardships; settlements; the discovery of gold; the life of miners; methods for extracting gold; and the impact of the Gold Rush.

Each of the teachers has created several lessons for this unit, beginning with a lesson plan (approximately 55 minutes) on routes and trails to the West. Specifically, the content of this lesson covers the Oregon Trail, the Overland Trail, and the route around Cape Horn.

Teaching Scenarios

To demonstrate how Ms. Chen, Mrs. Hargroves, and Mr. Hensen prepared their first lesson on the trails west, we visit them in their fourth-grade classrooms. As you read, think of the SIOP indicators for Preparation: Content Objectives, Language Objectives, Content Concepts, Supplementary Materials, Adaptation of Content, and Meaningful Activities.

Ms. Chen

As Ms. Chen began the first day's lesson on the Gold Rush, she referred students to the content objectives written on the board: 1) Find and label the three main routes to the west on a map; 2) Tell one or two facts about each of the three trails. After reading the content objectives aloud, Ms. Chen then read the language objectives from the whiteboard: 1) Write sentences explaining how the three routes to the west were given their names; 2) Tell how the structure of some words gives clues to their meaning.

Next, Ms. Chen asked the students to brainstorm why people would leave their comfortable homes and travel great distances to seek their fortunes. She listed their responses on the board, and then asked the students to categorize the words or phrases, using a List-Group-Label activity. The children determined the following categories: For Adventure, To Get Rich, For a Better Life. Examples of phrases under the first category included *riding in a wagon train, seeing new places, climbing mountains, becoming a gold miner*, etc.

Ms. Chen then assigned her students a quick-write about the Gold Rush. She distributed two to three picture books on the topic for each of the table groups (four to five children per group), and directed students to use their background knowledge, the brainstormed categories, and the books to generate a brief paragraph on the Gold Rush. Students were encouraged to work quietly together with a partner, and each pair was expected to have a brief paragraph written for later whole-class discussion.

While the rest of the class was preparing their quick-writes, Ms. Chen asked the six English learners with very limited English proficiency to meet her at the table in the back of the room. For seven to ten minutes, she provided the small group of students with a jump-start for the Gold Rush unit they were about to begin. She introduced key vocabulary with illustrations and simple definitions, led the students through a picture and text walk of two picture books and the textbook chapter, showed the trails on the U.S. map, and talked about where the pioneers began their journey and where they were heading in California. Ms. Chen showed the students some chunks of fool's gold (iron pyrite), and asked them how they thought the gold miners were able to get the gold from the earth. After the brief jump-start lesson, Ms. Chen convened the entire class for a brief discussion of the quick-writes and a whole-class introduction to the unit. Several of the groups volunteered to share their quick-writes with the entire class.

Ms. Chen then referred to the key vocabulary she had previously written on the board: Oregon Trail, Overland Trail, Route around Cape Horn. She asked students to think about the names of the trails they were going to be reading about, and she asked, "Why are streets given their names?" She then asked students to call out some of the names of streets on which they lived. They offered First Street, River Avenue, Main Street, and Mill Creek Road, among others. Ms. Chen then suggested that trails, routes, streets, avenues, and highways are often named after geographical landmarks. She explained that often we learn about places and surrounding areas by examining their names.

Following a shared reading of the social studies text, Ms. Chen asked the students to examine the map of the United States on the wall and try to determine why the three main trails to the west were named as they were. The children volunteered appropriate ideas for the first one, the Oregon Trail. Ms. Chen then wrote "Over + land = Overland." One child said, "I get it! They went over the land!" The teacher reinforced this by pointing out the "over the land" route on the wall map. She then wrote "Route around Cape Horn" on the board and asked students to think about the name's meaning while directing them to look at the map. One child said, "See, the land looks kind of like a horn. And, they had to sail around it!" To check understanding, Ms. Chen asked each student to tell another in a complete sentence why the three western routes were given their respective names. These reasons were shared with the others in their groups.

Next, Ms. Chen distributed a duplicated map of the United States to each group. She asked three students to come to the wall map and point to the Route around Cape Horn, the Overland Trail, and the Oregon Trail. She then modeled with transparencies how to color in the trails, and then directed the students to work together as a team to complete their groups' maps.

In the few remaining minutes, Ms. Chen distributed a skeleton outline of the chapter that students would complete individually the following day. The outline had subheadings labeled for each of the trails: "Location," "Characteristics," "Challenges," and "Advantages." She told the groups they would have about ten minutes to begin working on the outline, using their maps and their text chapter. Ms. Chen wrapped up the lesson by reviewing the content and language objectives, and by having several students report a number of facts about each of the trails.

On the SIOP form in Figure 2.1, rate Ms. Chen on each of the Preparation indicators.

FIGURE 2.1   Preparation Section of the SIOP: Ms. Chen

4	3	2	1	0	NA
1. Clearly defined **content objectives** for students		**Content objectives** for students implied		No clearly defined **content objectives** for students	

4	3	2	1	0	NA
2. Clearly defined **language objectives** for students		**Language objectives** for students implied		No clearly defined **language objectives** for students	

4	3	2	1	0	NA
3. **Content concepts** appropriate for age and educational background level of students		**Content concepts** somewhat appropriate for age and educational background level of students		**Content concepts** inappropriate for age and educational background level of students	

4	3	2	1	0	NA
4. **Supplementary materials** used to a high degree, making the lesson clear and meaningful (e.g., computer programs, graphs, models, visuals)		Some use of **supplementary materials**		No use of **supplementary materials**	

4	3	2	1	0	NA
5. **Adaptation of content** (e.g., text, assignment) to all levels of student proficiency		Some **adaptation of content** to all levels of student proficiency		No significant **adapatation of content** to all levels of student proficiency	

4	3	2	1	0	NA
6. **Meaningful activities** that integrate lesson concepts (e.g., surveys, letter writing, simulations, constructing models) with language practice opportunities for reading, writing, listening, and/or speaking		**Meaningful activities** that integrate lesson concepts, but provide little opportunity for language practice with opportunities for reading, writing, listening, and/or speaking		No **meaningful activities** that integreate lesson concepts with language practice	

Mrs. Hargroves

Mrs. Hargroves began her lesson on the trails west by stating, "Today, you'll learn about the Oregon Trail, the Overland Trail, and the Route around Cape Horn. We'll also be working on maps, and I want you to color the Overland Trail a different color from the color you use for the Cape Horn route. When you learn about the Oregon Trail, you'll complete the map with a third color. By the time you're finished, you should have all three routes drawn on the map using different colors." She held up a completed map for the students to see as an example.

Mrs. Hargroves then presented a brief lecture on the trails west, using the map in the textbook to point out where the pioneers traveled. She referred students to pictures in the book, and answered questions. She read the chapter title and the first few paragraphs about the trails west, and then assigned the remainder of the chapter as independent reading. She suggested that if students had difficulty with any words, they should hold up their hands and she would circulate to give assistance.

After about twenty minutes, Mrs. Hargroves asked students to stop reading. She distributed the U.S. maps and colored pencils, and asked the students to work with a partner to complete their maps by coloring in the three trails. When most were finished, Mrs. Hargroves asked three of the students to show and explain their maps to the other students. All maps were then submitted for a grade. At the conclusion of the lesson, students were given the following writing assignment for homework: "If you had been a pioneer, which trail would you have chosen? Why?"

On the SIOP form in Figure 2.2, rate Mrs. Hargroves on each of the Preparation indicators.

Mr. Hensen

Mr. Hensen began his lesson on westward expansion by introducing the topic and asking how many children had been to California. He then asked, "How did you get to California? Did you go by car? By plane? By boat? Or did you go by wagon train? Today, you're going to learn how the pioneers made their voyages to California." Mr. Hensen then showed a brief video on westward expansion. At the end of the video, he introduced the terms Oregon Trail, Overland Trail, and Route around Cape Horn, and then read aloud two paragraphs from the textbook that described the routes. Then, he numbered off the students to form six new groups, and quickly moved students into the groups. With their team members, students did a Jigsaw of the remainder of the chapter, and when they had finished reading, everyone returned to their original home groups to report on what they had read. The ELs with limited English proficiency were partnered with other students during the Jigsaw reading activity.

Mr. Hensen then wrote the names of the three trails on the board, and on his wall map he pointed out where the pioneers had traveled along the three routes. He directed the groups to divide the three trails, with one to two students in each group drawing the Oregon Trail, and the other students drawing either the Overland or Cape Horn trails. Their next task was to tell the other

FIGURE 2.2 Preparation Section of the SIOP: Mrs. Hargroves

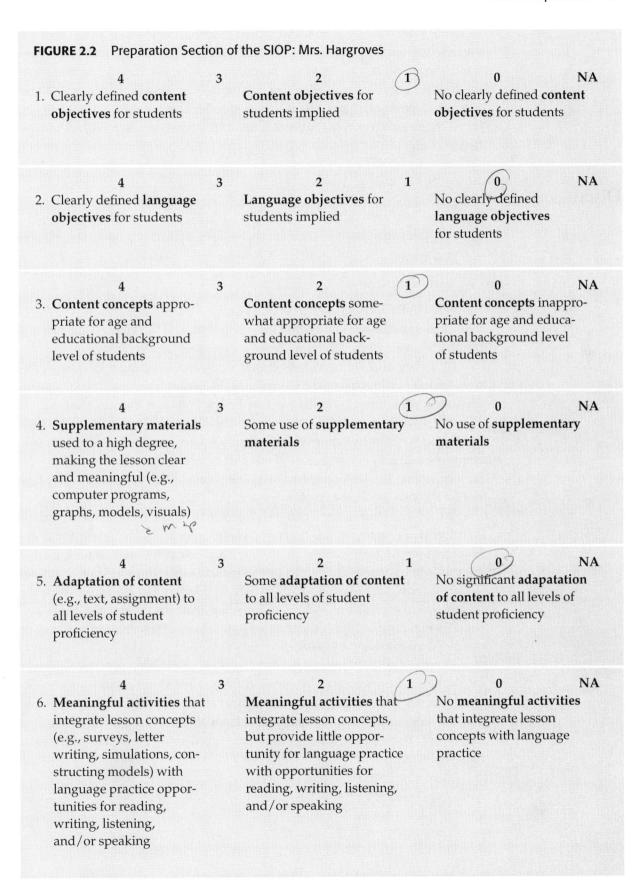

	4	3	2	1	0	NA
1.	Clearly defined **content objectives** for students		**Content objectives** for students implied	①	No clearly defined **content objectives** for students	

	4	3	2	1	0	NA
2.	Clearly defined **language objectives** for students		**Language objectives** for students implied		⓪ No clearly defined **language objectives** for students	

	4	3	2	1	0	NA
3.	**Content concepts** appropriate for age and educational background level of students		**Content concepts** somewhat appropriate for age and educational background level of students	①	**Content concepts** inappropriate for age and educational background level of students	

	4	3	2	1	0	NA
4.	**Supplementary materials** used to a high degree, making the lesson clear and meaningful (e.g., computer programs, graphs, models, visuals)		Some use of **supplementary materials**	①	No use of **supplementary materials**	

≥ m ɣ

	4	3	2	1	0	NA
5.	**Adaptation of content** (e.g., text, assignment) to all levels of student proficiency		Some **adaptation of content** to all levels of student proficiency		⓪ No significant **adapatation of content** to all levels of student proficiency	

	4	3	2	1	0	NA
6.	**Meaningful activities** that integrate lesson concepts (e.g., surveys, letter writing, simulations, constructing models) with language practice opportunities for reading, writing, listening, and/or speaking		**Meaningful activities** that integrate lesson concepts, but provide little opportunity for language practice with opportunities for reading, writing, listening, and/or speaking	①	No **meaningful activities** that integreate lesson concepts with language practice	

students in their group how to color their maps, using the map in the text and the language on the board as a guide. Mr. Hensen circulated through the room while the children completed the mapping activity, assisting as necessary. At the lesson's conclusion, students were directed to pass in their maps. Those maps that were not finished were assigned as homework.

On the SIOP form in Figure 2.3, rate Mr. Hensen on each of the Preparation indicators.

Discussion of Lessons

1. *Content Objectives*

   Ms. Chen: 4

   Mrs. Hargroves: 2

   Mr. Hensen: 1

During their planning, Ms. Chen, Mrs. Hargroves, and Mr. Hensen approached the task of writing and delivering content objectives in different ways.

A review of Ms. Chen's lesson plan book indicated the following objectives for her first lessons on the Gold Rush: "The learner will be able to: 1) identify the three main routes to the west on a map; 2) state at least one distinct fact about each of the three trails." She wrote the content objectives on the whiteboard and she clearly, explicitly, and simply stated then in a manner that was comprehensible to her students: "Find and label the three main routes to the west on a map; and tell one or two facts about each of the three trails." (See Figure 2.4 for Ms. Chen's lesson plan.)

Mrs. Hargroves wrote a content objective in her plan book but not on the board, and she orally stated what she wanted her students to learn and do. However, her English learners might have had difficulty understanding what the purpose was for the activities they were to do. She did state her objectives in simple terms and some students may have inferred that the purpose for the lesson was the coloring activity rather than learning where the trails and routes were. Further, the content objectives were not written on the board or overhead for the students to see.

A review of Mr. Hensen's lesson plan book revealed no content objectives for the Gold Rush lesson on routes and trails. He did not define any content objectives for the students, but just began the lesson with a brief discussion and the video. Some students may have been able to infer the purpose of the map work, but English learners may have been unaware of the purpose of these assignments.

FIGURE 2.3 Preparation Section of the SIOP: Mr. Hensen

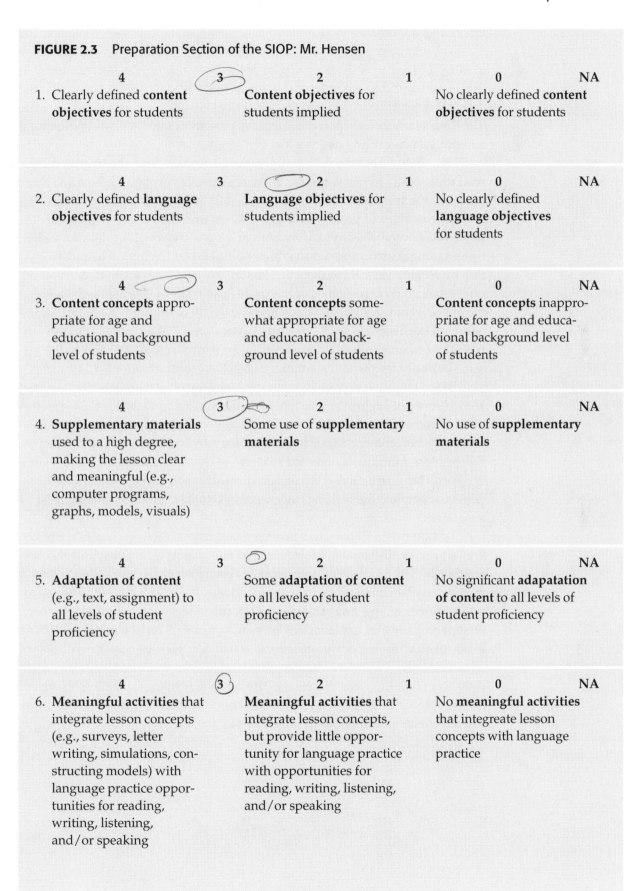

4	3	2	1	0	NA
1. Clearly defined **content objectives** for students		**Content objectives** for students implied		No clearly defined **content objectives** for students	

4	3	2	1	0	NA
2. Clearly defined **language objectives** for students		**Language objectives** for students implied		No clearly defined **language objectives** for students	

4	3	2	1	0	NA
3. **Content concepts** appropriate for age and educational background level of students		**Content concepts** somewhat appropriate for age and educational background level of students		**Content concepts** inappropriate for age and educational background level of students	

4	3	2	1	0	NA
4. **Supplementary materials** used to a high degree, making the lesson clear and meaningful (e.g., computer programs, graphs, models, visuals)		Some use of **supplementary materials**		No use of **supplementary materials**	

4	3	2	1	0	NA
5. **Adaptation of content** (e.g., text, assignment) to all levels of student proficiency		Some **adaptation of content** to all levels of student proficiency		No significant **adapatation of content** to all levels of student proficiency	

4	3	2	1	0	NA
6. **Meaningful activities** that integrate lesson concepts (e.g., surveys, letter writing, simulations, constructing models) with language practice opportunities for reading, writing, listening, and/or speaking		**Meaningful activities** that integrate lesson concepts, but provide little opportunity for language practice with opportunities for reading, writing, listening, and/or speaking		No **meaningful activities** that integreate lesson concepts with language practice	

2. *Language Objectives*

Ms. Chen: 4

Mrs. Hargroves: 0

Mr. Hensen: 2

The three teachers incorporated language objectives into their lesson planning and delivery to varying degrees.

Ms. Chen wrote the following language objectives on the board and she read them orally to her students: 1) Write sentences explaining how the three routes to the west were given their names; 2) Tell how the structure of some words gives clues to their meaning. Ms. Chen provided opportunities for students to meet the objective by encouraging class and small group discussion, by assigning sentences about the three trails, and by having each student convey important facts related to the lesson. Further, she scaffolded students' understandings of the names of the routes and trails by having them examine the names of familiar street names, and she led them through an analysis of the names of the historical routes, such as "over + land." She pointed out the compound word and supported students' approximations. At the end of the lesson, she orally reviewed the language objectives for the students.

Mrs. Hargroves did not include any language objectives in her lesson plan and she did not suggest any to the students. She did not discuss the meanings of the names or terms used in her demonstration and explanations, nor did she encourage her students to use the terminology and concepts during discussion. Further, Mrs. Hargroves expected students to read the textbook with very little support. Her instruction was conveyed mostly orally, and she expected students to complete the writing assignment as homework with no modeling or assistance.

Although Mr. Hensen had no stated language objectives, he did write key vocabulary on the board. He scaffolded the mapping activity and the text reading by having the children work in groups and by having each group member explain the map and key words to the others. This activity was appropriate for beginning English learners because they were supported by each other, and their oral explanations were not "public," for the entire class. The lesson would have been more effective had Mr. Hensen explained his language objectives to the children, emphasizing the importance of listening carefully and of giving clear directions. Though one purpose of the lesson was to build listening and speaking skills, the children were not informed of these objectives either orally or in writing.

FIGURE 2.4 Ms. Chen's SIOP Lesson Plan

Date: _Feb. 10-11_____ Grade/Class/Subject: _4 – SS_____

Unit/Theme: _Gold Rush_____ Standards: _____

Content Objective(s): _____Find / label 3 routes to West on map;_____

_Tell 1-2 facts about each trail_____

Language Objective(s): _____Write sentences explaining how 3 routes got_____

_their names; Tell how word structure gives clues to meaning_____

Key Vocabulary	Supplementary Materials
Oregon Trail	Picture books Outlines
Overland Trail	Iron Pyrite
Route around Cape Horn	Transp. w/ US map

Skel.
Outline
Jumpstart

SIOP Features

Preparation
- ✓ Adaptation of Content
- ✓ Links to Background
- ✓ Links to Past Learning
- ✓ Strategies incorporated
    List / Group / Label

Scaffolding
- ✓ Modeling Transp.
- ✓ Guided practice
- ___ Independent practice
- ✓ Comprehensible input

Grouping Options
- ✓ Whole class
- ✓ Small groups
- ___ Partners
- ✓ Independent

Integration of Processes
- ✓ Reading
- ✓ Writing
- ✓ Speaking
- ✓ Listening

Application
- ✓ Hands-on maps
- ✓ Meaningful
- ✓ Linked to objectives
- ✓ Promotes engagement

Assessment
- ✓ Individual
- ✓ Group
- ✓ Written
- ___ Oral

Min.	Lesson Sequence
	1. Content / lang. obj.
5	2. Brainstorm — Why would people leave their homes to seek fortunes?
	3. List – Group – Label
10	4. EOs — Quick Write: Gold Rush
	5. ELs — Jumpstart text / fool's gold / pictures
5	6. Quick Write Share Out
	7. Intro. Vocabulary: Why are streets given their names?
10	8. Shared reading — p. 124-128
10	9. On map — show trails - How did they get their names?
	10. Pass out U.S. maps —
	11. Model on transp. — Have kids color
5–10	12. Skeleton Outline — Work in groups - fill in categories – (Start, if time)

Reflections:

It felt a little rushed, but everyone finished the maps. Next time, save Skeleton outlines for 2nd day. Kids loved the fool's gold!

3. *Content Concepts*

Ms. Chen: 4

Mrs. Hargroves: 4

Mr. Hensen: 4

Each of the teaching scenarios indicates that the three fourth-grade teachers, Ms. Chen, Mrs. Hargroves, and Mr. Hensen were teaching a unit on the Gold Rush. The content concepts were appropriate because they are congruent with the fourth grade state and district standards for the Social Studies curriculum in the district where the teachers are employed.

4. *Supplementary Materials*

Ms. Chen: 4

Mrs. Hargroves: 1

Mr. Hensen: 3

Ms. Chen used the following supplementary materials: picture books on the Gold Rush, fool's gold, the wall map of the United States, and transparencies to model how students might color the trails on their maps.

Mrs. Hargroves, on the other hand, used only the wall map and the textbook during her lecture and when the students were coloring their maps. She did not demonstrate, model, or show visuals or other resources to support student learning other than the illustrations in the textbooks. Because Mrs. Hargroves delivered the content orally, some English learners may have had difficulty making connections between the lecture and the illustrations and maps in their books.

Mr. Hensen's video enabled his English learners and other students to connect with the pioneers in the Gold Rush and his use of the wall map enhanced student learning about the location of the three trails.

5. *Adaptation of Content*

Ms. Chen: 4

Mrs. Hargroves: 0

Mr. Hensen: 3

Ms. Chen adapted the grade-level content for her English learners and struggling readers in a number of ways. First, she had students brainstorm, categorize, and then quick-write information about the Gold Rush. She then provided a "jump-start" for her English learners by preteaching the lesson concepts and key vocabulary. She also had a variety of picture books that were easier to read and more comprehensible than the textbook. In addition, she used a skeleton outline that included key information. The students used this outline to organize their understanding of the content concepts.

Mrs. Hargroves did not adapt the content for her English learners, other than by lecturing on the topic. Without any supplementary support except the pictures in the textbook and her oral reading of the first few paragraphs, the ELs may have had difficulty learning key concepts just by listening and reading independently. Further, Mrs. Hargroves did not paraphrase or clarify important points during her lecture, nor did she explain or define key language or vocabulary before or during reading. Her lesson plans made no mention of other ways to adapt the content or text.

Mr. Hensen provided access to the textbook content through the Jigsaw activity and the video. He grouped the students for their reading so that they read with the support of others and then conveyed what they had learned to another group of students. He also had the students complete their work on the maps in small groups, and he encouraged them to help each other with the assignment.

6. *Meaningful Activities*

   Ms. Chen: 4

   Mrs. Hargroves: 2

   Mr. Hensen: 4

Recall that Ms. Chen asked students to brainstorm what they knew about the Gold Rush in order to activate and build background. She later asked them to name the streets they lived on. The purpose of this was to make meaningful the names of geographic locations, such as familiar street names, as well as routes to California. Her jump-start activity for the English learners included picture walks and discussion of key vocabulary, and the students were able to see and hold fool's gold, which simulated the feel and look of gold. The picture books supported their learning, and the skeleton outline provided a meaningful way to summarize the key concepts. Students colored in the trails on the U.S. maps after watching modeling by Ms. Chen.

Mrs. Hargroves's lesson plans included her lecture, the mapping activity, and the independent reading. Locating the trails by coloring the map was meaningful for students if they understood what they were doing; however, if they were unable to access the text or the lecture, the mapping activity may have been irrelevant. Mrs. Hargroves's lesson was teacher-centered with lecture and independent seat-work the predominant activities. She expected students to complete the homework assignment based only on the information they could gather from the lecture and text. If students did not understand the lecture or comprehend the chapter, it is unlikely they were able to write a meaningful essay on what they learned.

Mr. Hensen activated prior knowledge and background when he asked which students had traveled to California. He also showed the video on westward expansion, incorporated a Jigsaw reading activity, and had the students complete and explain their maps in triads. All of these activities helped make the content concepts more comprehensible for his English learners, and are thus considered to be meaningful and appropriate.

Summary

Separating "preparation" from "instruction" is difficult because they are closely linked. Hopefully, thoughtful planning leads to effective teaching—but a great plan does not always guarantee a great lesson for English learners. ELs require sensitive teachers who realize that curriculum must be grade-level appropriate, based on content standards and learning outcomes. If children lack background knowledge and experience with content concepts, effective sheltered teachers provide it through explicit instruction and they enhance student learning with appropriate supplementary materials. They provide scaffolded support by adapting dense and difficult text. They situate lessons in meaningful real-life activities and experiences that involve students in reading, writing, and discussion of important concepts and ideas.

These principles of effective sheltered instruction should be reflected in teachers' lesson plans. As we explore the other indicators on the Sheltered Instruction Observation Protocol and see how teachers apply many other important principles in their classrooms, remember that the first step in the instructional process is comprehensive and thoughtful lesson design.

Discussion Questions

1. What are some advantages to writing both content objectives and language objectives for students to hear and see? How might written objectives affect teacher and student performance in the classroom?
2. Think of a lesson you have recently taught or one you might teach. What would be an appropriate content objective and language objective for that lesson?

3. What are some ways that curriculum intended for younger learners can be used effectively as a supplement for teaching grade-level content concepts? Give examples.

4. Many teachers in sheltered settings rely on paper-and-pencil tasks or lectures for teaching concepts. Think of a curricular area (e.g., science, language arts, math, social studies) and discuss some meaningful activities that could be used to teach a concept in that area. What makes each of these activities "meaningful?"

3 Building Background

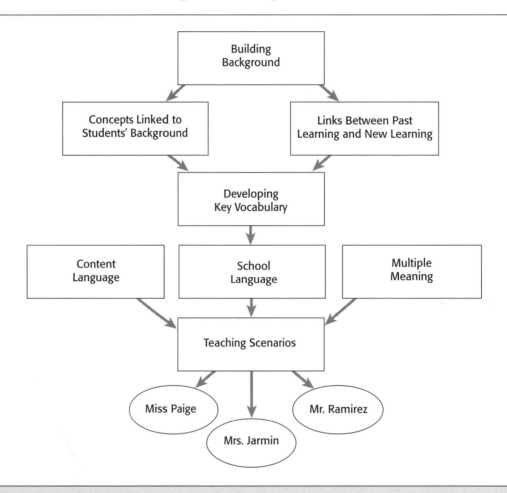

OBJECTIVES

After reading, discussing, and engaging in activities related to this chapter, you will be able to meet the following content and language objectives.

Content Objectives:

Recognize the importance of connecting students' personal experiences to lesson concepts

Identify strategies for linking past learning with new information

Language Objectives:

Examine text to determine key vocabulary for students to learn

Incorporate a variety of vocabulary development activities into lessons

Describe the difference between content language and school language

In our work in classrooms, we have seen teachers with good intentions go through the motions of a lesson. They have a lesson plan and follow the plan, but fail to connect with the students. The features of the SIOP are designed, in part, to encourage teachers of English learners (ELs) to pay attention to some very important aspects of teaching that can be overlooked. Effective teaching takes students from where they are and leads them to a higher level of understanding (Krashen, 1985; Vygotsky, 1978). Students learning English must have ample opportunity to use the target language (English); to hear and see comprehensible English; and to read, write, and speak the new language within the context of subject matter learning. But there is a caveat to this: *the language must be meaningful.* It is not only the amount of exposure to English that affects learning, but the quality as well (Wong-Fillmore & Valadez, 1986). As we will discuss in the next few chapters of this book, effective sheltered teachers present information in a way that students can understand, bearing in mind their language development needs and the gaps in their educational experiences. New information is tied to students' background and experiences, and strategies are used to scaffold students' acquisition of knowledge and skills (see Chapter 5 for a detailed discussion). All students benefit from scaffolded instruction, but it is a necessity for English learners. This chapter focuses on *Building Background* which is closely tied to Lesson Preparation and the teacher's assessment of the students' knowledge and experience of the topic at hand.

Background

During the past two decades, researchers have investigated how highly proficient readers and writers process new information (Carrell, 1987; Dole, Duffy, Roehler & Pearson, 1991). It is a widely accepted notion among experts that a reader's "schema"—knowledge of the world—provides a basis for understanding, learning, and remembering facts and ideas found in stories and texts. Individuals with knowledge of a topic have better recall and are better able to elaborate on aspects of the topic than those who have limited knowledge of the topic (Chiesi, Spilich, & Voss, 1979).

The importance of background experiences are expressed in the following ways:

> Schemata are the reader's concepts, beliefs, expectations, processes—virtually everything from past experiences—that are used in making sense of things and actions. In reading, schemata are used in making sense of text; the printed work evoking the reader's associated experiences, and past and potential relationships. (John McNeil)
>
> When reading, the learner forms meaning by reviewing past experiences that given images and sounds evoke. (Edmund Huey)

Christen & Murphy (1991) have suggested that when readers lack the prior knowledge necessary to read, three major instructional interventions need to be considered: (1) teach vocabulary as a prereading step; (2) provide experiences; and (3) introduce a conceptual framework that will enable students to build appropriate background for themselves.

In this chapter we will present a number of ways to preteach vocabulary prior to reading the text, as well as ways for developing vocabulary throughout a lesson. Some studies suggest that a limited number of words should be taught per lesson or per week, and those words must be key words in the text (Beck, Perfetti, & McKeown, 1982). In sheltered lessons, teachers select words that are critical for understanding the text or material and provide a variety of ways for students to learn, remember, and use those words. In that way, students develop a core vocabulary over time (Blachowicz & Fisher, 2000).

The second intervention is to provide experiences for students. In this chapter you will see how teachers used a videotape of the story to build some background experience before actually reading the novel. There are innumerable ways that background experiences can be created or ways that teachers can use the experiences the students bring. Connecting the students' own background experiences to the text, activating their background knowledge, and presenting background information about the text to be read are all effective ways of increasing comprehension.

A third intervention is to provide a way for students to build background for themselves. This can be accomplished by teaching them to use graphic organizers such as those shown in this chapter. As students begin to develop a conceptual framework for their own learning and understanding, they build a repertoire of background experiences from which to draw.

One of the challenges of teaching English learners is that students in the same class vary in the amount of prior knowledge they possess. Christen and Murphy (1991) suggest that students generally fall into three categories: much, some, or little prior knowledge. Based on their level, the teacher makes specific instructional decisions and differentiates instruction for each level. Some ideas for differentiation include using and teaching superordinate concepts, definitions, analogies, and linking words for students who have much prior knowledge; using and teaching examples, attributes, and defining characteristics for students who have some prior knowledge; and using and teaching associations, morphemes (e.g., base words and word roots), sound-alikes, and first-hand experiences for students who have little prior knowledge (Christen & Murphy, 1991).

Children from culturally diverse backgrounds may struggle with comprehending a text or concept presented in class because their schemata do not match those of the culture for which the text was written (Jimenez, Garcia, & Pearson, 1996; Anderson, 1984). In the United States, most school reading material, such as content area texts, relies on the assumption that students' prior knowledge is knowledge that is common to all children. Many English learners emigrate from other countries and bring an array of experiences that are quite different from those of the majority culture in the United States, and many have gaps in their education. Even for those students born in the United States, culture has strong effects on reading comprehension. As a teacher reads, "The man walked briskly down the dark alley, glancing from side to side," do all children get a sense of fear or danger? Anderson (1994) questions whether we can assume that, "when reading the same story, children from every subculture will have the same experience with the setting, ascribe the same goals and motives to characters, imagine the same sequence of actions, make predictions with the same emotional reactions, or expect the same outcomes" (pp. 480–481).

An actual example of cultural mismatch of schemata occurred in a middle school's self-contained special education class with a small group of students for whom English was their second language. The teacher was participating in a project using instructional conversations, an approach that, among other features, explicitly links students' background to text (Echevarria, 1995a). The teacher read a passage from a grade-level novel about a young man who was reading a magazine (his favorite subscription) while riding a public bus home. He left the magazine on the bus and as he exited, he spoke a quick Russian greeting to some passengers whom he had overheard speaking Russian. The story states that the young man, Mike, had learned a few phrases from his brother-in-law who is Russian. After Mike got off the bus, he heard the bus make its next stop with quite a commotion. He turned to see the Russians running toward him with guns! After taking a circuitous route home, he got to his second-floor apartment, breathing a sigh of relief. He had no idea why the Russians were so angry with him, but he was relieved that he had lost them. A half-hour later he heard a noise outside, looked out the window and saw the Russians coming into his building.

The teacher paused and asked the students about how the Russians could possibly have found where Mike lived when the story made it clear that he had lost them. The teacher expected that the students would remember that Mike had left the magazine, which had his address label on it, on the bus. However, one student volunteered that the Russians found Mike by asking his brother-in-law. The teacher admitted that she found the answer to be "out in left field" and would ordinarily have tactfully asked someone else for the answer. But the nature of instructional conversations is to discuss ideas, drawing out students' thoughts and linking them to the text. So the teacher asked the student to elaborate. He explained that in their community, which was 99 percent Latino with a small population of Samoans, if he needed to know where a certain Samoan person lived, he'd simply ask someone from the Samoan neighborhood.

The teacher admitted that she had learned an important lesson: the students' schemata were different from hers yet just as valid. Moreover, she nearly dismissed his excellent contribution because she was looking for a specific answer that matched her schemata. In reality, none of the students in her group would have had any idea about magazine subscriptions and address labels. In the students' experience, if one wanted a magazine, one merely walked to the store and bought it.

The example clearly demonstrates that the student and teacher had very different ideas and assumptions about the characters and events in the story and a different "magazine" schema. Some of the differences can be attributed to cultural variation and a difference in home environments.

Teachers of English learners need to be aware that what may appear to be poor comprehension and memory skills, may in fact be a lack of, or failure to activate, the background knowledge that was assumed by a message or a text (Bransford, 1994). Through the SIOP model, we urge teachers to activate students' background knowledge explicitly and provide linkages from their experiences to the concepts or text. The interactive emphasis of the SIOP model (see Chapter 6 for specific features) enables teachers to elicit students' background knowledge and discuss ideas, issues, concepts, or vocabulary that are unfamiliar to them.

Concepts Linked to Students' Background

Tying new information to students' own background experiences, both personal (including cultural) and academic, makes the information take on new meaning. Teachers may provide explicit links to students' background by asking questions that preview an upcoming topic—such as, "Have you ever seen a rat?" or "How do people usually feel about rats? Why?" or "Have you ever been sick?"—and then directly relating it to the text by saying, "Well, today we're going to read about some rats. Let's see how similar the rats in the story are to the ones you've just described from your experience."

Links Made between Past Learning and New Concepts

It is also important for teachers to make explicit connections between new learning and the material, vocabulary, and concepts previously covered in class. Research clearly emphasizes that in order for learning to occur, new information

must be integrated with what the learner already knows (Rumelhart, 1980). The teacher must build a bridge from previous lessons to new learning for students to cross over. Many students do not automatically make such connections, and all students benefit from having the teacher explicitly point out how past learning is related to the information at hand (Tierney & Pearson, 1994).

Links between past learning and new learning can be made through a discussion—such as, "Who remembers what we learned about ____? How does that relate to our story?"—or by reviewing graphic organizers or other written reminders about the information. By preserving and referring to word banks, outlines, charts, maps, and graphic organizers, teachers have tools for reminding students of previous learning. This is particularly important for ELs who receive so much input through the new language. A review of prior lessons indicates the key information they should remember.

Key Vocabulary Emphasized

Vocabulary development is critical for English learners because we know that there is a strong relationship between vocabulary knowledge in English and academic achievement (Saville-Troike, 1984). To be most effective, vocabulary development should be closely related to the subject matter students are studying. As you will see, the one teacher in this chapter, Miss Paige, who taught vocabulary well, embedded the new words within the context of the text, providing students with a rich contextual environment in which to learn new terms and expand their English vocabulary.

In a synthesis of twenty years of research on vocabulary instruction, Blachowicz & Fisher (2000) determined four main principles that should guide instruction:

1. *Students should be active in developing their understanding of words and ways to learn them.* Such ways include use of semantic mapping, word sorts (see Figures 3.1a and 3.1b), use of a Concept Definition Map (see Figure 3.2), and developing strategies for independent word learning.
2. *Students should personalize word learning* through such practices as Vocabulary Self-Collection Strategy (VSS) (Ruddell, 2001), mnemonic strategies, and personal dictionaries.
3. *Students should be immersed in words* by providing rich language environments that focus on words and draw students' attention to the learning of words. Word walls, personal word study notebooks and dictionaries, and comparing/contrasting words with the same morphemic element (e.g., photograph, photosynthesis, photogenic) aid students in recognizing and using the words around them.
4. *Students should build on multiple sources of information to learn words through repeated exposures.* Letting students see and hear new words more than once and drawing on multiple sources of meaning is important for vocabulary development.

FIGURE 3.1A Word Sorts: American Revolution—Example 1

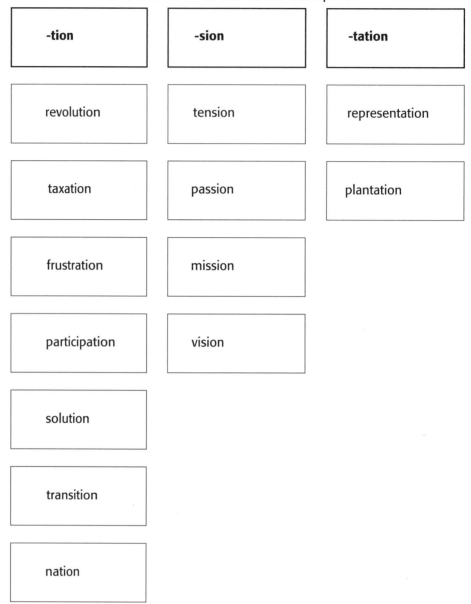

There are two aspects to vocabulary development to attend to when using the SIOP. One involves selecting several key terms on which to focus from the lesson's material, and the other is explicitly teaching "school language"—or the vocabulary associated with activities such as identify, define, compare, and summarize—the kinds of terms that are typically used in classroom tasks and discussions.

Developing Content Language

There is little benefit to selecting twenty-five to thirty isolated vocabulary terms and asking ELs to copy them from the board and look up their defini-

FIGURE 3.1B Word Sorts: American Revolution—Example 2

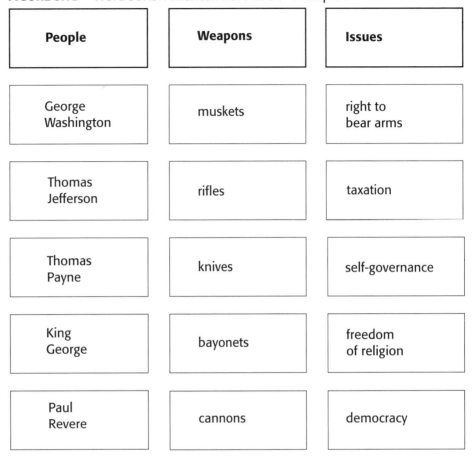

People	Weapons	Issues
George Washington	muskets	right to bear arms
Thomas Jefferson	rifles	taxation
Thomas Payne	knives	self-governance
King George	bayonets	freedom of religion
Paul Revere	cannons	democracy

tions in the dictionary. Many of the words in the definitions are also unfamiliar to these students, rendering the activity meaningless. Although using the dictionary is an important school skill to learn, the task must fit the students' learning needs. The number of terms should be tailored to the students' English and literacy levels, and they should be presented in context, not in isolation. The *Oxford Picture Dictionary for Content Areas* (Kauffman & Apple, 2002) is an excellent resource for contextualizing terms. For students with minimal literacy skills, using the dictionary to find words can serve to reinforce the concept of alphabetizing and it familiarizes them with the parts of a dictionary; however, defining words should not be the only activity used. Effective sheltered instruction teachers support the understanding of dictionary definitions so that the task is meaningful for students. In fact, many effective teachers introduce dictionary skills to students by using words that are already familiar to them.

There are a myriad of meaningful and useful ways that vocabulary can be taught to English learners. The following section describes approaches to vocabulary development and word study that are especially helpful to ELs. When used regularly, they provide students with multiple exposures to key language and vocabulary through meaningful practice and review.

Contextualizing Key Vocabulary   Sheltered teachers peruse the material to be learned and select several key terms that are critical to understanding the lesson's most important concepts. The teacher introduces the terms at the outset of the lesson, systematically defining or demonstrating each and showing how that term is used within the context of the lesson. Experienced SI teachers know that having students understand the meaning of several key terms completely is more effective than having a cursory understanding of a dozen terms.

Another way of contextualizing words is to read with students in small groups and, as they come across a term they do not understand, pause and explain it to them, using as many examples, synonyms, or cognates as necessary to convey the meaning.

Vocabulary Self-Collection Strategy (VSS)   Following the reading of a content text, according to Ruddell (2001), students self-select key vocabulary that is essential to understanding content concepts. Words may be selected by individuals, partners, or small groups, and they are eventually shared and discussed by the entire class. A class list of vocabulary self-collection words for a particular lesson or unit is mutually agreed on by the teacher and the students, and these are reviewed and studied throughout. They also may be entered into a word study notebook and students may be asked to demonstrate their knowledge of these words through written or oral activities. Ruddell (2001) has found that when students are shown how to identify key content vocabulary, they become adept at selecting and learning words they need to know, and, given opportunities to practice VSS, comprehension of the text improves (Shearer, Ruddell, & Vogt, 2001).

The Vocabulary Self-Collection Strategy is an effective method for teaching and reviewing content vocabulary because students learn to trust their own judgments about which content words are the most important to learn. This approach is most appropriate for students who are high-intermediate and advanced English learners.

Personal Dictionaries   Similar to VSS, personal dictionaries are created as an individual vocabulary and spelling resource for students at all levels of English proficiency. Generally used with students who have intermediate and advanced English proficiency, ELs read together in partners or small groups and write unknown words they encounter in their personal dictionaries. The teacher works with each group and discusses the words students have written in their dictionaries, providing correction or clarity as needed.

Word Wall   During a lesson, key vocabulary is reviewed by directing students to a Word Wall where relevant content vocabulary words are listed alphabetically, usually on a large poster, sheet of butcher paper, or pocket chart (Cunningham, 1995). Originally designed as a method for teaching and reinforcing sight words for emergent readers, Word Walls are also effective for displaying content words related to a particular unit or theme. The words are revisited frequently throughout the lesson or unit and students are encouraged to use them in their writing and discussions.

Cunningham (1995) recommends that teachers judiciously select words for a Word Wall and that the number be limited to those of greatest importance. We would add that teachers should resist the temptation to have multiple Word Walls in one classroom because the walls quickly become cluttered with words that are difficult to sort through, especially for ELs. One Word Wall, carefully maintained and changed as needed, is what we recommend. Some teachers, with students' input, regularly remove words from a Word Wall to keep the number of words at a reasonable number. Every Friday, or every other Friday, for example, the students jointly decide which words they no longer need on the wall. Word Wall posters can also be kept and stored for later reference or review.

Concept Definition Map   The Concept Definition Map is a great way to learn and remember content vocabulary and concepts (Buehl, 1995). Even though it is a simple graphic, it can be used to discuss complex concepts. For example, a class is studying the American Revolution in social studies. To clarify the meaning of "revolution," the class could complete a Concept Definition Map, as shown in Figure 3.2.

FIGURE 3.2   Concept Definition Map

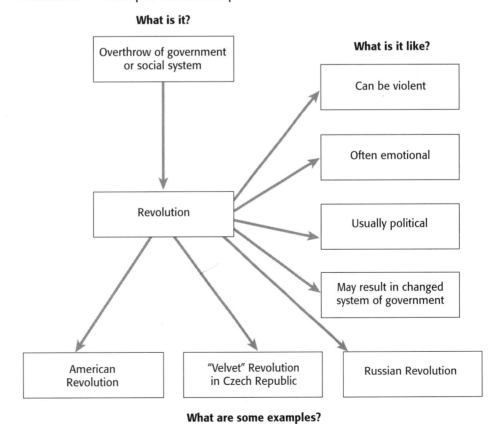

Cloze Sentences   Cloze sentences can be used to teach and review content vocabulary. Students read a sentence that has strong contextual support for the vocabulary word that has been omitted from the sentence. Once the meaning of the word is determined and possible replacement words are brainstormed, the teacher (or a student) provides the correct word. For example, "During a _____, which can be violent or peaceful, a group of people tries to overthrow an existing government or social system." *(revolution)*

Word Sorts   During a Word Sort, students categorize words or phrases, which have been previously introduced, into groups predetermined by the teacher (Bear, Invernizzi, Templeton, & Johnston, 2000). Words or phrases are typed on a sheet of paper (46-point type on the computer works well). Students cut the paper into word strips and then sort the words according to meaning, similarities in structure (e.g., words ending in -tion, -sion, or -tation), derivations, or sounds.

For example, words related to the American Revolution are listed in mixed order on a sheet of paper: revolution, tension, frustration, taxation, representation, vision, plantation, mission, participation, solution, passion, transition, nation, and so on. After you discuss the meanings of the words, have students cut out each of the words and sort them according to spelling pattern (see Figure 3.1a). The objectives here would be twofold: to introduce words related to content concepts and to reinforce spellings and word structure.

Another example of a Word Sort for the American Revolution might involve words and phrases related to content concepts such as right to bear arms, muskets, George Washington, rifles, Thomas Jefferson, democracy, Thomas Payne, knives, taxation, King George, bayonets, freedom of religion, Paul Revere, self-governance, cannons. After students cut apart the words and phrases, they sort them into groups and identify an appropriate label for each (e.g., People, Weapons, Issues) (see Figure 3.1b).

This categorizing activity also can be completed as a List–Group–Label activity (Vacca & Vacca, 2001) when students brainstorm words related to the topic and then determine possible categories or labels for the words. The brainstormed words are then reviewed when they are rewritten under the various labels.

Word Generation   This activity helps EL students and others learn and/or review new content vocabulary through analogy. For example, write "-port" on the board. Invite students to brainstorm all the words they can think of that contain "port." Examples might include report, import, export, important, portfolio, Port-a-Potty, Portland, deport, transport, transportation, support, airport, and so on. Analyze the meaning of each brainstormed word and ask students to figure out what words containing "-port" might mean ("to carry"). If they cannot figure it out, it's fine to tell them the meaning. Then, go back and revisit each word to see if the definition "to carry" has something to do with the word's meaning. Note that we did not define "port" first; rather, we recommend that students generalize meanings of content words from words that they already know that contain the same syllable or word-part.

Word Study Books   A Word Study Book is a student-made personal notebook containing frequently used words and concepts. Bear et al. (2000) recommend that the Word Study Book be organized by English language structure, such as listing together all the words studied so far that end in -tion, -sion, and -tation. We support this notion and believe that Word Study Books can also be used for content study where words are grouped by meaning (e.g., American Revolution-related words).

Vocabulary Games   Playing games like Pictionary and Scrabble can help students recall vocabulary terms. Word searches for beginning students and crossword puzzles for more proficient students are additional vocabulary development tools. Software programs are available for teachers or students to create crossword puzzles.

Developing School Language

The issue of making "school language" comprehensible to students is an important one. Teachers often give students instructions and assume the terms used in the instructions are meaningful to the students. In a science class, we observed that a teacher did an excellent job of preparing a hands-on lesson that incorporated many of the features of the SIOP. However, as the lesson was introduced, the teacher said, "The purpose of this lesson is for you to better understand why some things float while others sink. Before we're done, you'll be able to calculate and predict whether something will be buoyant enough to float." The teacher did well in stating the objective of the lesson in a way the students could understand, but the students were lost when the teacher used unfamiliar terms such as "calculate," "buoyant," and "predict."

Multiple Meaning Words   Another issue for teachers of ELs to be aware of is the use of words with multiple meanings. Students may know the meaning of words like power (as in Power Ranger) or rational (sane) as used in a non-academic environment, but not know their more technical meanings in a mathematics course. Therefore, teachers should assess student understanding and teach the technical meanings to prevent possible misconceptions.

The Lesson

Unit: Mrs. Frisby and the Rats of NIMH (6th grade)

The lessons described in this chapter take place in a large urban middle school with a large population of English learners. The number of ELs in this school enables classes to be grouped homogeneously by student English proficiency level. Students in all three classes described here are advanced beginners, which means their English proficiency is beyond the beginning stages of acquisition, but not quite at an intermediate level. Most of the students emigrated from rural areas in Latin America and have low literacy levels due to interrupted schooling experiences.

continued

Unit: Mrs. Frisby and the Rats of NIMH (6th grade)   *continued*

As part of a literature course, Miss Paige, Mrs. Jarmin, and Mr. Ramirez are required to teach a variety of American literature. The first book in the series is *Mrs. Frisby and the Rats of NIMH,* and the teachers will spend one week to ten days on the unit. The story is about Mrs. Frisby, a field mouse, who is worried about her younger son, Timothy. He has had pneumonia and is too weak and frail to be moved. But if the Frisbys don't move immediately, they'll all be killed. Mrs. Frisby hears about the wonderful Rats of NIMH who are strong, smart, and able to do almost anything. The story chronicles the adventures of the family and the Rats of NIMH.

The goals for this unit include 1) students will read an extended text, and 2) students will use their prior knowledge as a tool for understanding the text. Although these may seem somewhat vague, the teachers felt strongly that these students need to have the experience of reading an extended text since materials written at their literacy levels tend to be short, simple stories. The teachers are planning to introduce the novel by showing the video version of the story. Seeing the video prior to reading the text will provide students with an overall understanding of the story, and will provide exposure to new vocabulary associated with the text. Following the viewing of the video, the teachers will introduce the text, which the class will read together. The teachers may provide activities of their choosing to reinforce the concepts and vocabulary covered in the story.

Teaching Scenarios

The teachers have prepared their own plans for teaching the unit on *Mrs. Frisby and the Rats of NIMH.* Their individual approaches to teaching the unit and SIOP scores are described below.

Miss Paige

Miss Paige began the first lesson of the unit by asking, "Have you ever seen a rat?" and showing the class a picture of one. The students were quite interested in this topic and readily shared their experiences. Students brainstormed a variety of characteristics of the rats they had had experience with, either personal experiences or through other means such as television and movies. Miss Paige then drew a semantic map and, with the students' input, categorized the various characteristics of rats they had knowledge about. When they had completed the semantic map and the students had a good understanding of rats, Miss Paige then directly related the discussion to the text by showing the book and saying, "Well, in this book we're going to read about some rats. Let's see how similar the rats in the story are to the ones you've just described from your experience." Then she explained to the students that prior to reading the book, they would see a video, *The Secret of NIMH.*

After watching the video, Miss Paige showed a transparency listing ten key terms from the story that she was certain the students did not understand. As she pointed to each word, she asked the class if they knew what the word meant. At least one student knew the meaning of two of the ten vocabulary terms, indicating that Miss Paige had done an adequate job of selecting key

FIGURE 3.3   Building Background Section of the SIOP: Miss Paige

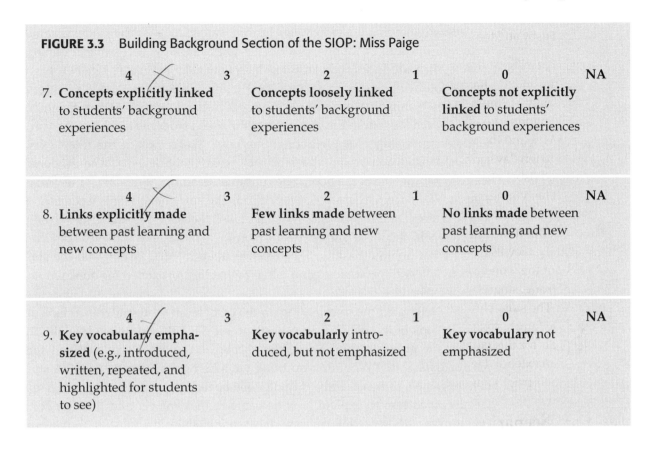

4	3	2	1	0	NA
7. **Concepts explicitly linked** to students' background experiences		**Concepts loosely linked** to students' background experiences		**Concepts not explicitly linked** to students' background experiences	

4	3	2	1	0	NA
8. **Links explicitly made** between past learning and new concepts		**Few links made** between past learning and new concepts		**No links made** between past learning and new concepts	

4	3	2	1	0	NA
9. **Key vocabulary emphasized** (e.g., introduced, written, repeated, and highlighted for students to see)		**Key vocabularly** introduced, but not emphasized		**Key vocabulary** not emphasized	

vocabulary words for which the students needed direct instruction. She discussed each term and wrote a brief definition next to the word on the transparency. Next, Miss Paige began reading the first chapter of the book with her students. While reading chapters in the book throughout the course of the unit, she made it a practice to pause every few paragraphs to check for understanding, elaborate, define words, and paraphrase parts of the story. Occasionally she reminded students of something they had discussed in another lesson. For example, when Mrs. Frisby is described as a widow, Miss Paige said, "Who remembers what a widow is? We talked about that word when we read *The Witches* by Roald Dahl. Remember the grandma who was a widow? What does that mean?" Then Miss Paige wrote the word on a piece of chart paper that she continued to use as a Word Wall throughout the unit, adding words the students identified as unfamiliar throughout the course of the unit.

On the SIOP form in Figure 3.3, rate Miss Paige for each of the Building Background indicators.

Mrs. Jarmin

At the beginning of the first lesson of the unit, Mrs. Jarmin began by telling the class that they would be reading an interesting book in which the main characters were rats. Then Mrs. Jarmin asked, "Who has ever seen a rat?" Several students told of their experiences seeing rats or having them as pets. Then Mrs. Jarmin told the class that they would see a video based on the novel, *Mrs. Frisby and the Rats of NIMH,* and that they would read the book after seeing the video.

Before showing the video, Mrs. Jarmin wanted to teach the students some terms they would encounter during the unit. Working with small, rotating groups, she introduced reciprocal teaching (Palinscar & Brown, 1984) by posting the following words on a chart: "predicting," "clarifying," and "questioning." Mrs. Jarmin distributed three index cards that described each of the three terms to each student in the group. First she asked students to look at the card that gave guidelines for predicting. She read, "Let's look at the title." Mrs. Jarmin paused and asked the students what the title was. The students showed her the title of the book. She continued reading, "Look at all the visual clues on the page." Again she stopped to make sure the students understood and she asked the meaning of "visual clues." Because the students weren't sure, she told them the phrase means pictures, graphs, and the like. Then she read, "What do you think we'll be reading about?" Mrs. Jarmin told the students to follow the guidelines and tell her what they predicted the book would be about. (See Figure 3.4.)

She reiterated the information on the card, telling the students to look at the title, look at the pictures, and think about what they'd be reading about. She left the group to think while she checked on another group. When she returned she said, "What do you think we'll be reading about? I. . . ." A student began his sentence with, "I think we'll be reading about some rats." Mrs. Jarmin asked him to explain how he came to that answer and then replied, "Good. Who has more information they want to share?" One student made a comment about the mice. The teacher wrote the words "mice" and "rats" on the board and asked what the story would be about. Some students seemed confused about those words so the teacher asked them to look at the title. They

FIGURE 3.4 Activity Based on *Reciprocal Teaching* (Palinscar and Brown, 1984)

Predicting

Let's look at the title. Look at all the visual clues on the page. What do you think we'll be reading about?

Clarifying

One of the words I wasn't sure about was _____.

Questioning

What is the story about?

had a brief discussion about how mice and rats differ. Once the distinction was made, they moved on to the card about clarifying.

Mrs. Jarmin read, "One of the words I wasn't sure about was _____." She then distributed a photocopy of the summary of the story to the students and told them to use a highlighter to identify the words they didn't understand. The teacher circulated among other groups as the students read the summary and highlighted unfamiliar words. When she returned, she asked the students to tell her their highlighted words as she wrote them on the board. She said, "Let's see if there are other words that can be used in place of the highlighted words. We'll see which words we already know and the ones we don't know we'll look up in the thesaurus. A thesaurus is a book that is like a dictionary that helps us clarify words." The words the students didn't know were:

Vocabulary Word List

NIMH–   a place

Scarce–   _____

Asparagus–   a vegetable

Frail–   _____

Abandoned– left behind

The group went through the list, with Mrs. Jarmin asking if anyone knew the meaning of the words. One student recognized that NIMH is the name of a place and that asparagus is a vegetable, so the teacher wrote those definitions beside the words. Since nobody knew the meaning of "frail" and "scarce," Mrs. Jarmin drew a line, indicating that the students would find those words in the thesaurus. Then the students looked up each word together. The first student to find the word called out to the others the page number on which the word was found. As a group, the students decided on a word or two to denote meaning. When they finished defining all the words, the teacher drew their attention to the final card about questioning. She read, "What is the story about?" and said, "Now that we have made some predictions about the story and we've clarified some terms, what do you think this story will be about?"

The students were now familiar with making predictions about a story and knew one way to clarify words they didn't understand. So, before starting the video, Mrs. Jarmin showed a transparency on the overhead projector that listed ten words she identified as key vocabulary. Each group of students was asked to look up two of the words in their thesaurus. The class discussed the definitions that the students read and Mrs. Jarmin wrote a short definition next to each word on the overhead. She then told the students to copy the words on a piece of paper and to put a check next to each word as they heard it while watching the video. At the conclusion of the video, she asked students which vocabulary words they had heard and marked. Mrs. Jarmin wrote those words on a Word Wall and then reviewed with the class the meaning of each word, providing synonyms and drawing a picture, if necessary, to convey meaning as they had done in the clarifying exercise. (The Word Wall remained posted throughout the reading of the novel and Mrs. Jarmin often drew students' attention to one of the posted words as they came across it in the text.)

After viewing the video, Mrs. Jarmin and the class began reading the story. Mrs. Jarmin paused after the first chapter and brought out a Venn diagram from an earlier lesson that illustrated the way fiction and fantasy are similar, although not all fiction involves fantasy. She asked the students how they would describe this story so far, as fiction or as fantasy. Looking at the descriptors listed on the Venn diagram, they decided the story was fantasy. Mrs. Jarmin then told the students that, especially because fantasy can sometimes be confusing, they would construct a graphic organizer as they proceeded through the story to keep track of the characters, as well as to provide visual clues for plot events and vocabulary in the story. She asked students to think of words to describe the characters Timothy, Martin, Cynthia, Teresa, and Mrs. Frisby, from the first chapter. As students mentioned adjectives describing the characters, Mrs. Jarmin began writing them on chart paper as a graphic organizer.

Mrs. Jarmin and the class continued this same type of process until they had completed the novel.

On the SIOP form in Figure 3.5, rate Mrs. Jarmin on each of the Building Background indicators.

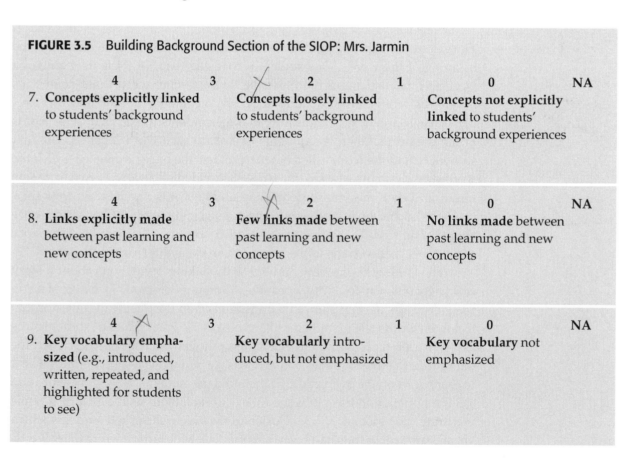

FIGURE 3.5 Building Background Section of the SIOP: Mrs. Jarmin

4	3	2	1	0	NA
7. **Concepts explicitly linked** to students' background experiences		**Concepts loosely linked** to students' background experiences		**Concepts not explicitly linked** to students' background experiences	

4	3	2	1	0	NA
8. **Links explicitly made** between past learning and new concepts		**Few links made** between past learning and new concepts		**No links made** between past learning and new concepts	

4	3	2	1	0	NA
9. **Key vocabulary emphasized** (e.g., introduced, written, repeated, and highlighted for students to see)		**Key vocabularly introduced, but not emphasized**		**Key vocabulary not emphasized**	

Mr. Ramirez

Mr. Ramirez began the first lesson of the unit by distributing the text to the students. He asked what the students thought the book would be about and they suggested that it would be something about rats. He told them that they would first watch a video based on the book before actually reading the text. He gave an oral summary of the video to provide some background before showing it. He showed the video, then told the students they would begin reading the book the next day.

Mr. Ramirez began the second day's lesson by writing (twenty) vocabulary terms on the board. He told the students that they were to copy each term in their notebooks and look up the definition of each term in the dictionary. The students spent the second day completing this activity. Most students worked independently, although sometimes they would ask a friend for help.

The third day of the unit Mr. Ramirez read the first chapter with the students. While reading, he asked a number of comprehension questions, cleared up one student's confusion about which character was ill, and reviewed the chapter completely after reading it with the students. He continued this process throughout the book. At the conclusion of the unit, he gave the class an exam to check their understanding.

On the SIOP form in Figure 3.6, rate Mr. Ramirez on each of the Building Background indicators.

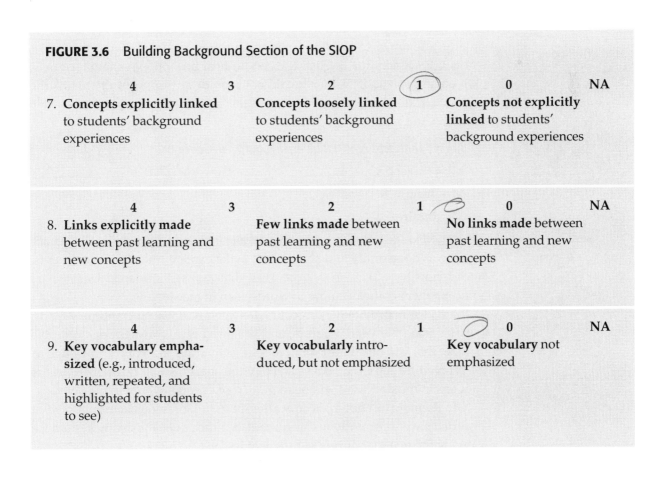

FIGURE 3.6 Building Background Section of the SIOP

4	3	2	1	0	NA
7. **Concepts explicitly linked** to students' background experiences		**Concepts loosely linked** to students' background experiences		**Concepts not explicitly linked** to students' background experiences	

4	3	2	1	0	NA
8. **Links explicitly made** between past learning and new concepts		**Few links made** between past learning and new concepts		**No links made** between past learning and new concepts	

4	3	2	1	0	NA
9. **Key vocabulary emphasized** (e.g., introduced, written, repeated, and highlighted for students to see)		**Key vocabularly introduced**, but not emphasized		**Key vocabulary** not emphasized	

Discussion of Lessons

7.   *Concepts Linked to Background*

Miss Paige: 4

Mrs. Jarmin: 2

Mr. Ramirez: 1

Miss Paige received a "4" on the SIOP for this indicator. She spent time eliciting students' background knowledge about rats, creating an interest level that would facilitate learning. A novel such as *Mrs. Frisby and the Rats of NIMH* may be difficult for English learners to understand, yet by linking the topic to their own experiences the teacher helped to enhance student comprehension.

Mrs. Jarmin received a "2" on the SIOP for this indicator. She made an effort to activate the students' prior knowledge but it was not done in an explicit or systematic way. While Miss Paige organized the information using a semantic map for students to see and make reference to later, Mrs. Jarmin merely conducted a verbal discussion of a few students' experiences. English learners benefit from visual clues given during a discussion and Mrs. Jarmin did not provide any visual assistance for those learners with limited English proficiency. Further, she did not organize the information in a useful way that would make the information accessible and meaningful to all the students in class.

Mr. Ramirez received a "1" on the SIOP for this indicator. Although the video did provide background information for the students, Mr. Ramirez did not provide students with an adequate introduction to the video or the book. While he attempted to provide some background before showing the video, there is little benefit for English learners to hear an oral explanation of new, unknown information. Further, he did not provide any opportunity to link the students' background or experiences to the unit by tapping into what they already knew.

8.   *Links Made between Past Learning and New Concepts*

Miss Paige: 2

Mrs. Jarmin: 4

Mr. Ramirez: 0

Although Miss Paige made a few links between past learning and new vocabulary, it was done orally and she did not make explicit links to new concepts. She did, however, develop a Word Wall that assisted students' learning by reminding them of the meaning of words used in the story.

Mrs. Jarmin provided a direct link between past learning and new learning by showing the Venn diagram, and she also began constructing a graphic organizer that will be an important tool for activating students' knowledge as they proceed through the book. Each day the students will be oriented to the characters in the story, and will be reminded of events covered in the book.

Mr. Ramirez did not make any attempt to link previous learning to what the students were currently reading about, nor did he establish any system for reviewing the material during subsequent lessons.

9. *Key Vocabulary*

Miss Paige: 1

Mrs. Jarmin: 4

Mr. Ramirez : 0

Although Miss Paige wrote on a transparency a number of key vocabulary terms and discussed them, there was no further reference to the list nor did she have students copy the list for their own reference. It became a vocabulary building activity done in isolation of any context, rendering it less effective than if she had used the transparency throughout the unit, reviewing and repeating the words, and having them available for students to see.

Mrs. Jarmin took time to introduce students not only to the story and associated vocabulary, but also to ways of "doing school." The introduction took only fifteen minutes or so, and it presented some valuable skills that are required in school, but not always explicitly taught. Also, she made new vocabulary words meaningful by defining terms before watching the video, then asking students to identify the terms within the context of the video. The words were written, posted, and referred to frequently. In this way, the key vocabulary terms became an integral part of the unit.

Mr. Ramirez did a poor job of developing students' vocabulary in any authentic way. First, rather than selecting a manageable number of key terms, he simply selected twenty words he assumed the students didn't know. He didn't discuss the terms with the students or support their understanding of new vocabulary. Given these students' low literacy and English proficiency levels, an optimal number of new terms would range from five to twelve. The large number of terms, coupled with the vocabulary contained within the definitions, becomes overwhelming. Secondly, considering the students' academic and English proficiency levels, copying terms from the board and looking up their definitions in the dictionary is not very meaningful. Frequently this type of exercise results in papers filled with misspelled words and incomplete sentences since the majority of words—both the vocabulary terms and their definitions—are unfamiliar to these students. Finally, the more decontextualized the activity, the more problematic learning becomes. That is, the more directly related the activity is to the learning objective, the more likely it is that student learning will take place. In this lesson, the activity was not closely aligned to the context of the story. Both the vocabulary terms and their multiple definitions were unfamiliar to the students, as was the formal lexicon of the dictionary that was supposed to clarify the terms. The activity, although probably well-intentioned, had little or no meaning for these students.

Summary

The importance of building background has been well established and is one of the easier components of the SIOP to incorporate into teaching. Taking a few minutes to jump-start students' schema, finding out what they know or have experienced about a topic, and linking their knowledge directly to the lesson's objective will result in greater understanding for English learners. Finally, the scenarios presented in this chapter demonstrate the importance of developing students' vocabulary in meaningful ways. The traditional approach of copying words and writing their definitions is less effective than preteaching key words, highlighting them in context, and using some type of visual to provide repeated exposure to those key words.

Discussion Questions

1. Some educators argue the importance of connecting new information to English language learners' own cultural backgrounds in order to make content concepts meaningful. Others disagree, stating that students relate more to popular American influences (e.g., "adolescent culture") than they do to their parents' traditional cultural practices. What are some merits and problems with both positions? What about ELs born in the United States who have never lived in their native cultural setting?

2. Reflect on how you learn new vocabulary. In what settings and around which people are you most comfortable using the new word(s)? What happens if you don't frequently use the word(s)? What are the implications of this process of learning new words to teaching key vocabulary to ELs?

3. Was the concept of developing "school language" a new idea to you? Discuss the importance of explicitly teaching school language to English language learners, and give specific examples of the kinds of terminology teachers frequently assume students know. Draw from the language of classroom routines and the language of specific subjects.

4. Think about a joke or cartoon that you didn't understand, such as from a late-show monologue or a political cartoon. Why was it confusing or unamusing? What information would you have needed for it to make sense? What are the implications for teaching content to all students, including English language learners?

4 Comprehensible Input

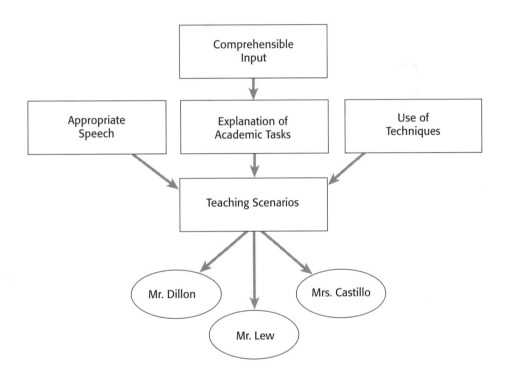

OBJECTIVES

After reading, discussing, and engaging in activities related to this chapter, you will be able to meet the following content and language objectives.

Content Objectives:

Explore techniques for presenting content information in ways that students comprehend

Review various ways to model and provide directions for academic tasks

Language Objectives:

Give examples of modifications to teacher speech that can increase student comprehension

Identify the language needed for students to perform academic tasks and techniques to introduce that language to students

This section of the SIOP reflects one of the components that distinguishes effective sheltered instruction from high-quality nonsheltered instruction. As you have seen in the SIOP items discussed so far, it is true that sheltered instruction shares many of the features of high-quality nonsheltered instruction. However, an effective sheltered teacher takes into account the unique characteristics of English learners. For these students, the teacher makes verbal communication more understandable by consciously attending to students' linguistic needs. Making adjustments to speech so that the message to the student is understandable is referred to as *comprehensible input* (Krashen, 1985). Comprehensible input is important and should be measured throughout the lesson to ensure that students are taking in and understanding what is being communicated to them.

Background

One way that communication is made more understandable is by using speech that is appropriate to students' proficiency levels. The teacher enunciates and speaks more slowly, but in a natural way, for students who are beginning English speakers. More repetition may be needed for beginners and, as students gain more proficiency in English, the teacher adjusts her speech for the students' levels.

These linguistic modifications are made in concert with a variety of techniques that make the message clear. The teacher also avoids jargon and idiomatic speech as much as possible. Effective sheltered teachers use gestures, body language, pictures, and real objects to accompany their words; for example, when saying, "We're going to learn about the three forms of water," the teacher holds up three fingers. Showing one finger she says, "One form is liquid," and shows a glass of water. Holding up two fingers she says, "the second form is ice," and shows an ice cube. Holding up three fingers she says, "and the third form is steam," and shows a picture of a steaming cup of coffee. These simple gestures and visual aids assist students in organizing and making sense of information that is presented verbally.

Another technique that facilitates English learners' comprehension of the message is to provide a model of a process or of what is expected of students. For example, as the teacher discusses the process of water taking on the form of ice, she shows or draws a model of the process as it is being described. When students are later instructed to record conditions under which the change in ice from a solid to a liquid is accelerated or slowed, the teacher shows an observation sheet that is divided into three columns on the overhead projector. The teacher has a number of pictures (e.g., lamp, sun, and refrigerator), which depict various conditions such as heat and cold. She demonstrates the first condition, heat, with a picture of the sun. She models how students will describe the condition in the first column (e.g., _____ heats). Then she asks students what effect the sun, or heat, has on ice. They answer and in the second column she records how the ice changed (e.g., _____ melted), and in the third column she indicates if the process was accelerated or slowed by the condition (e.g., _____ *accelerated*). Providing a model as the students are taken through the task verbally eliminates ambiguity and gives the message in more than one way. Students are then able to complete the rest of the worksheet.

Hands-on activities provide students with an alternative form of expressing their understanding of information and concepts. Oftentimes ELs have learned the lesson's information but have difficulty expressing their understanding in English, either orally or in writing. Further, hands-on activities can be used to reinforce the concepts and information presented, with a reduced linguistic demand on these students.

As mentioned in Chapter 3, vocabulary development is critical for English language learners. There is a correlation between vocabulary development and academic achievement, so it behooves SI teachers to present content vocabulary to students in a way that can be comprehended and retained.

In the scenarios that follow later in the chapter, you will see examples of teachers who use comprehensible input strategies to varying degrees of effectiveness.

Appropriate Speech for ELs

For this item, speech refers to (1) rate and enunciation and (2) complexity of speech. The first aspect addresses *how* the teacher speaks and the second aspect refers to *what* is said, such as level of vocabulary used, complexity of sentence structure, and use of idioms.

Students who are at the beginning levels of English proficiency benefit from teachers who slow down their rate of speech and enunciate clearly while speaking. As students become more comfortable with the language and acquire higher levels of proficiency, a slower rate isn't as necessary. In fact, for advanced and transitional students, teachers should use a rate of speech that is normal for a regular classroom. Effective sheltered teachers adjust their rate of speech and enunciation to their students' levels of English proficiency.

Also, sheltered teachers carefully monitor the vocabulary and sentence structure they use with ELs in order to match the students' proficiency levels, especially with students at beginning levels of English proficiency. Idioms—sayings that cannot be translated exactly such as, "He's gone head over heels for her"—creates difficulty for students who are trying to make sense of a new language. English learners are better served when teachers use language that is straightforward and clear, and is accompanied by a visual representation. Paraphrasing and repetition are useful techniques. Cognates are often useful in promoting comprehension for students whose native language has a Latin base. For example, using "calculate the mass/volume ratio" (*calcular* in Spanish) may be easier for some students to understand than "figure out the mass/volume ratio." Furthermore, teachers should use simple sentence structures like subject–verb–object with beginning students and reduce or eliminate embedded clauses.

Explanation of Academic Tasks

English learners at all levels (and native English speakers) perform better in academic situations when the teacher gives clear instructions for assignments and activities. The more practice students have with the types of tasks found in content classes, the better prepared they will be when they exit the language support program. It is critical for ELs to have instructions presented in a step-by-step manner, preferably accompanied by a visual representation or demonstration of what is expected. Oral directions should always be accompanied by written ones so ELs can refer to them in the future. According to case study data collected from ELs in sheltered classes (Echevarria, 1998), teachers *do* present information differently to students. The following are some student comments:

- "She doesn't explain it too good. I don't understand the words she's saying because I don't even know what they mean."
- "She talks too fast. I don't understand the directions."
- "He talks too fast. Not patient."
- "It helps when he comes close to my desk and explains stuff in the order that I have to do it."

These students' comments illustrate the importance of providing a clear explanation of teachers' expectations for lessons, including delineating the steps of academic tasks. This point cannot be overstated. In our observations of classes, many "behavior problems" are often the result of students not being sure what they are supposed to do. A cursory oral explanation of an assignment can leave many students without a clue as to what to do to get started. The teacher, frustrated with all the chatter, scolds students, exhorting them to get to work. However, students do not know *how* to get to work and oftentimes do not know how to articulate that fact to the teacher.

Use of Techniques

Effective SI teachers make content concepts clear and understandable for English learners through the use of a variety of techniques that make content comprehensible. We have observed some teachers who teach the same way for English learners as they do for native English speakers, except that they use pictures for ELs. We believe that the actual teaching techniques a teacher uses have a greater impact on student achievement than having a lot of pictures illustrating content concepts. High-quality sheltered lessons offer students a variety of ways for making the content accessible to them. Although it might be impossible for teachers to present a variety of interesting hands-on lessons that include visuals to illustrate every concept and idea in the curriculum each period of every day, there does need to be sufficient planning to incorporate such techniques and activities throughout the week's lessons.

The techniques we suggest in the SIOP are critical for providing meaningful, understandable lessons to students learning English, including adapting the content to students' proficiency levels (Chapter 2); highlighting key vocabulary (Chapter 3); using scaffolding techniques and providing opportunities for students to use strategies (Chapter 5); and providing activities that allow students to apply newly acquired content and language knowledge (Chapter 7).

Many ESL techniques are applicable to content classrooms with slight modifications. For example, use of sentence strips, a common technique to review events in a story, can be applied in science to sequence steps in an experiment. Several resources offer teachers techniques for integrating language and content instruction and are suited for the SIOP model (e.g., Brinton & Master, 1997; Chamot & O'Malley, 1994; McLaughlin & Vogt, 2000; Short, 1991).

Teachers should also use multimedia and other technologies in their lessons as well. Teachers may use overhead transparencies, Powerpoint slides, or relevant websites as supplements to a presentation. In so doing, they not only provide more visual support but also model the use of the technology.

Unit: Buoyancy (9th grade)

The following lessons take place in an urban high school where English learners comprise 35 percent of the school population. In the classrooms described, all the students are beginning to advanced-beginning speakers of English, and they have varying levels of literacy in their native languages.

Ninth-grade teachers Mr. Dillon, Mr. Lew, and Mrs. Castillo are all teaching a unit on *buoyancy,* the ability to float. The science standard that each of the three teachers is teaching requires that students understand why some objects float while others sink. In addition, they review the concepts of *mass,* which is a quantity of matter of nonspecific shape, and *volume,* which is the capacity of a three-dimensional object. The goal is for students to understand that an object will float as long as the mass doesn't exceed the object's capacity, or volume. Students have calculated mass/volume ratios previous to this unit, although the application of these concepts to buoyancy is new. You will see in the scenarios that the teachers have their own way of helping students understand that an object's ability to float is based on its mass/volume ratio.

Teaching Scenarios

Mr. Dillon

Mr. Dillon began the lesson by having students open their science texts to the chapter on buoyancy. He told them that in this unit they would learn what makes objects buoyant. He gave a five-minute oral introduction to the concepts behind buoyancy, discussing the fact that if the object's mass exceeds its volume, then it will sink. Mr. Dillon used his normal, somewhat rapid manner, the same speaking style he used with all his classes. He then directed the students' attention to 13 vocabulary terms written on the board and told the class to copy each word, look up the definition in the glossary, and copy the definition onto their papers. After students looked up vocabulary words in the glossary, Mr. Dillon asked them to put the papers in their homework folders. He told them that they needed to take the words home and their homework assignment was to use each word in a sentence. He emphasized that students needed to complete their homework since he had been frustrated by low homework response rates in this class.

Then Mr. Dillon turned to the science text, telling students to open their books to the beginning of the chapter. He proceeded to lecture from the text, asking students questions to stimulate a class discussion. Most students were reluctant to speak up. After lecturing on the material in the first five pages of the text, Mr. Dillon gave students a worksheet about buoyancy. He told them they could work in pairs or alone, calculating the mass/volume ratio of the objects shown on the worksheet. He said, "You remember how to calculate mass/volume ratios? First you determine the volume of the object, and then you take the mass and divide it by the volume. Ok, just calculate the ratios for each object shown on the worksheet, and when you finish, you may begin doing your homework."

After the class completed the worksheet for calculating mass/volume ratios, Mr. Dillon went over the answers as a whole group. He began by demonstrating how to calculate the first problem. He wrote the numbers on the overhead and went through the process. When he finished he said, "If you got the same answer as I did, raise your hand." About half of the students raised their hands. Mr. Dillon determined that he needed to demonstrate a few more problems so that more students would understand the process. He continued with the next three problems, asking students what they did differently.

Finally, he told the class to work in pairs to review their work, checking the final problems against the process he demonstrated.

On the SIOP form in Figure 4.1, rate Mr. Dillon on each of the Comprehensible Input indicators.

Mr. Lew

As Mr. Lew began the lesson, he drew students' attention to the objective written on the board and told students that the purpose of the unit was to understand why some objects float and others sink. As he said the word "float," he

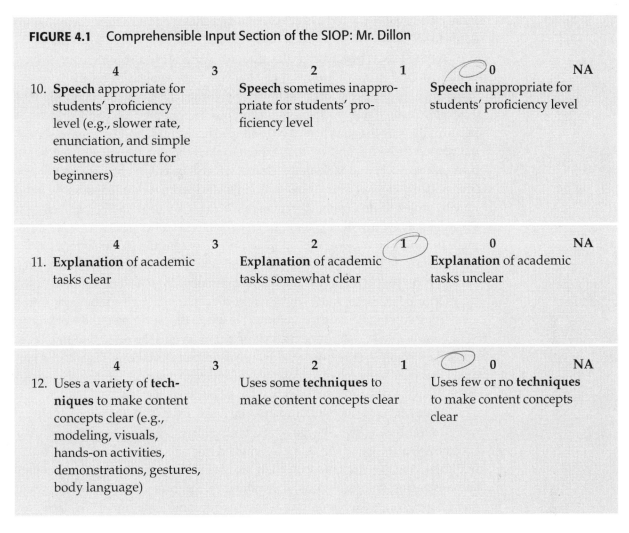

FIGURE 4.1   Comprehensible Input Section of the SIOP: Mr. Dillon

4	3	2	1	0	NA
10. **Speech** appropriate for students' proficiency level (e.g., slower rate, enunciation, and simple sentence structure for beginners)		**Speech** sometimes inappropriate for students' proficiency level		**Speech** inappropriate for students' proficiency level	

4	3	2	1	0	NA
11. **Explanation** of academic tasks clear		**Explanation** of academic tasks somewhat clear	*(1)*	**Explanation** of academic tasks unclear	

4	3	2	1	0	NA
12. Uses a variety of **techniques** to make content concepts clear (e.g., modeling, visuals, hands-on activities, demonstrations, gestures, body language)		Uses some **techniques** to make content concepts clear		Uses few or no **techniques** to make content concepts clear	

demonstr pointed at an orange floating in the aquarium at the front of the room, and as he said the word "sink," he dropped a peeled orange into the water, which sank to the bottom. Then he repeated while pointing at the corresponding object, "Some things float and others sink." He went on to tell the students that at the end of the unit they would be able to calculate and predict whether something has buoyancy. The words, "float," "sink," "calculate," "predict," and "buoyant" were written in the Word Bank for students to see. The word list included content vocabulary (buoyant, float, and sink) as well as functional language (calculate and predict). Since many of Mr. Lew's students were recent immigrants and had gaps in their educational backgrounds, Mr. Lew was careful to make sure students not only knew the meaning of content vocabulary, but also knew the meaning of words associated with academic tasks, such as predict and calculate.

Throughout the lesson, Mr. Lew used language structures and vocabulary that he believed the students could understand at their level of proficiency. He spoke slowly, often contextualizing vocabulary words, and enunciated clearly. Also, he avoided the use of idioms, and when he sensed that students did not understand him, he paraphrased to convey the meaning more clearly. He repeated important words frequently and wrote them for students to see.

As the lesson progressed, the students were told to complete an activity while working in small groups. Mr. Lew was very explicit in his instructions. As he gave students instructions orally, he wrote each step on the overhead projector. He said, "First, you will get into your assigned groups and prepare to perform the role that has been assigned to you. Second, you will make shapes out of aluminum foil and try to get them to float (he put a small aluminum foil boat on the water and it floated). Third, you will calculate the object's volume (the students already know how to do this) and write it on the worksheet, and fourth, you will determine the maximum mass the boat will hold before it sinks. Finally, you will calculate the mass/volume ratio. You will write all of these numbers on the worksheet." Then Mr. Lew told the students to watch as he demonstrated. He took a piece of aluminum foil and shaped it into a long, narrow boat. He pointed to #2 on the transparency. Then he took the boat, filled its interior space with water and then poured the water from the boat into a measuring cup to calculate the volume. He wrote the amount on the worksheet. Mr. Lew went on to determine the maximum mass and the mass/volume ratio, writing each step on the overhead as he made the calculations. He told the students that they must make at least five different boat shapes during the experiment. He wrote the number 5 next to step #2 on the overhead.

After Mr. Lew showed students the steps for calculating mass/volume ratios described above, he gave students thirty seconds to get into their assigned group, get their items organized for the experiments, and begin working. Mr. Lew circulated through the classroom, supervising the students and answering their questions. After about five minutes, Mr. Lew determined that all the groups except one were clear about their assignment. To clarify for the other group, Mr. Lew drew that group's attention to another group that was doing well. He asked one student to stand and explain the steps of what they were doing. As the student talked, Mr. Lew pointed to the step-by-step instructions on the overhead projector. When the student finished explaining, Mr. Lew asked a volunteer from the confused group to explain what they were going to do.

After all groups had calculated at least five boats' mass/volume ratios, Mr. Lew showed a table on the overhead with columns for mass and volume figures. He asked students to pool their data by selecting two boats per group and reporting their mass and volume. A representative from each group wrote their figures in the appropriate columns on the overhead transparency. Then Mr. Lew told the class that they would use these data to construct a graph, plotting the maximum mass held by the boat on the y-axis and the boat's volume on the x-axis. Each student then plotted the mass to volume ratios on their individual graphs. At the end of the lesson, Mr. Lew asked the students to look at the objective written on the board and asked each student to write on his or her paper why some objects float and others sink.

On the SIOP form in Figure 4.2, rate Mr. Lew on each of the Comprehensible Input indicators.

FIGURE 4.2 Comprehensible Input Section of the SIOP: Mr. Lew

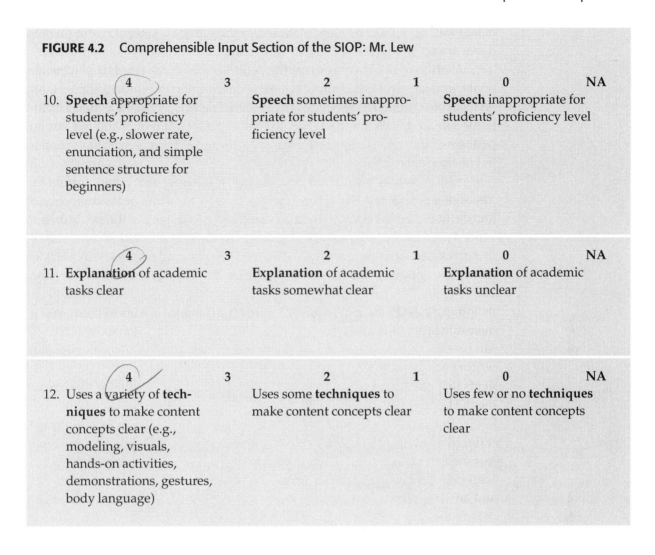

4	3	2	1	0	NA
10. **Speech** appropriate for students' proficiency level (e.g., slower rate, enunciation, and simple sentence structure for beginners)		**Speech** sometimes inappropriate for students' proficiency level		**Speech** inappropriate for students' proficiency level	
11. **Explanation** of academic tasks clear		**Explanation** of academic tasks somewhat clear		**Explanation** of academic tasks unclear	
12. Uses a variety of **techniques** to make content concepts clear (e.g., modeling, visuals, hands-on activities, demonstrations, gestures, body language)		Uses some **techniques** to make content concepts clear		Uses few or no **techniques** to make content concepts clear	

Mrs. Castillo

As is her practice, Mrs. Castillo wrote the objective, "Find the mass/volume ratio for objects that float," on the board. She began the lesson by discussing the fact that some things float and others sink, giving examples of objects that float, such as a large ship, and others that sink, such as a small coin. Then she asked the class if they knew what makes some objects float and others sink. A few students guessed, but nobody was able to give an accurate explanation. During the discussion, Mrs. Castillo's rate of speech was normal for her speech style, with a mix of both simple and slightly complex sentences. When the discussion was completed, she noticed that some of the students still seemed confused.

Mrs. Castillo told the students to read the first three pages of their text to themselves and stated that they would discuss it when they'd finished. After the students indicated that they were done reading, Mrs. Castillo asked students if there were any words in the text they did not know. Several students called out unfamiliar words, and the teacher wrote them on the overhead. Then she assigned students at each table a word to look up in the glossary. After several minutes, she asked the students what they had found. Only about half of the words were included in the glossary, since the other words were not science terms per se, but words such as "therefore," and "principle." Mrs. Castillo orally gave students the definitions of those words that were not in the glossary, and then summarized the information the students had read in the text. As she talked, she occasionally spoke rapidly, using long, detail-laden sentences in her summary. When she noticed that students were not paying attention, she slowed her rate of speech to make it understandable and to regain students' interest.

Mrs. Castillo continued the lesson following the same format as described previously. She asked students to read a portion of the text, paused to clarify unknown vocabulary, and summarized the part of the text students read. When they completed the chapter, Mrs. Castillo selected several end-of-chapter questions for students to answer. She let students work in pairs or groups to complete the questions, and then the class discussed the answers together.

On the SIOP form in Figure 4.3, rate Mrs. Castillo on each of the Comprehensible Input indicators.

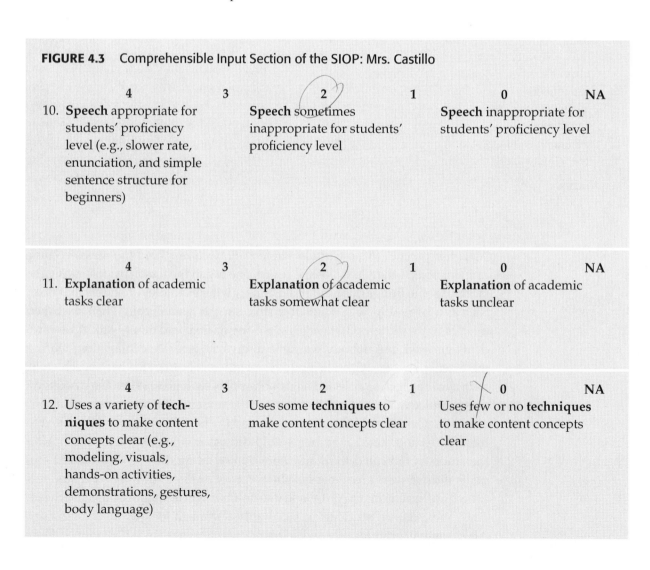

FIGURE 4.3   Comprehensible Input Section of the SIOP: Mrs. Castillo

4	3	2	1	0	NA
10. **Speech** appropriate for students' proficiency level (e.g., slower rate, enunciation, and simple sentence structure for beginners)		**Speech** sometimes inappropriate for students' proficiency level		**Speech** inappropriate for students' proficiency level	

4	3	2	1	0	NA
11. **Explanation** of academic tasks clear		**Explanation** of academic tasks somewhat clear		**Explanation** of academic tasks unclear	

4	3	2	1	0	NA
12. Uses a variety of **techniques** to make content concepts clear (e.g., modeling, visuals, hands-on activities, demonstrations, gestures, body language)		Uses some **techniques** to make content concepts clear		Uses few or no **techniques** to make content concepts clear	

Discussion of Lessons

10. *Speech Appropriate for Students' Proficiency Level
     (Rate and Complexity)*

     Mr. Dillon: 0

     Mr. Lew: 4

     Mrs. Castillo: 2

As you can see in the lesson descriptions, the teachers varied in their attention to the unique language needs of the English learners in their classes.

Mr. Dillon seemed unaware that his students would understand more if he adjusted his oral presentation to accommodate the proficiency levels of English learners in his class. He lectured about new, complex concepts without regard to his rate of speech or complexity of speech, variables that impact ELs' ability to comprehend information in class. Also, copying definitions for new terms and creating original sentences are inordinately difficult tasks for ELs. Unwittingly, Mr. Dillon set the students up for failure and then was frustrated by the low number of completed homework assignments. While he believed students chose not to complete assignments, in reality they *could not* complete the type of assignment he gave.

Mr. Dillon did not discuss the lesson content, or the class or homework assignments in any meaningful or understandable way for ELs. He thought that discussing the material in the chapter and asking questions during his lecture would make the concepts clear for his students, but the type of language he used did little to facilitate learning for them. His efforts were lost on the English learners who needed richer, comprehensible development of the lesson's concepts to understand the text or lecture. The few students who participated in the discussion gave Mr. Dillon the inaccurate impression that the class was following along.

Mr. Lew was the most attuned to the benefit of modulating his speech to make himself understood by the students. He slowed his rate of speech and enunciated clearly when he addressed beginning speakers; he adjusted his speech for the other, more proficient speakers of English. He used a natural speaking voice, but paid attention to his rate of speed and enunciation. Further, Mr. Lew adjusted the level of vocabulary and complexity of the sentences he used so that students could understand. Since most students were beginning English speakers, he selected words that were appropriate to their proficiency level. Although the science book highlighted nearly fifteen terms for the unit on buoyancy, Mr. Lew learned from experience that it is better for his students to learn a smaller number of vocabulary words thoroughly than to give superficial treatment to dozens of content-associated vocabulary. His students will be able to use and apply the selected words and their concepts since they have a complete understanding of their meaning.

Mrs. Castillo's rate of speech and enunciation vacillated between that used with native speakers and a rate that her students could understand. She didn't consistently adjust her speech (rate or complexity) to the variety of proficiency levels in the class. She was aware that her EL students needed extra attention in understanding the language, but she only addressed their needs by asking for unfamiliar vocabulary. She could have paraphrased, using simpler sentence structure, and she could have used synonyms for words that appeared too difficult for students to understand.

11. *Clear Explanation of Academic Tasks*

    Mr. Dillon: 1

    Mr. Lew: 4

    Mrs. Castillo: 1

Making your expectations crystal clear to students is one of the most important aspects of teaching, and when working with English learners, explicit, step-by-step directions can be critical to a lesson's success. It is difficult for almost any student to remember directions given only orally, and oral directions may be incomprehensible to many English learners. A lesson is sure to get off to a rocky start if students don't understand what they are expected to do. Written procedures provide students with a guide.

As an experienced teacher, Mr. Lew understood the value of being explicit in what he wanted the students to do. He walked them through each step of the buoyancy experiment, demonstrating what they were expected to do. When a group hadn't gotten started, he had other students model the steps of the assignment for the class, drawing their attention again to the instructions on the overhead. The effort that Mr. Lew put into making sure students knew what to do contributed to the success of the lesson and enhanced learning.

Mrs. Castillo, on the other hand, did not explain to the students what was expected during the lesson, although the expectation was inferred by the format she used: read material, discuss unknown terms, summarize material. Since Mrs. Castillo followed the same format whenever the class read from the text, the students knew what was expected, however uninteresting the format made the class.

Mr. Dillon had a tendency to be unclear about his expectations but then blamed the students for not completing work. It is obvious that he doesn't understand the importance of making sure students are given explicit instructions at their level of understanding. First, he made unsubstantiated assumptions about the students' knowledge and ability to complete tasks. He said, "You remember how to calculate mass/volume ratios? . . . Ok, just calculate the ratios for each object. . . ." and left them to work independently. Some student did not know how to calculate the ratios but were left on their own.

Second, while he did demonstrate how to calculate ratios, Mr. Dillon should have done that kind of demonstration *before* asking students to do it independently. Teaching is more effective when a good model is demonstrated prior to the exercise, rather than a post hoc review of student work, correcting their mistakes after completion. The process of explaining the assignment *after* students completed the worksheet was particularly confusing for the English learners in his class who struggled to make sense of the assignment, only to find out that they had calculated most of the problems incorrectly.

Third, Mr. Dillon did not make his expectations—for in-class assignments and for homework—clear by modeling and discussing what students were to do. He should have provided a step-by-step explanation of the academic tasks he asked the students to complete.

12. *Uses A Variety of Techniques*

Mr. Dillon: 2

Mr. Lew: 4

Mrs. Castillo: 0

Concepts become understandable when teachers use a variety of techniques, including modeling, demonstrations, visuals, and body language. Throughout his lesson, Mr. Lew did an excellent job of providing visuals through the use of the tanks and aluminum foil, as well as by using the overhead projector. Not only did he write the vocabulary and assignment for students to see, he consistently referred back to the visual information. In addition to providing a clear explanation of the assignment, this technique teaches students to use visual clues to gain understanding.

Also, Mr. Lew used graphing and writing effectively to review the concepts of the lesson. Notice that these academic tasks came after students were already familiar with the lesson's concepts, which increased the likelihood that students would be able to successfully complete the academic tasks.

Finally, students were able to apply their knowledge through the hands-on activity, making the concepts of mass, volume, and buoyancy tangible, and thus more understandable. Measuring a boat's actual volume and determining maximum mass by adding to the mass by hand makes the concepts come alive for students. Compare the benefit of this hands-on activity to the other scenarios where the students simply went through a paper-and-pencil task. Surely those students learned and remembered less about buoyancy and mass-to-volume ratios than did the students in Mr. Lew's class.

Mrs. Castillo is a compassionate teacher who is concerned about the academic success of the English learners in her class. Her effort to help ELs included clarifying unknown vocabulary (in a somewhat random fashion), paraphrasing or summarizing the chapter (done orally, without visuals or other contextual clues), reducing the number of end-of-chapter questions (done independently by students) and having the students work together in answering questions (with no systematic checks for understanding). Although she had good intentions and wanted her students to understand the concept of buoyancy, Mrs. Castillo did not use the kinds of techniques that facilitate conceptual understanding for these students.

The atmosphere in Mrs. Castillo' classroom was warm and nonthreatening for ELs. She chatted with students throughout the class, and showed genuine interest in their well-being. Although it is clear that she enjoys working with students from diverse cultural backgrounds, she needs to develop effective techniques and strategies to further students' learning. The lesson was presented almost entirely orally, which was difficult for the beginning English speakers in her class to follow. Having students read a portion of the text followed by her summary was a good idea, except that there were no techniques used to ensure students understood the text, which was likely too difficult for them to read independently. Also, she did not teach them the necessary skills so that eventually they could read texts on their own. The summary was given orally, which makes it likely that beginning English speakers got little understanding from it. Mrs. Castillo should have had a more structured approach to reading the text and discussing the concepts therein. Finally, she should have adjusted the number of questions students had to answer according to their ability level. The students worked diligently on the assignment because they liked Mrs. Castillo and wanted to please her, but they needed assistance in making the information meaningful—assistance beyond that which Mrs. Castillo provided.

Mr. Dillon attempted to use a number of techniques to make concepts clear, such as using the text as a basis for discussion, providing a worksheet that showed different sized boats and other objects, and some demonstration of the calculations. Also, he let students work in pairs to calculate the mass-to-volume ratios. However, Mr. Dillon should have used more visuals, modeled what he expected from the students *before* he asked them to work independently, and provided a hands-on activity for this lesson. Some lessons, like this one, lend themselves easily to hands-on activities, but Mr. Dillon did not take advantage of the opportunity.

Summary

English learners often report that teachers talk too fast and do not explain things well. We need to pay attention to these informants' comments, for they are our "customers." The effective SI teachers constantly modulate and adjust their speech when teaching English learners to ensure that the context is comprehensible. Concepts are taught using a variety of techniques, including modeling, gestures, hands-on activities, and demonstrations, so that students understand and learn the content material. Finally, effective sheltered teachers provide explanations of academic tasks in ways that make clear what students are expected to accomplish and that promote student success.

Discussion Questions

1. Have you recently been in a situation where you were not an "insider," and therefore you didn't understand what was being said? Compare that situation and your feelings about it to the use of jargon and idiomatic speech within classrooms where there are English learners. As a teacher, what can you do to make sure all students are able to follow a lecture or discussion?

2. It has been said that humans can "hold on" to no more than three oral directions at a time. Think of an academic task you might ask students to do and explain it clearly and simply in no more than three steps. What should you do if the task requires more than three steps?

3. Many times in classrooms, discipline problems can be attributed to students not knowing what they're supposed to be doing. What are some ways that a teacher can avoid having students confused about accomplishing academic tasks?

4. If you have traveled in another country, or if you are an English learner, reflect on difficulties you had in understanding basic and academic information. What are some techniques people used to try to communicate with you? What could people have done to make their messages more clear?

5 Strategies

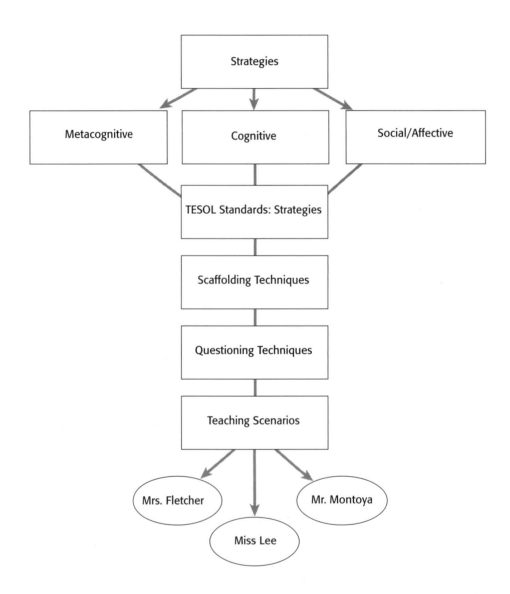

OBJECTIVES

After reading, discussing, and engaging in activities related to this chapter, you will be able to meet the following content and language objectives.

Content Objectives:

Select learning strategies appropriate to a lesson's objectives

Incorporate explicit instruction and student practice of metacognitive and cognitive strategies in lesson plans

Recognize the value of scaffolding instruction and identify techniques to scaffold for verbal, procedural, and instructional understanding

Language Objectives:

Identify language learning strategies to use with students

Discuss the importance of asking higher-order questions to students of all proficiency levels

Write a set of questions with increasing levels of difficulty on one topic

To this point, we have discussed elements of effective planning, background building, and content instruction for English learners (ELs). This chapter examines how we teach students to access information in memory, how we help them make connections between what they know and what they are learning, how we assist them in problem solving, and how we promote retention of newly learned information. This involves the explicit teaching of strategies that facilitate the learning process. Techniques and methods for learning and retaining information are systematically taught, reviewed, and assessed in effective sheltered classrooms.

The lessons on the tropical rain forest found later in this chapter illustrate how three seventh-grade science teachers incorporate the teaching of strategies into their classrooms.

Background

As introduced in Chapter 3, researchers have learned that information is retained and connected in the brain through "mental pathways" that are linked to an individual's existing schema (Anderson, 1984; Barnhardt, 1997). If the schemata for a particular topic are well developed and personally meaningful, new information is easier to retain and recall, and proficient learners initiate and activate their associations between the new and old learning.

In cognitive theory, this initiation and activation are described as the mental processes that enhance comprehension, learning, and retention of information. Competent language learners actively engage these cognitive skills, and researchers know these learners are effective, in part, because they have special ways of processing the new information they are learning. These mental processes are called *learning strategies* because they are "the special thoughts or behaviors that individuals use to help them comprehend, learn, or retain new information" (O'Malley & Chamot, 1990, p. 1).

Strategies

There is considerable evidence that teaching students a variety of self-regulating strategies improves student learning and reading (Fisher, Frey, & Williams, 2002; Pressley, 2000; Shearer, Ruddell, & Vogt, 2001; Slater & Horstman, 2002). Self-regulated learning "emphasizes autonomy and control by the individual who monitors, directs, and regulates actions toward goals of information acquisition, expanding expertise, and self-improvement" (Paris, 2001, p. 89).

Three types of learning strategies have been identified in the research literature (O'Malley & Chamot, 1990). These include:

1. **Metacognitive Strategies.** The process of purposefully monitoring our thinking is referred to as metacognition (Baker & Brown, 1984). Metacognition is characterized by (1) matching thinking and problem-solving strategies to particular learning situations, (2) clarifying purposes for learning, (3) monitoring one's own comprehension through self-questioning, and (4) taking corrective action if understanding fails (Dermody & Speaker, 1995). The use of metacognitive strategies implies awareness, reflection, and interaction; and strategies are used in an integrated, interrelated, and recursive manner (Dole, Duffy, Roehler, & Pearson, 1991; Pressley, 2000). Studies have found that when metacognitive strategies are taught explicitly, reading comprehension is improved (Duffy, 2002).

2. **Cognitive Strategies.** Along with metacognitive strategies, cognitive strategies help students organize the information they are expected to learn through the process of self-regulated learning (Paris, 2001). Cognitive strategies are directly related to individual learning tasks and are used by learners when they mentally and/or physically manipulate material, or when they apply a specific technique to a learning task (Pressley, Johnson, Symons, McGoldrick, & Kurita, 1989; Slater & Horstman, 2002). Previewing a story prior to reading, establishing a purpose for reading, consciously making connections between personal experiences and what is happening in a story, taking notes during a lecture, completing a graphic organizer, and creating a semantic map are all examples of cognitive strategies that learners use to enhance their understandings (McLaughlin & Allen, 2002a).

3. **Social/Affective Strategies.** These are identified in the research literature on cognitive psychology as the social and affective influences on learning (O'Malley & Chamot, 1990). For example, learning can be enhanced when people interact with each other to clarify a confusing point or when they participate in a group discussion or cooperative learning group to solve a problem.

In a somewhat different scheme, Muth and Alvermann (1999, p. 233) suggest there is a continuum of strategies that occurs during the teaching–learning process (see Figure 5.1)—from teacher-centered, teacher-assisted, peer-assisted, and student-centered.

FIGURE 5.1 Continuum of Strategies (Muth and Alvermann, 1999)

Teacher-Centered	*Teacher-Assisted*	*Peer-Assisted*	*Student-Centered*
Lecture	Drill and practice	Role playing	Rehearsal strategies
Direct instruction	Discovery learning	Peer tutoring	Repeated readings
Demonstration	Brainstorming	Reciprocal teaching	Selective underlining
Recitation	Discussion	Cooperative learning	Two-column notes
			Elaboration strategies
			Mental imagery
			Guided imagery
			Creating analogies
			Organizational strategies
			Clustering
			Graphic organizers
			Outlining

The ultimate goal is for students to develop independence in self-monitoring and self-regulation through practice with peer-assisted and student-centered strategies. Many English learners, however, have difficulty initiating an active role in using these strategies because they are focusing mental energy on their developing language skills. Therefore, SI teachers must scaffold ELs by providing many opportunities for them to use a variety of strategies that have been found to be especially effective.

ESL Standards and Strategies

The national ESL Standards for Pre-K–12 Students (TESOL, 1997) recognize the importance of EL's learning strategies. One standard for each of the three goals—to use English in social settings, to use English to achieve academically in all content areas, and to use English in socially and culturally appropriate ways—highlights strategic knowledge:

> **Goal 1, Standard 3:** Students will use learning strategies to extend their communicative competence.
>
> **Goal 2, Standard 3:** Students will use appropriate learning strategies to construct and apply their academic knowledge.
>
> **Goal 3, Standard 3:** Students will use appropriate learning strategies to extend their sociolinguistic and sociocultural competence.

The ESL Standards' document (TESOL, 1997) provides guidance to teachers in terms of the types of behaviors students should exhibit in order to meet the standards. Our interest relates primarily to Goal 2, Standard 3, which refers to academic achievement. The following are some suggested behaviors for teachers to foster:

- Focusing attention selectively; that is, focusing on the "big picture" and most important information
- Situating new learning in context; that is, building on what students already know and what is familiar
- Applying self-monitoring and self-corrective strategies to build and expand a knowledge base; that is, knowing how to "fix-it" when comprehension is impeded
- Evaluating one's own success in a completed learning task; that is, self-assessing one's competence and knowledge
- Recognizing the need for and seeking assistance appropriately from others
- Imitating the behaviors of native English speakers to complete tasks successfully
- Knowing when to use native language resources (human and material) to promote understanding (TESOL, 1997, p. 91).

Whatever strategies are emphasized, learned, and used, it is generally agreed that they should be taught through explicit instruction, careful modeling, and scaffolding (Duffy, 2002). Additionally, Lipson and Wixson (2003) suggest that teaching a variety of strategies is not enough. Rather, learners need not only *declarative* knowledge (What is a strategy?) but they also need *procedural* knowledge (How do I use it?), and *conditional* knowledge (When and why do I use it?). When teachers model strategy use and then provide appropriate scaffolding while children are practicing strategies, they are likely to become more effective strategy users (Fisher, Frey, & Williams, 2002; Pressley & Woloshyn, 1995).

When teaching strategies, effective sheltered teachers employ a variety of approaches, such as the following:

- **Mnemonics:** A memory system often involving visualization and/or acronyms
- **SQP2RS:** An instructional framework for teaching content with expository texts, that includes these steps (Vogt, 2000, 2002):
  1. **S**urveying (scanning the text to be read for 1–2 minutes)
  2. **Q**uestioning (having students generate questions likely to be answered by reading the text, with teacher guidance)
  3. **P**redicting (stating 1–3 things students think they will learn based on the questions that were generated)
  4. **R**eading (searching for answers to questions and confirming/disconfirming predictions)
  5. **R**esponding (answering questions and formulating new ones for the next section of text to be read)
  6. **S**ummarizing (orally or in writing summarizing the text's key concepts)
- **PENS:** Students are taught to **P**review ideas, **E**xplore words, **N**ote words in a complete sentence, and **S**ee if the sentence is okay (Deshler, Ellis, & Lenz, 1996).

- **GIST:** This summarization procedure assists students in "getting the gist" from extended text (Muth & Alvermann, 1999). Together, students and teacher read a section of text printed on a transparency. After reading, assist students in underlining ten or more words or concepts that are deemed "most important" to understanding the text. List these on the board and together write a summary statement or two using as many of the listed words as possible. Repeat the process through subsequent sections of the text. When finished, write a topic sentence to precede the summary sentences; the end result is a summary paragraph.
- **Rehearsal strategies:** Rehearsal is used when verbatim recall of information is needed (McCormick & Pressley, 1997; Muth & Alvermann, 1999). Visual aids, such as flashcards, engage students during rehearsal; and strategies, such as underlining and note-taking, help students commit information to memory.
- **Graphic organizers:** These are graphic representations of key concepts and vocabulary. Teachers present them as schematic diagrams of information being taught and students use them to organize the information they are learning. Barton, Heidama, & Jordan (2002) recommend the use of graphic organizers to help students comprehend math and science textbooks. Examples include Venn diagrams, timelines, flow charts, semantic maps, and so forth.
- **Comprehension strategies:** Dole, Duffy, Roehler, and Pearson (1991) recommend that students' comprehension of text is enhanced when teachers incorporate instruction that includes strategies such as prediction, self-questioning, monitoring, determining importance, and summarizing. These strategies were identified in what has come to be known as the "proficient reader research" because: (1) proficient readers use them in all kinds of text; (2) they can be taught; and (3) the more they are taught explicitly and practiced, the more likely students are to use them independently in their own reading. In their studies involving diverse readers, Keene and Zimmerman (1997) and Fisher, Frey, & Williams (2002) report that reading test scores can be elevated through scaffolded instruction of these and other similar strategies.

One of the most widely accepted methods for teaching strategies to English learners is the Cognitive Academic Language Learning Approach (CALLA) created by Chamot and O'Malley (1987, 1994). It is an instructional model for content and language learning that incorporates student development of learning strategies. Developed initially for intermediate and advanced ESL students in content-based ESL classes, it has had wider application over the years in sheltered classes as well. The CALLA method incorporates the three previously identified categories of learning strategies: metacognitive, cognitive, and socio-affective. Through carefully designed lesson plans tied to the content curriculum, teachers explicitly teach the learning strategies and have students apply them in instructional tasks. These plans are based on the following propositions (O'Malley & Chamot, 1990, p. 196):

1. Mentally active learners are better learners
2. Strategies can be taught
3. Learning strategies transfer to new tasks
4. Academic language learning is more effective with learning strategies

Scaffolding Techniques

Scaffolding is a term associated with Vygotsky's (1978) notion of the Zone of Proximal Development (ZPD). In essence, the ZPD is the difference between what a child can accomplish alone and what he or she can accomplish with the assistance of a more experienced individual. In the classroom, teachers scaffold instruction when they provide substantial amounts of support and assistance in the earliest stages of teaching a new concept or strategy, and then decrease the amount of support as the learners acquire experience through multiple practice opportunities (Vacca, 2000).

There are two types of scaffolding that can be used effectively with English learners. One is *verbal scaffolding,* in which teachers, aware of ELs' existing levels of language development, use prompting, questioning, and elaboration to facilitate students' movement to higher levels of language proficiency, comprehension, and thinking. Effective teacher–student interaction promotes confidence when it is geared to a student's language competence. The following are examples of verbal scaffolding:

- **Paraphrasing**—restating a student's response in order to model correct English usage
- **Using "think-alouds"**—carefully structured models of how effective strategy users think and monitor their understandings (Baumann, Jones, & Seifert-Kessell, 1993)
- **Reinforcing contextual definitions**—an example is: "Aborigines, the people native to Australia, were being forced from their homes." The phrase "the people native to Australia" provides a definition of the word "Aborigines," within the context of the sentence.

In addition to this important verbal scaffolding, effective teachers incorporate instructional approaches that provide *procedural scaffolding.* These include, but are not limited to, the following:

1. Using an instructional framework that includes explicit teaching, modeling, and practice opportunities with others, and expectations for independent application (see Figure 5.2)
2. One-on-one teaching, coaching, and modeling
3. Small group instruction with children practicing a newly learned strategy with another more experienced student (see Figure 5.3)
4. Partnering or grouping students for reading activities, with more experienced readers assisting those with less experience (Nagel, 2001)

FIGURE 5.2   Scaffolding Model: Teach, Model, Practice, Apply

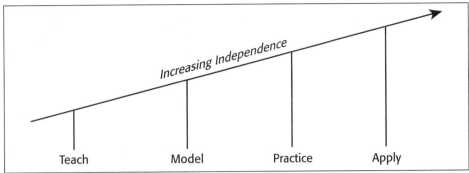

Increasing Independence

Teach   Model   Practice   Apply

FIGURE 5.3   Scaffolding Model: Grouping

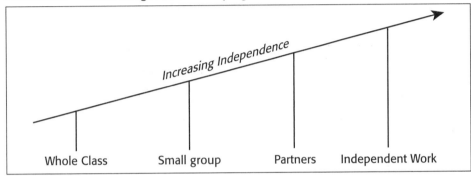

Increasing Independence

Whole Class   Small group   Partners   Independent Work

In addition, teachers can use *instructional scaffolding* to enhance student learning. For example, graphic organizers can be used as a prereading tool to prepare students for the content of a textbook chapter. The organizer can also be used to illustrate a chapter's text structure, such as comparative or chronological. Think of how the graphic organizers are used in this book and how they assist you in comprehending and organizing the text content.

Questioning

Another way that teachers can promote strategy use is by asking questions that promote critical thinking. More than 40 years ago, Bloom and colleagues (1956) introduced a taxonomy of educational objectives that includes six levels: Knowledge, Comprehension, Application, Analysis, Synthesis, Evaluation. This taxonomy was formulated on the principle that learning proceeds from concrete knowledge to abstract values, or from the denotative to the connotative (Nagel, Vogt, & Kaye, 1998). Educators adopted this taxonomy as a hierarchy of questioning that, when used in the classroom, elicits varied levels of student thinking. A similar hierarchy of comprehension collapsed the six levels into three, referred to as Literal, Interpretive, and Applied (Ruddell, 2001).

Over the years, teachers have been encouraged to vary the levels of oral and written questions with special attention to those at the top four levels of Bloom et al.'s taxonomy. However, researchers have found that of the approximately 80,000 questions the average teacher asks annually, 80 percent of them are at the Literal or Knowledge level (Gall, 1984; Watson & Young, 1986). This is especially problematic with English learners. As children are acquiring proficiency in English, it is tempting to rely on simple questions that result in yes/no or other one-word responses.

It is possible, however, to reduce the linguistic demands of responses while still promoting higher levels of thinking. For example, in a study of plant reproduction, the following question requires little thought: "Are seeds sometimes carried by the wind?" A nod or one-word response is almost automatic if the question is understood. A higher-level question such as the following requires analysis: "Which of these two seeds would be more likely to be carried by the wind: the round one or smooth one? Or this one that has fuzzy hairs?" Encouraging students to respond with higher levels of thinking requires teachers to consciously plan and incorporate questions at a variety of levels.

Teachers can also assist students in becoming strategic when they teach them how to determine levels of questions they are asked. For example, if a student recognizes that a question is at the literal level, he'll know the answer can be found right in the text. Similarly, if he identifies a question as inferential, he'll know he'll have to "read between the lines" to find the answer. This process has been named QAR (Question-Answer Relationships) (Raphael, 1984).

When students are able to determine levels of questions, they can be taught to ask their own questions of varying levels. This complements the goal of developing hypotheses using the scientific method, and it also benefits the research skills students must learn and practice. For example, Burke (2002) explains the importance of students writing their own research questions *before* they use the Internet to find information so that they "steer" rather than "surf" for answers.

Successful learners know how to use question-asking to help them construct meaning while they read. They ask questions and challenge what the author says if something does not make sense to them. Beck and McKeown (2002) recommend using the instructional approach, Questioning the Author (QtA), to develop students' comprehension of textbook material, which sometimes can be disjointed and lacking in connections between ideas and key concepts. QtA values the depth and quality of students' interactions with texts, and their responses to authors' intended meanings. It assists students in developing the ability to read text closely, as if the author were there to be questioned and challenged. We encourage you to learn more about both QAR and QtA in order to enhance your students' comprehension of text material, and to assist them in developing self-regulating strategies related to questioning.

The Lesson

The lesson described in this chapter is taken from a seventh grade unit on the tropical rain forest.

Unit: The Rain Forest (7th grade)

The three classrooms described in the teaching scenarios in this chapter are heterogeneously mixed with native English speakers and English learners who have intermediate fluency. The middle school is in a suburban community and Hispanic English learners comprise approximately 75 percent of the student population.

Mrs. Fletcher, Miss Lee, and Mr. Montoya are each teaching a unit on the tropical rain forest. They are all using the same article taken from a science news magazine designed for middle school students.

District content standards for seventh-grade science include the following guiding questions:

1. Where are the tropical rain forests on Earth?
2. Why are rain forests needed to support life on Earth?
3. What is the effect of the destruction of the rain forests?
4. What can we do to protect our rain forests?

The following teaching scenarios take place during the first day of the unit on the rain forest.

Teaching Scenarios

To demonstrate how Mrs. Fletcher, Miss Lee, and Mr. Montoya planned instruction for their students, including their English learners, we look at how each designed a lesson on the rain forest.

Mrs. Fletcher
Mrs. Fletcher began her lesson by distributing the rain forest article to the students and asking them to read the title, "Our Burning Forests," together. She then directed them to predict from the title and opening photograph what they thought the article would be about. One boy said, "It looks like the jungle." Another said, "I think it's about parrots." One of the girls responded, "I think it's about burning forests." Mrs. Fletcher then began reading the article, stopping once to ask the class, "What do you think will happen to the animals in

FIGURE 5.4 Strategies Section of the SIOP: Mrs. Fletcher

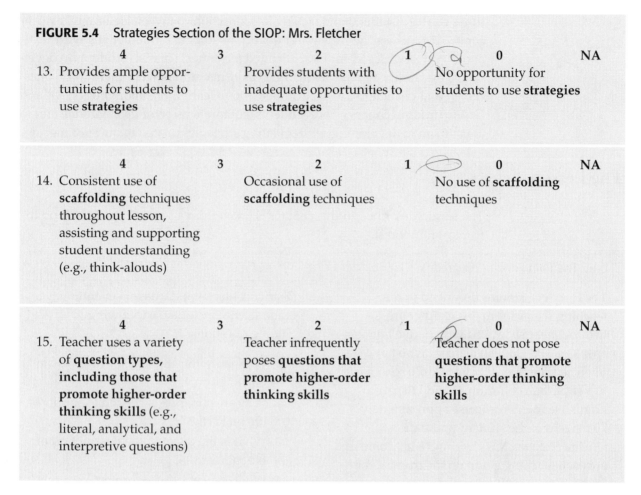

4	3	2	1	0	NA
13. Provides ample opportunities for students to use **strategies**		Provides students with inadequate opportunities to use **strategies**		No opportunity for students to use **strategies**	

4	3	2	1	0	NA
14. Consistent use of **scaffolding** techniques throughout lesson, assisting and supporting student understanding (e.g., think-alouds)		Occasional use of **scaffolding** techniques		No use of **scaffolding** techniques	

4	3	2	1	0	NA
15. Teacher uses a variety of **question types, including those that promote higher-order thinking skills** (e.g., literal, analytical, and interpretive questions)		Teacher infrequently poses **questions that promote higher-order thinking skills**		Teacher does not pose **questions that promote higher-order thinking skills**	

this rain forest?" When she had finished orally reading the article, she asked the students if they had any questions.

One of the children asked, "Why do people burn the rain forests if it's so bad?" Mrs. Fletcher replied that the wood is very valuable and people want to make money from the sale of it. Because there were no further questions, she asked each student to write a letter to the editor of the local newspaper explaining why we should save the rain forests. Several of the students began writing, while others re-read the article. A few appeared confused about how to start and Mrs. Fletcher helped them individually. When they had finished writing their letters, Mrs. Fletcher asked for volunteers to read their papers aloud. After a brief discussion of the letters, Mrs. Fletcher collected them and dismissed the students for lunch.

On the SIOP form in Figure 5.4, rate Mrs. Fletcher on each of the Strategies indicators.

Miss Lee

Miss Lee introduced the magazine article by presenting a brief lecture on the rain forest and by showing a variety of photographs. She then divided the students into groups of four and asked one person in each group to read the article to the other group members. When the students were finished reading,

no explanation on letter writing or what was/should be included

Miss Lee distributed worksheets. The children were instructed to independently write the answers to the following questions:

1. How much of the Earth's surface is covered by rain forests?
2. What percent of the Earth's species are found in the rain forest?
3. What are three products that come from the rain forests?
4. Why are the rain forests being burned or cut?
5. Who are the people who are doing the burning and cutting?
6. One of the birds found in the rain forest is a _____.
7. Global warming is believed to be caused by _____.
8. I hope the rain forests are not all cut down because _____ _____.

In addition to their rain forest article, Miss Lee encouraged students to use the class computers to search the Internet for the answers to these questions. She told them to type in "rain forest" on a search engine to begin their search.

When the students were finished writing their responses, they were to compare them to those of their group members. Miss Lee directed them to use the article to fix any answers the group thought were incorrect. She explained that they needed to come to agreement and record their group answer on a

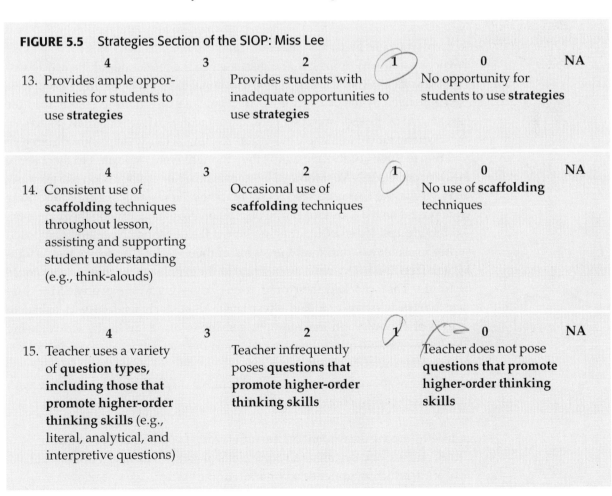

FIGURE 5.5 Strategies Section of the SIOP: Miss Lee

4	3	2	1	0	NA
13. Provides ample opportunities for students to use **strategies**		Provides students with inadequate opportunities to use **strategies**		No opportunity for students to use **strategies**	

4	3	2	1	0	NA
14. Consistent use of **scaffolding** techniques throughout lesson, assisting and supporting student understanding (e.g., think-alouds)		Occasional use of **scaffolding** techniques		No use of **scaffolding** techniques	

4	3	2	1	0	NA
15. Teacher uses a variety of **question types, including those that promote higher-order thinking skills** (e.g., literal, analytical, and interpretive questions)		Teacher infrequently poses **questions that promote higher-order thinking skills**		Teacher does not pose **questions that promote higher-order thinking skills**	

clean worksheet. For question #8, students were to decide which of the students' responses in their group was the best.

On the SIOP form in Figure 5.5, rate Mrs. Lee on each of the Strategies indicators.

Mr. Montoya

After distributing the magazine article on the tropical rain forest to his class, Mr. Montoya engaged his students in a SQP2RS activity (known as "Squeepers"). First, students were directed to preview and think about the article. He asked them to take one to two minutes individually, or with a partner, to preview the text material by examining illustrations, photographs, bold or italicized print, charts, and chapter questions (**Survey**). This was a familiar process for his students, and all engaged in the preview. After one minute, Mr. Montoya stopped the survey and directed the students to work with a partner to write three questions they thought they would find answers to by reading the article (**Question**). When finished, the partners shared their questions with the class, and from the questions, the class predicted five important things they thought they would learn from the article (**Predict**).

Mr. Montoya then read aloud the first section of the article while the students followed along in their copies of the text. After he had read four paragraphs, Mr. Montoya referred students to the list of predictions on the board. Next to each prediction that had been confirmed so far in the reading, a "+" was written, while one prediction that was disconfirmed was marked with a "–." One prediction that was unlikely to be discussed in the remainder of the article was marked with a question mark. A few additional questions and predictions were then generated by the class prior to Mr. Montoya's directions to quietly read the next section of the text (about six paragraphs) with a partner or a triad (**Read**).

When students finished the group reading activity, they were directed to find two to three vocabulary words they thought were important to the topic of the rain forest (VSS). Mr. Montoya led the class in a brief discussion of the vocabulary words and the class voted on ten that they felt were most important. These were posted on the board for future discussion during the unit on the rain forest.

In groups, the students then reviewed the questions that had been posed earlier to see if they had found answers in their reading, and they used Highlighter Tape and sticky notes to indicate in the article where the answers could be found. They checked their predictions according to the process Mr. Montoya had previously modeled (**Respond**). Next, each student was asked to write a brief paragraph that summarized the information in the article, using the VSS words, the questions/answers, and the predictions as a guide to writing (**Summarize**).

Toward the end of the class, Mr. Montoya displayed a transparency with the following questions:

1. Why are we dependent on the rain forests for our survival on Earth?
2. Compare and contrast the arguments of foresters and environmentalists. With which argument do you most agree? Why?

3. Imagine the Earth in one hundred years. How would you describe it if the present rate of deforestation continues?

4. Pretend you are the President of the United States. You are writing a letter to the president of the lumber company that is responsible for the overseas burning of many acres of rain forest. What would you say in your letter to convince her to stop destroying the rain forest and practice sustainable lumber development?

After reading the questions aloud, Mr. Montoya briefly asked each student to select one. For homework, he asked students to copy the question they chose and to discuss it with parents or caregivers that evening. Students were asked to jot notes as to how they would answer the question, using the information from the article and any insights they had gained through their discussions at home. He announced that these questions would be debated during the next day's class.

On the SIOP form in Figure 5.6, rate Mr. Montoya on each of the Strategies indicators.

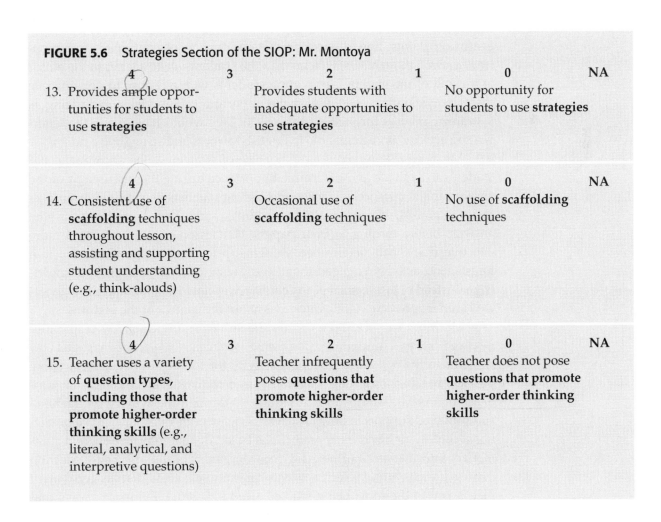

FIGURE 5.6 Strategies Section of the SIOP: Mr. Montoya

4	3	2	1	0	NA
13. Provides ample opportunities for students to use **strategies**		Provides students with inadequate opportunities to use **strategies**		No opportunity for students to use **strategies**	

4	3	2	1	0	NA
14. Consistent use of **scaffolding** techniques throughout lesson, assisting and supporting student understanding (e.g., think-alouds)		Occasional use of **scaffolding** techniques		No use of **scaffolding** techniques	

4	3	2	1	0	NA
15. Teacher uses a variety of **question types, including those that promote higher-order thinking skills** (e.g., literal, analytical, and interpretive questions)		Teacher infrequently poses **questions that promote higher-order thinking skills**		Teacher does not pose **questions that promote higher-order thinking skills**	

Discussion of Lessons

13. *Provides Ample Opportunities for Students to Use Strategies*

Mrs. Fletcher: 2

Miss Lee: 2

Mr. Montoya: 4

Mrs. Fletcher received a "2" for her use and teaching of strategies. She began the lesson by asking her students to make predictions from the title of the article, and three students responded. As typically happens with predictions based on titles, one girl repeated the title of the article in her prediction ("I think it will be about burning forests"), but Mrs. Fletcher did not probe the response to elicit deeper thinking about the topic. Further, she didn't build upon or reinforce the other two students' predictions, nor did she seek other predictions during the text reading. We often see teachers ask for predictions, accept them, and move on without expanding on them or coming back to revisit them later in a lesson.

Mrs. Fletcher's lesson would have been strengthened if she had included additional strategies, and perhaps a graphic organizer or other means for students to organize the information they were learning. She also could have periodically stopped her oral reading to reinforce important concepts, clarify confusing points, and discuss predictions that were confirmed or disconfirmed. Even though Mrs. Fletcher had the students write a letter to the editor at the end of the reading—providing students with a chance to demonstrate their understanding—she missed the opportunity to model summarizing as a strategic process throughout the article. This would have made the letter-writing activity more accessible to English learners and struggling readers.

Miss Lee also received a "2" for use of strategies. She encouraged her students to evaluate and determine importance during the discussions of the answers to the questions on the worksheet. Students were required to support their responses, clarify misunderstandings, and have consensus on the answers before turning in their papers. Her lesson would have been more effective if she had determined students' prior knowledge about the rain forests, and actively engaged them in drawing on their background knowledge. Instead of just lecturing, she could have shown photographs and generated student predictions and questions about the content of the pictures.

Mr. Montoya received a "4" on the strategies indicator. He taught and modeled several important processing strategies when he engaged his students in the SQP2RS/Squeepers activity for the expository text selection: prediction, self-questioning, monitoring and clarifying, evaluating, and summarizing. As Mr. Montoya led his students through the activity, he modeled and provided support in how to survey text, generate questions, make predictions, confirm or disconfirm predictions based on text information, and summarize information. Further, he incorporated Vocabulary Self-Collection Strategy (VSS), during which students carefully select and discuss vocabulary that is key to the topic being studied (Ruddell, 2001). Evidence shows that when students are guided in how to select important vocabulary, and in how to apply strategies through SQP2RS, their comprehension is enhanced (Blachowicz & Fisher, 2000; Shearer, Ruddell, & Vogt, 2001; Vogt, 2000; 2002).

14. *Consistent Use of Scaffolding Techniques*

    Mrs. Fletcher: 1

    Miss Lee: 3

    Mr. Montoya: 4

Mrs. Fletcher received a "1" for scaffolding. She attempted to scaffold student learning by having the class orally read the title together and by reading the article to the students. This significantly reduced the reading demands of the text. However, if she continues to read everything aloud to the students, she won't be gradually reducing her support, and the students will be less likely to become independent. Therefore, her scaffolding might have been more effective if she had begun reading the article to the students and then had them complete the reading with a partner or group. Obviously, this presumes that the text difficulty is such that the students could successfully read it with help from one another.

Miss Lee received a "3" for scaffolding. She effectively scaffolded student learning in three ways. First, the photographs she displayed during her lecture provided additional support for students who had little background knowledge about the topic of rain forests. Second, by having the students complete the reading in their groups, the reading demands were reduced. Depending on the length of the article, she might have encouraged the reading involvement of more than one student in each group if she had suggested, for example, a "Page, Paragraph, or Pass" approach. With this activity, each student decides whether he or she wishes to read a page, a paragraph, or pass on the oral reading. English learners and reluctant readers may feel more comfortable having the option of choosing whether and how much they'll read aloud to their peers.

Miss Lee also scaffolded the students' answering of the questions on the worksheet. They had to answer the questions independently, but then were allowed to compare their responses to the other students' and decide on the correct answers together. This provided students the opportunity to demonstrate individual learning of the rain forest material, but also the chance to compare their understandings with those of their peers.

Mr. Montoya received a "4" for scaffolding. He incorporated a variety of techniques that provided support with the expectation that his students eventually would be able to apply the various strategies independently. He used several grouping configurations during the lesson, including whole class, small groups, triads, and partners. Students had the opportunity to confer with each other, receiving support and assistance if necessary. Mr. Montoya also carefully modeled the strategies for the students prior to requiring application. The reading demands of the article were reduced when students were allowed to read it in pairs or triads. Choice also played a critical role in this lesson when students were encouraged to select key vocabulary and the question for homework that most interested them.

15. *Variety of Question Types, Including Those that Promote Higher-Order Thinking Skills*

Mrs. Fletcher: 0

Miss Lee: 1

Mr. Montoya: 4

Mrs. Fletcher received a "0" for questioning. She missed several opportunities to use questioning to engage her students' thinking. When the three children made their predictions, she could have probed with questions such as, "What made you think that?" or "Why do you think it's about parrots?" Toward the end of the lesson, when one student asked why people still burn the rain forests, Mrs. Fletcher could have used the student's question to develop inquiry skills in her students, and these questions could then have motivated the letters to the editor. Instead, the letter-writing activity, while potentially meaningful, seemed somewhat removed from the article and brief discussion about the rain forests.

Miss Lee received a "1" for questioning. Although she incorporated questioning into her lesson by using the worksheet, the questions were essentially written at the literal level, with answers that could be found easily in the rain forest article. The activity would have required greater cognitive work on the part of the students if Miss Lee had written questions at various levels. Question 8 was the only one that required actual application and evaluation of the content concepts.

In addition, although Miss Lee tried to incorporate technology into her lesson, she did not provide enough guidance to the students to help them find the information they needed in a timely fashion. She could have worked with students interested in using the Internet to: refine their search procedures; generate some of their own questions about the rain forest; and use several key words to yield the information they were seeking while narrowing the resulting prospective websites.

Mr. Montoya received a "4" for questioning. He incorporated questioning throughout the lesson, first during the SQP2RS activity, when students generated their own questions based on the text information, and then with the debate/discussion questions. Note the varied levels of the questions: The first is a literal-level question, the second requires analysis and evaluation, the third requires application and synthesis, and the fourth requires synthesis and evaluation. Mr. Montoya effectively reduced the text's difficulty through the SQP2RS activity, not by lowering the cognitive demand of the questions.

Summary

In some of our classes we frequently tell preservice candidates preparing to be teachers, "Just because the students can't read doesn't mean they can't think!" A similar adage to this might be said of English learners, "Just because they can't speak English proficiently doesn't mean they can't think!"

In this chapter, we have described how to promote critical and strategic thinking for all students, but most especially for ELs. Learning is made more effective when teachers actively assist students in developing metacognitive, cognitive, and social/affective strategies, those that promote self-monitoring, self-regulation, and problem solving. We believe that students with developing English proficiency should not be denied effective, creative, and generative teaching while they are learning the language. By conscientiously sheltering instruction through strategy teaching and modeling, by appropriately scaffolding support, and by thoughtfully asking questions that require students to interpret, apply, and synthesize, we increase the chances that English learners will become critical thinkers.

Discussion Questions

1. Describe a learning situation you participated in in which the teacher modeled how to do something through demonstration. What worked and what didn't? How could the teacher have made things more clear?

2. Strategies are an important part of a teacher's repertoire. What are effective ways to explicitly teach students the use of strategies to enhance their learning? With a partner, demonstrate how to teach effectively a mnemonic strategy to English learners.

3. The concept of scaffolding may be confusing. Consider the term to represent the construction process in which scaffolds are put in place to support a building. As the building becomes more complete, less scaffolding is necessary. When the building can stand on its own, the scaffolding is completely removed. The same may be said for teaching. How does the building analogy apply to teaching new information to English learners?

4. Here's a factual question a teacher might ask based on a social studies text: "Who was the first President of the United States?" Given the topic of the presidency, what are several additional questions you could ask that promote higher-order thinking? Why is it important to use a variety of questioning strategies with English learners?

6 Interaction

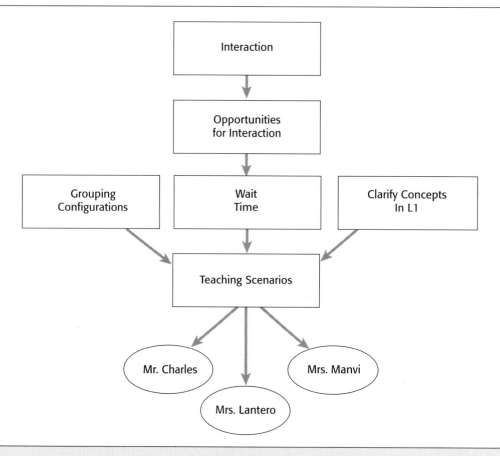

OBJECTIVES

After reading, discussing, and engaging in activities related to this chapter, you will be able to meet the following content and language objectives.

Content Objectives:

Select from a variety of activities that promote interaction and incorporate into lesson plans

Design grouping patterns that support lesson content and language objectives

Identify strategies to increase wait time

Language Objectives:

Explain the purpose of student–student interaction for language development

Describe strategies to reduce the amount of teacher talk in a lesson

Adjust teacher questioning techniques to promote student elaboration of responses

Identify resources to support student clarification in the native language

English learners benefit from structured opportunities to use the target language (English) in multiple settings and across content areas. Because of the large number of English learners in schools today, *all* teachers are teachers of English, even if their content specialization is science, math, or social studies. For students learning English, teachers must create ample opportunities to practice using *academic* language, not simply social uses of language. And the language must be meaningful to students; it is not just the quantity of exposures to English that affects learning, but it is the quality as well (Wong-Fillmore & Valadez, 1986).

Background

Studies have indicated that, in most classrooms, teachers dominate the linguistic aspect of the lesson, leaving students severely limited in terms of opportunities to use language in a variety of ways (Goodlad, 1984; Marshall, 2000). In a study of programs for ELs (Ramirez, Yuen, Ramey & Pasta, 1991), it was found that the classes were characterized by excessive teacher talk. When students were given an opportunity to respond, it usually involved only simple information-recall statements, restricting students' chance to produce language and develop complex language and thinking skills. Instead of teachers talking and students listening, sheltered content classes should be structured so that students are interacting in their collaborative investigation of a body of knowledge (Diaz, 1989). Further, interaction with others is an important component of reading instruction for increasing motivation and comprehension (Guthrie & Ozgungor, 2002).

We find that it is interesting and helpful to analyze actual transcripts from lessons to demonstrate the kind of teacher dominance that is so prevalent in classrooms. The following transcripts are from a pilot study (Echevarria, Greene & Goldenberg, 1996) in middle school social studies classes. The teachers were videotaped teaching the same content about consumerism to English learners, the first using a typical approach found in mainstream classes and the other using a sheltered approach. Both classes had approximately 25 students and in this lesson students were learning how to read labels on clothing and on a bottle of antiseptic.

Mainstream Lesson

TEACHER: Look at the piece of clothing at the bottom. It says *(he reads),* "This shirt is flame-resistant," which means what?

STUDENT: Could not burn.

STUDENT: Won't catch fire.

TEACHER: It will not burn, won't catch fire. Right *(continues reading).* "To retain the flame-resistant properties"—what does "to retain" mean?

STUDENT: *(unintelligible)*

TEACHER: To keep it. All right. "In order to keep this shirt flame-resistant *(he reads)*, wash with detergent only." All right *(he reads)*. "Do not use soap or bleach. Tumble dry. One hundred percent polyester." Now, why does it say, "Do not use soap or bleach"?

STUDENT: 'Cause it'll take off the . . .

TEACHER: It'll take off the what?

STUDENTS: *(fragmented responses)*

TEACHER: It'll take off the flame-resistant quality. If you wash it with soap or bleach, then the shirt's just gonna be like any old shirt, any regular shirt, so when you put a match to it, will it catch fire?

STUDENT: No.

TEACHER: Yes. 'Cause you've ruined it then. It's no longer flame-resistant. So the government says you gotta tell the consumer what kind of shirt it is, and how to take care of it. If you look at any piece of clothing: shirt, pants, your shirts, um, your skirts, anything. There's always going to be a tag on these that says what it is made of and how you're going to take care of it. OK. And that's for your protection so that you won't buy something, and then treat it wrong. So labeling is important. All right. Let's review. I'll go back to the antiseptic. What did we say indications meant? Indications? Raise your hands, raise your hands. Robert?

STUDENT: What's it for.

TEACHER: What is it for, when do you use this? OK. What do directions, what is that for, Victor?

STUDENT: How to use . . .

TEACHER: How to use. OK, so indications is when you use it *(holds one finger up)*, directions is how you use it *(holds another finger up)*, and warnings is what?

STUDENTS: *(various mumbled responses)*

TEACHER: How you don't use it. This is what you don't do.

The teacher in this case tended to finish sentences for the students and accept any form of student comment without encouraging elaborated responses.

Sheltered Instruction

TEACHER: Most clothing must have labels that tell what kind of cloth was used in it right? Look at the material in the picture down there *(points to picture in text)*.[1] What does it say, the tag right there?

---

[1]The teacher explained then that they would be doing an activity in which they would read labels for information.

STUDENT: The, the, the . . .

TEACHER: The tag right there.

STUDENT: *(Reading)* "Flame-resis . . ."

TEACHER: Resistant.

STUDENT: "Flame-resistant. To retain the flame-resistant properties, wash with detergent only. Do not use soap or bleach. Use warm water. Tumble dry."

TEACHER: "One hundred percent . . ."

STUDENT: "Polyester."

TEACHER: Now, most clothes carry labels, right? *(pointing to the neck of her sweater)*. They explain how to take care of it, like dry clean, machine wash, right? It tells you how to clean it. Why does this product have to be washed with a detergent and no soap or bleach?

STUDENT: Because clothes . . .

TEACHER: Why can't you use something else?

STUDENTS: *(several students mumble answers)*

STUDENT: *(says in Spanish)* Because it will make it small.

TEACHER: It may shrink, or *(gestures to a student)* it may not be . . . what does it say?

STUDENT: It's not going to be able to be resistant to fire.

TEACHER: Exactly. It's flame-resistant, right? So, if you use something else, it won't be flame-resistant anymore. How about the, uh, look at the *antiseptic (holds hands up to form a container)*—the picture above the shirt, the antiseptic?

STUDENT: Read it?

TEACHER: Antiseptic *(Teacher reads)*, and other health products you buy without a prescription often have usage and warning labels. So what can you learn from this label? Read this label quietly please, and tell me what you can learn from the label. Read the label on that antiseptic. *(Students read silently.)*

TEACHER: What can you learn from this label?

STUDENT: It kills, oh I know.

TEACHER: Steve?

STUDENT: It kills germs.

STUDENT: Yeah, it kills germs.

TEACHER: It kills germs. You use it for wounds, right? What else?

STUDENTS: *(various enthusiastic responses)*

TEACHER: One person at a time. OK, hold on. Veronica was saying something.

STUDENT: It tells you in the directions that, you could use it, that like that, 'cause if you use it in another thing, it could hurt you.

TEACHER: It could hurt you. OK, what else? Ricardo?

STUDENT: If you put it in your mouth, don't put it in your mouth or your ears or your eyes.

TEACHER: Very good. Don't put it in your mouth, ears, and eyes. OK, for how many days should you use it? No more than what?

STUDENT: No more than ten days.

STUDENT: Ten days.

TEACHER: So don't use it—you have to follow what it says so don't use it more than ten days. Now, the next activity you're going to do . . .

The sheltered teacher allowed for a balance of teacher-to-student talk and encouraged student participation. She asked questions, waited for students' responses, and restated or elaborated on the responses.

Opportunities for Interaction

This SIOP element emphasizes the importance of balancing linguistic turn-taking between the teacher and students, and among students. As mentioned previously, we have clear evidence that teachers tend to do most of the talking in class. While teachers certainly have knowledge to share and discuss with students, learning is more effective when students have an opportunity to participate fully in lessons by discussing ideas and information. Students benefit from using and practicing English as a means of expressing their ideas, opinions, and answers. Effective SI teachers structure their lessons in ways that

promote student discussion and they strive to provide a more balanced linguistic exchange between themselves and their students. It can be particularly tempting for teachers to do most of the talking when students are not completely proficient in their use of English, but these students are precisely the ones who need opportunities to practice using English the most.

Effective sheltered teachers also encourage elaborated responses from students when discussing the lesson's concepts. The teacher elicits more extended student contributions by using a variety of techniques that will take students beyond simple yes or no answers and short phrases (Echevarria, 1995b; Goldenberg, 1992–1993). Some of these techniques include asking students to expand on their answers by saying, "Tell me more about that"; and by asking direct questions to prompt more language use such as, "What do you mean by . . ." or "What else. . . ." Another technique is to provide further information through questions such as: "How do you know?" "Why is that important?" "What does that remind you of?" Other techniques include offering restatements such as, "In other words . . . is that accurate?" and by frequently pausing to let students process the language and formulate their responses. Some teachers often call on other students to extend a classmate's response.

It takes time and practice for these techniques to become a natural part of a teacher's repertoire. The teachers with whom we've worked report that they had to consciously practice overcoming the temptation to speak for students or to complete a student's short phrase. The preceding transcript showed how the first teacher spoke for students instead of encouraging students to complete their thoughts. The following segment from the transcript provides another example:

TEACHER: What do "directions," what is that for, Victor?

STUDENT: How to use . . .

TEACHER: How to use. OK, so "indications" is when you use it, "directions" is how you use it, and "warnings" is what?

STUDENTS: *(various mumbled responses)*

TEACHER: How you don't use it. This is what you don't do.

In this segment, the mainstream teacher could have encouraged a more balanced exchange between himself and the students. First, he did not encourage students to completely express their thoughts; he accepted partial and mumbled answers. Secondly, he answered for the students, dominating the discussion. It is easy to imagine how students could become disinterested, passive learners in a class in which the teacher accepts minimal participation and does the majority of the talking.

The sheltered teacher approached students–teacher interaction differently:

TEACHER: What can you learn from this label?

STUDENT: It kills, oh I know.

> **TEACHER:**   Steve?
>
> **STUDENT:**   It kills germs.
>
> **STUDENT:**   Yeah, it kills germs.
>
> **TEACHER:**   It kills germs. You use it for wounds, right? What else?
>
> **STUDENTS:**   *(various enthusiastic responses)*
>
> **TEACHER:**   One person at a time. OK, hold on. Veronica was saying something.
>
> **STUDENT:**   It tells you in the directions that, you could use it, that like that, 'cause if you use it in another thing, it could hurt you.
>
> **TEACHER:**   It could hurt you. OK, what else? Ricardo?
>
> **STUDENT:**   If you put it in your mouth, don't put it in your mouth or your ears or your eyes.
>
> **TEACHER:**   Very good. Don't put it in your mouth, ears, and eyes. OK, for how many days should you use it? No more than what?
>
> **STUDENT:**   No more than ten days.
>
> **STUDENT:**   Ten days.
>
> **TEACHER:**   So don't use it—you have to follow what it says, so don't use it more than ten days. Now, the next activity you're going to do . . .

The sheltered teacher let the students have time to express their thoughts (e.g., student says, "It kills . . . It kills germs."). The teacher could have completed the sentence for the student, but she waited for him to complete his answer. Also, the sheltered teacher encouraged and challenged the students more than the mainstream teacher did by asking twice, "What else?" Finally, the teacher nominated students who volunteered to talk and repeated what they said so that the class could hear a full response (e.g., Veronica).

Effective sheltered teachers plan instruction so that students have opportunities to work with one another on academic tasks, using English to communicate. Through meaningful interaction, students can practice speaking and making themselves understood. That implies asking and answering questions, negotiating meaning, clarifying ideas, giving and justifying opinions, and more. Students may interact in pairs, triads, and small groups. Literature circles, think-pair-share, Jigsaw readings, debates, and science experiments are only a sample of the types of activities teachers can include in lessons to foster student–student interaction.

Furthermore, interaction need not always be oral. Students can interact with teachers through dialogue journals, sharing ideas and learning from the teacher, who models appropriate written text. Using technology, students can interact with each other through a class electronic list, shared research files on a school network, or through a planned pen pal email exchange with another class elsewhere in the world.

Grouping Configurations

Over the years, we have learned that homogeneous grouping for instruction (low group, average group, high group) has serious academic and social effects for students who are not in the top group (Hiebert, 1983). Frequently referred to as "tracking," the practice of providing instruction to students in instructional groups segregated by ability or performance level has been found to be inequitable because it often differentiates across socioeconomic and ethnic lines, and it promotes differentiated expectations for students' success. When working with low-achieving groups, teachers have been found to talk more, use more structure, ask lower-level questions, cover less material, spend more time on skills and drills, provide fewer opportunities for leadership and independent research, encourage more oral than silent reading, teach less vocabulary, and allow less wait time during questioning, plus they spent twice as much time on behavior and management issues.

In many schools, it has become common practice to group English learners with low-achieving students regardless of academic ability and performance. However, all students, including ELs, benefit from instruction that frequently includes a variety of grouping configurations. Whole-class groups are beneficial when they develop classroom community and provide a shared experience for everyone. Flexible small groups promote the development of multiple perspectives and encourage collaboration. Partnering encourages success because it provides practice opportunities, scaffolding, and assistance for classmates (Flood, Lapp, Flood, & Nagel, 1992; Nagel, 2001; Tompkins, 2001).

Effective sheltered classes are characterized by a variety of grouping structures, including individual work, partners, triads, small groups of four or five, cooperative learning groups, and whole-group. Groups also vary in that they may be homogeneous or heterogeneous by gender, language proficiency, language background, and/or ability. There are times that it may be most effective to have students grouped by language-proficiency level. For example, if a teacher's goal is for students at beginning levels of English proficiency to practice using a particular language structure within the context of a social studies lesson, such as present progressive (*-ing* form), then it may be useful to have those students grouped together for that lesson. Likewise, when developing the skills of students with low levels of literacy, it makes sense to have those with similar ability grouped together for a particular lesson. Grouping all ELs together regularly is *not* good practice, especially when a bilingual aide teaches them almost exclusively. In SI classes, ELs are given the same access to the curriculum and the teacher's expertise as native English speaking students.

Using a variety of grouping configurations also facilitates learning in a couple of ways. One, the variety of groups helps to maintain students' interest. It is difficult for some students to stay focused when the classroom is always set up the same way with the teacher talking to the whole class or having students work individually. Moving from a whole group to cooperative groups or partners adds variety to the learning situation and increases student involvement in the learning process.

Second, varying grouping structures increases the chance that a student's preferred mode of instruction will be matched. For instance, some students work best with a partner, getting somewhat distracted in a large group. Other students are stimulated by the many perspectives shared in a large group and do well in that setting.

It is recommended that at least two different grouping structures be used during a lesson, depending on the activity and objectives of the lesson.

Wait Time

Wait time is the length of time between utterances during an interaction. In classroom settings, it refers to the length of time that teachers wait for students to respond before interrupting, answering a question themselves, or calling on someone else to participate. Wait time varies by culture; it is appropriate in some cultures to let seconds, even minutes, lag between utterances, while in other cultures utterances can even overlap one another. In U.S. classrooms, the average length of wait time is clearly *not* sufficient. Imagine the impact of wait time on ELs who are processing ideas in a new language and need additional time to formulate the phrasings of their thoughts.

Effective sheltered teachers consciously allow students to express their thoughts fully, without interruption. Many teachers in U.S. schools are uncomfortable with the silence that follows their questions or comments, and they immediately fill the void by talking themselves. This situation may be especially pertinent in sheltered classes where ELs need extra time to process questions in English, think of an answer in their second language, and then formulate their responses in English. Although teachers may be tempted to fill the silence, ELs benefit from a patient approach to classroom participation, in which teachers wait for students to complete their verbal contributions.

While effective sheltered teachers provide sufficient wait time for ELs, they also work to find a balance between wait time and moving a lesson along. Some students may become impatient if the pace of the class lags. One strategy for accommodating impatient students is to have the more advanced students write down their responses while waiting, and then they check their answers against the final answer.

Another way to help ELs is to allow the techniques made popular by a television show: "50-50" and "phone a friend." Students who are unsure of an answer or are unable to articulate it well might ask to choose between two possible responses provided by the teacher (50-50) or ask a classmate for help (phone a friend). However, to ensure practice with the language, the original student must give "the final answer" to the teacher.

Clarify Key Concepts in L1

Best practice indicates that English learners benefit from opportunities to clarify concepts in their native language (L1). Although sheltered instruction involves teaching subject-matter material in English, students are given the opportunity to have a concept or assignment explained in their L1 as needed. Significant controversy surrounds the use of L1 for instructional purposes, but we believe that clarification of key concepts in students' L1 by a bilingual instructional aide, peer, or through the use of materials written in the students' L1 provides an important support for the academic learning of those students who are not yet fully proficient in English.

This item on the SIOP may have NA circled as a score because not all sheltered classes need to use (especially for advanced ELs) students' L1 to clarify concepts for them.

However, with websites offering word translation capabilities, and the availability of bilingual dictionaries in book and computer program formats, all sheltered classrooms should have some resources in most of the students' native languages.

The Lesson

Unit: Addition and Subtraction (1st grade)

The first-grade teachers in this chapter, Mr. Charles, Mrs. Lantero, and Mrs. Manvi, work in a suburban school that has a 24 percent EL population. Their classes have an even distribution of English learners, each with approximately 10 percent ELs. Most of those students are at the intermediate to advanced-intermediate levels of English proficiency, and still benefit from having teachers use sheltered techniques to increase their understanding of lessons.

The teachers in this school plan math units around the district's content standards. The lessons described in the scenarios that follow are part of a unit on addition and subtraction sums to twelve. The standards in this lesson are related to number sense and mathematical reasoning. Students are to know the addition facts (sums to twenty) and the corresponding subtraction facts and commit them to memory. The teachers each have their own methods for teaching addition, as seen in the lessons that follow.

Teaching Scenarios

Mr. Charles

Mr. Charles began the lesson by explaining to the first-grade children that they were going to learn about different ways to do addition. He reviewed vocabulary that had been taught previously, such as addends and sums. He then engaged the children in a discussion about what information they knew about addition that had been learned previously, and he provided an adequate amount of time for the children to respond. He then asked the children when they would use addition in their everyday lives. Some of the children volunteered information about going to the grocery store or the bank and how they might have to use addition to solve problems. Mr. Charles then showed the children an addition problem on the overhead and asked them to work with a partner to figure out how they might solve the problem. He picked a student to come up to the overhead to solve one of the problems. (He chose the student by picking a name that had been written on a tongue depressor to ensure that he would call on a variety of children—not just the ones who raised their hands.) He also asked the student to underline the addends and circle the sums in the problem. To engage the whole class, Mr. Charles asked the children to raise their hands if they thought the student had the correct answer.

Mr. Charles continued the lesson by asking a volunteer to give a number from one to eight. He then had the children write the number on their paper, then draw the same number of shapes as the number they had written, using the color blue. Mr. Charles checked to make sure the children understood the directions and he stopped at each child's desk to see how each was doing. He then asked the children to draw two more shapes, using the color yellow. He checked all students' work by circulating around the room. He asked the children to count all the blue and yellow shapes and to write an addition problem to illustrate what they had done. Mr. Charles asked the children to check with a partner to see if their problem was done correctly. He then engaged the children in a discussion of how pictures can help you find the answer to "how many in all." The discussion was balanced between the teacher and the students and Mr. Charles asked for some examples of the kinds of pictures that they might draw to help them solve addition problems. He reminded the children to check for the addends and the sums in their problems.

Mr. Charles then had the children work in pairs. He distributed a paper plate and clothespins to each pair of students. He told the children to clip four clothespins on the top edge of a paper plate and three on the bottom. He then instructed the students to write an addition sentence for the clothespins and solve it (4 + 3 = 7). Mr. Charles called on children to explain how they found the answer. He asked a child who understood the concept to model putting clothespins on the plate and writing a corresponding addition sentence. He then asked another child to answer the addition problem provided by the previous child.

Next, Mr. Charles told the children that they would be taking the clothespins off their plates and making up a new problem using a different number of clothespins. He explained that he would like one partner in the group to tell the other partner how many clothespins to place on the top and how many to place on the bottom thus giving the children an opportunity to practice their English with each other. The children exchanged paper plates and one partner was responsible for writing the addition problem.

Mr. Charles finished the lesson with a review of what the students had learned about addition and asked for volunteers from the class to give some examples of addends and sums.

On the SIOP form in Figure 6.1, rate Mr. Charles on each of the Interaction indicators.

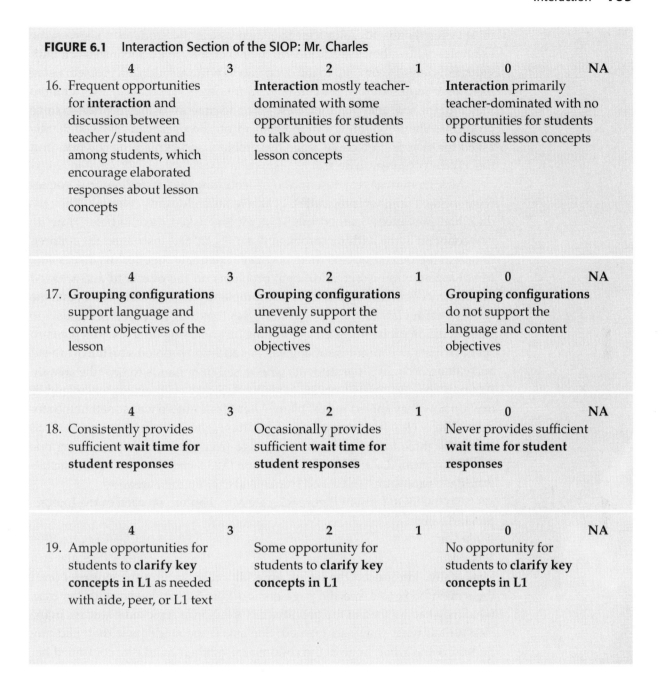

FIGURE 6.1   Interaction Section of the SIOP: Mr. Charles

4	3	2	1	0	NA
16. Frequent opportunities for **interaction** and discussion between teacher/student and among students, which encourage elaborated responses about lesson concepts		**Interaction** mostly teacher-dominated with some opportunities for students to talk about or question lesson concepts		**Interaction** primarily teacher-dominated with no opportunities for students to discuss lesson concepts	

4	3	2	1	0	NA
17. **Grouping configurations** support language and content objectives of the lesson		**Grouping configurations** unevenly support the language and content objectives		**Grouping configurations** do not support the language and content objectives	

4	3	2	1	0	NA
18. Consistently provides sufficient **wait time for student responses**		Occasionally provides sufficient **wait time for student responses**		Never provides sufficient **wait time for student responses**	

4	3	2	1	0	NA
19. Ample opportunities for students to **clarify key concepts in L1** as needed with aide, peer, or L1 text		Some opportunity for students to **clarify key concepts in L1**		No opportunity for students to **clarify key concepts in L1**	

Mrs. Lantero

Mrs. Lantero introduced the lesson on addition by giving an example of how she used addition to count and add the playground equipment that they had in their classroom. On an overhead projector transparency she drew a picture of five balls, three jump ropes, and three hula hoops. She called on students to come up to the overhead to solve the problem and demonstrate how they counted all the objects that she drew. She made an effort to call on a wide variety of students to respond and explain their answers. She asked students to explain how they answered the question, "How many in all?" Several students raised their hands to volunteer. She then asked the students to give some examples of how they use addition in their everyday lives. She instructed individual students to come up to the overhead to write an addition problem using pictures to represent the numbers (e.g., four flowers + two trees). Mrs. Lantero then told the students that they were going to practice using addition to solve problems. She wrote an addition problem on the overhead (3 + 4 = 7). She asked the class if they could solve the problem and explain their work, then called on a volunteer to do so.

Mrs. Lantero gave a description of "counting on," a strategy that teaches what the next number is regardless of where the child starts counting. The children had previously learned this strategy. She asked the children "How do you count on in the addition problem (9 + 1= __)?" She instructed the children to talk to the person next to them and gave adequate time for the discussion. Mrs. Lantero wrote some additional problems on the overhead and showed the students how to solve the various problems. Mrs. Lantero then gave the class a brief review of some of the strategies that they had used previously to solve addition problems, such as counting on and using doubles. Mrs. Lantero spent the next five minutes solving various addition problems on the overhead and calling on individual students who raised their hands to give the answer. At times she encouraged the students to elaborate on their responses and to explain how they solved the problem. After Mrs. Lantero was sure that the students had a clear understanding of addition, she had the children get into groups of three to complete the workpage from their textbook, helping one another as needed. At the end of the lesson the teacher reviewed the concepts of addends and sums and asked students to explain their answers.

On the SIOP form in Figure 6.2, rate Mrs. Lantero on each of the Interaction indicators.

Mrs. Manvi

Mrs. Manvi introduced the lesson on addition by having the students open their math book to a specific page on addition. She reviewed with the class what they had learned in the previous day's lesson and picked a student in the class to tell what they had learned. She asked the students if they had any questions and when none of the children raised their hand, she continued her lesson. Mrs. Manvi had the children count in unison from one to thirty. Then she asked the students to come up with some examples using addition facts to add numbers and called on two volunteers to provide examples. Next, Mrs. Manvi demonstrated some addition problems on the overhead. To engage the students in prior learning, she asked the students to provide descriptions of the word "addition." She reviewed the strategies of counting on and drawing pictures to help determine the correct answers to the problems. Mrs. Manvi tried to encourage the children to raise their hands if they did not understand how to do the addition problems. She continued the lesson, providing many examples to the children.

Mrs. Manvi had the students take out their workbooks and told them to do two pages of addition. She walked around the room to make sure that

FIGURE 6.2 Interaction Section of the SIOP: Mrs. Lantero

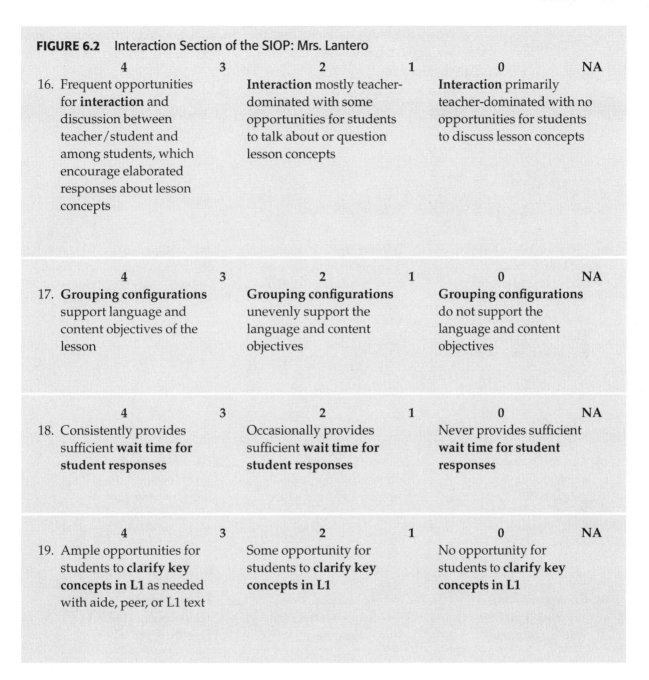

4	3	2	1	0	NA
16. Frequent opportunities for **interaction** and discussion between teacher/student and among students, which encourage elaborated responses about lesson concepts		**Interaction** mostly teacher-dominated with some opportunities for students to talk about or question lesson concepts		**Interaction** primarily teacher-dominated with no opportunities for students to discuss lesson concepts	

4	3	2	1	0	NA
17. **Grouping configurations** support language and content objectives of the lesson		**Grouping configurations** unevenly support the language and content objectives		**Grouping configurations** do not support the language and content objectives	

4	3	2	1	0	NA
18. Consistently provides sufficient **wait time for student responses**		Occasionally provides sufficient **wait time for student responses**		Never provides sufficient **wait time for student responses**	

4	3	2	1	0	NA
19. Ample opportunities for students to **clarify key concepts in L1** as needed with aide, peer, or L1 text		Some opportunity for students to **clarify key concepts in L1**		No opportunity for students to **clarify key concepts in L1**	

the students were on task and to see if anyone needed extra support. Mrs. Manvi realized that the students were having difficulty so she drew some examples on the board using pictures and asked the children if they had any questions. She again encouraged the children to raise their hands if they were having problems. Mrs. Manvi then worked through the problems one at a time on the overhead, and had the children check their work. She noticed that one student in particular was coming up with incorrect responses so she focused her attention on that child and tried to help the child solve the problem correctly.

When she was confident that the students understood addition, Mrs. Manvi assigned homework that night so they could practice some more addition problems.

On the SIOP form in Figure 6.3, rate Mrs. Manvi on each of the Interaction indicators.

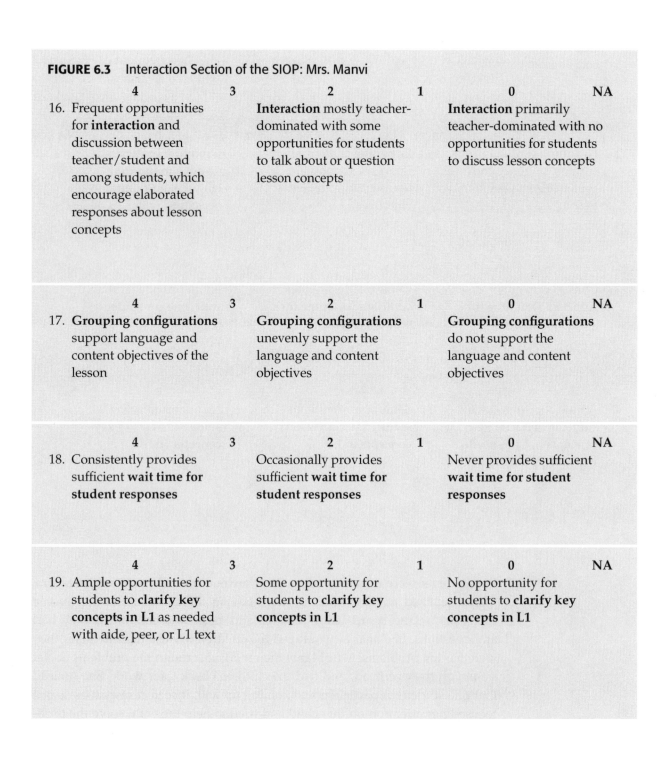

FIGURE 6.3   Interaction Section of the SIOP: Mrs. Manvi

4	3	2	1	0	NA
16. Frequent opportunities for **interaction** and discussion between teacher/student and among students, which encourage elaborated responses about lesson concepts		**Interaction** mostly teacher-dominated with some opportunities for students to talk about or question lesson concepts		**Interaction** primarily teacher-dominated with no opportunities for students to discuss lesson concepts	

4	3	2	1	0	NA
17. **Grouping configurations** support language and content objectives of the lesson		**Grouping configurations** unevenly support the language and content objectives		**Grouping configurations** do not support the language and content objectives	

4	3	2	1	0	NA
18. Consistently provides sufficient **wait time for student responses**		Occasionally provides sufficient **wait time for student responses**		Never provides sufficient **wait time for student responses**	

4	3	2	1	0	NA
19. Ample opportunities for students to **clarify key concepts in L1** as needed with aide, peer, or L1 text		Some opportunity for students to **clarify key concepts in L1**		No opportunity for students to **clarify key concepts in L1**	

Discussion of Lessons

16. *Opportunities for Interaction*

    Mr. Charles: 4

    Mrs. Lantero: 2

    Mrs. Manvi: 0

Although interaction among students is important for learning new concepts and practicing English, the teachers varied in the opportunities they provided to their students. Mr. Charles planned a lesson that had frequent opportunities for interaction so he received a "4" on the SIOP. He used a variety of techniques that ensured participation from the whole class, such as calling on children by selecting their names on written sticks (tongue depressors); asking students to work with partners to solve problems; involving students in a discussion; and having students work in pairs for practice with addition sentences represented by clothespins, writing the sentence, and coming up with the sum.

Mrs. Lantero's lesson was heavily teacher-controlled, although she did attempt to involve the children in discussion and did call on volunteers to come to the overhead. (Often it is the students who least need the practice using English that are called upon to participate in the lesson.) She also had students work in groups of three, although completing a workpage from the textbook isn't an optimal activity for interaction since it is basically an individual paper and pencil activity.

Mrs. Manvi used a traditional whole-group format for teaching her first graders. This format severely restricted opportunities for students to discuss the concepts and ask for clarification as needed. It is very difficult to determine the needs of students and gauge their understanding when teaching the way Mrs. Manvi did.

17. *Grouping Configurations*

    Mr. Charles: 4

    Mrs. Lantero: 2

    Mrs. Manvi: 0

Rather than having students in structured groups interact to solve problems, Mrs. Lantero and Mrs. Manvi solved problems on the overhead in front of the whole class. Whole group instruction has a role to play, but it should not be used extensively because it limits opportunities for students to ask questions, discuss ideas, and clarify information. English learners and students who struggle academically may find whole group instruction intimidating, as undoubtedly was the case with Mrs. Manvi's lesson. Although she asked several times if students had questions, nobody was willing to speak up in the whole group setting.

Mr. Charles, on the other hand, was aware of the importance of having students interact with the material (creating problems and solving them) and one another (practicing English). He had students work in pairs and small groups throughout the lesson, which provided optimal opportunity for interaction.

18.   *Wait Time*

Mr. Charles: 4

Mrs. Lantero: 4

Mrs. Manvi: 0

Both Mr. Charles and Mrs. Lantero interacted with students in such a way as to allow them time to formulate their thoughts and express them in English. These teachers recognized English learners' need to have a little extra time when participating in class. Mrs. Manvi, on the other hand, had students count in unison so the pace was set by the more proficient speakers, leaving the others with no time to think about the next number. Also, when she did call on students, she was looking for specific answers to be given quickly to the whole class. Therefore, she received a "0" on the SIOP for Wait Time.

19.   *Opportunities to Clarify Key Concepts in L1*

Mr. Charles: N/A

Mrs. Lantero: 3

Mrs. Manvi: 0

The students in Mr. Charles' class had enough contextual clues throughout the lesson—coupled with intermediate English proficiency—so they did not need to use their primary language (L1). Therefore, Mr. Charles received a NA on the SIOP. Mrs. Lantero permitted the students to complete the worksheet together, which provided the opportunity for discussing and clarifying concepts in the students' native language if necessary. However, since opportunities for interaction were limited, there may have been a need for students to use L1 more extensively, which is why Mrs. Lantero received a "3" on the SIOP. Mrs. Manvi did not provide opportunities for students to interact with one another so their L1 could not be used even if it would have helped scaffold their understanding.

Summary

Teachers need to create ample opportunities for English learners to practice using academic English, among themselves and with teachers. Incorporating a number of grouping configurations into lessons often facilitates using English in ways that support the lessons' objectives.

The evidence is clear that for most teachers, it is challenging to balance the interchange between themselves and their students. Effective sheltered teachers plan for and incorporate structured opportunities for students to use English in a variety of ways.

Discussion Questions

1. Think of a content concept that you might be teaching. Describe three different grouping configurations that could be used for teaching and learning this concept. How would you organize the members of each group? How would you monitor student learning? What would you want students to do while working in their groups? How would the grouping configurations facilitate learning for ELs?

2. Either videotape your own classroom while you're teaching a lesson or observe another teacher's classroom for a 15-minute segment. Estimate the proportion of teacher talk and student talk. Given the ratio of teacher–student talk, what are some possible ramifications for English learners in the class?

3. English learners are often reticent to contribute to class discussions. An important role for a sheltered teacher is to encourage ELs to participate in nonthreatening ways. What are some specific techniques you can use to encourage students to elaborate on their responses and express their thoughts fully? What can you do to ensure sufficient wait time for students to formulate and express their thoughts?

4. The use of primary language (L1) instruction is controversial today. What are the pros and cons of primary language support in sheltered classrooms? Why do you think this is such a contentious issue?

7 Practice/Application

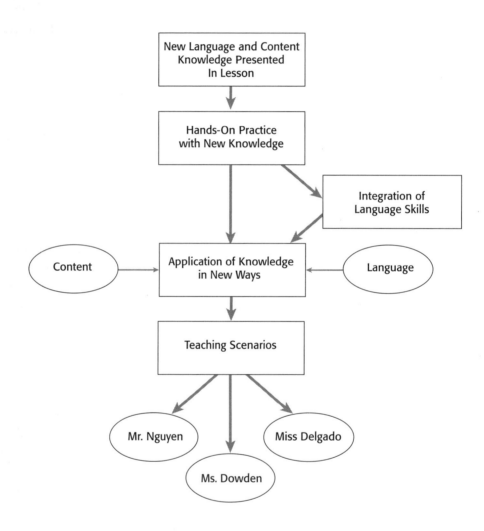

OBJECTIVES

After reading, discussing, and engaging in activities related to this chapter, you will be able to meet the following content and language objectives.

Content Objectives:

Identify a variety of ways for students to enhance their learning through hands-on practice

Create application activities that extend the learning in new ways and relate to multiple standards or content objectives

Language Objectives:

Design activities that require integrated use of different language skills for students to practice new content knowledge

Discuss the importance of linking practice and application activities to specific lesson objectives

Recognize the need for academic vocabulary practice

One common memory that most adults share is of learning to ride an adult bike. Even after riding smaller bicycles with training wheels, most of us were unprepared for the balancing act required for us not to fall down when riding a "big" bike. If you had an older brother or sister who talked you through the process, showed you how to balance, and perhaps even held onto the bike while you were steadying yourself, your independent practice time with the big bike was probably enhanced. Talking about the experience, listening to someone else describe it, observing other riders, and then practicing for yourself all worked together to turn you into a bicycle rider. That feeling of accomplishment, of mastering something new through practice and application, is a special feeling that most of us have experienced as learners.

Background

In this chapter, we discuss how sheltered teachers provide English learners (ELs) with the types of hands-on experiences, guidance, and practice that can lead to mastery of content knowledge. The teaching vignettes demonstrate how three high school general biology teachers, all of whom have large numbers of ELs in their classes, designed biology lessons on ecosystems.

Hands-On Materials and/or Manipulatives for Practice

As previously mentioned, riding a bike is usually preceded by practicing with training wheels and working with a more experienced bike rider. Obviously, the more practice one has on the bike the more likely one is to become a good bike rider. Now, think about learning to play a musical instrument.

Some years ago, an entrepreneur decided to market a piano-teaching course that included a cardboard sheet printed with piano keys. Students were supposed to practice the piano on the paper keyboard by following the directions printed in the course manual. The black-and-white keys on the keyboard were printed and dotted lines represented where students were supposed to place their fingers during practice sessions. It was little surprise that the paper keyboards didn't catch on even though the course manual clearly described in incremental steps how to play the piano, because even with hours of practice on the paper keyboard, students were still unable to play the piano well. In this case, it wasn't just the *practice* that was important. Without hearing the sounds during practice, learning to play the piano was an artificial and nearly impossible task.

When learning to ride a bicycle, play the piano, or articulate how convex lenses differ from concave, students have a greater chance of mastering content concepts and skills when they are given multiple opportunities to practice in relevant, meaningful ways. When this practice includes "hands-on" experiences including manipulatives, practice sessions are enhanced. Madeline Hunter (1982), a renowned expert in teaching methods, coined the term "guided practice" to describe the process of the teacher leading the student through practice sessions prior to expecting independent application. She suggested that we keep the following four questions (and their answers) in mind as we plan lessons involving hands-on practice for students (pp. 65–68):

1. How much material should be practiced at one time? *Answer:* A short meaningful amount. Always use meaning to divide your content into parts.
2. How long in time should a practice period be? *Answer:* A short time so the student exerts intense effort and has intent to learn.
3. How often should students practice? *Answer:* New learning, massed practice. Older learning, distributed practice. [Hunter explains that massed practice means several practice periods scheduled close together. Distributed practice means spacing practice periods farther and farther apart, such as when we review previously learned material.]
4. How will students know how well they have done? *Answer:* Give specific knowledge of results (i.e., specific feedback).

Although all students benefit from guided practice, English learners make more rapid progress in mastering content objectives when they are provided with multiple opportunities to practice with hands-on materials and/or manipulatives. These may be organized, created, counted, classified, stacked, experimented with, observed, rearranged, dismantled, and so forth. Manipulating learning materials is important for ELs because it helps them connect abstract concepts with concrete experiences.

Obviously, the type of manipulative employed for practice depends on the subject being taught. For example, in a tenth-grade geometry class in which students are learning how to solve proofs, content objectives might justify paper-and-pencil practice. However, if it is possible to incorporate hands-on practice with manipulatives, students' learning will probably be enhanced.

Being told how to ride a bike or play the piano, reading about how to do so, or watching a video of someone else engaged in bike riding or piano playing is much different from riding down the sidewalk or listening to musical sounds you have produced yourself. Whenever possible and appropriate, use hands-on manipulatives for practice.

Application of Content and Language Knowledge

Think again about the relationship between actually riding a bicycle and just watching someone else ride it, or about actually playing a piano and just reading step-by-step piano-playing instructions. As Hunter (1982) said:

> The difference between knowing how something should be done and being able to do it is the quantum leap in learning . . . new learning is like wet cement, it can be easily damaged. A mistake at the beginning of learning can have long-lasting consequences that are hard to eradicate (p. 71).

We all recall our own learning experiences in elementary, middle, and high school, and the university. For many of us, the classes and courses we remember best are the ones in which we applied our new knowledge in meaningful ways. These may have included activities such as writing a diary entry from the perspective of a character in a novel, creating a semantic map illustrating the relationships among complex concepts, or completing comprehensive case studies on children we assessed and taught. These concrete experiences forced us to apply new information and concepts in a personally relevant way. We remember the times when we "got it," and we remember the times when we gave it our all but somehow still missed the point.

For students acquiring a new language, the need to apply new information is critically important because discussing and "doing" make abstract concepts concrete. Application can occur in a number of ways, such as clustering, using graphic organizers, solving problems in cooperative learning groups, writing a journal, engaging in discussion circles, or a variety of other meaningful activities (Peregoy & Boyle, 1997). Mainly we must remember that we learn best by involving ourselves in relevant, meaningful application of what we are learning.

For English learners, application must also include opportunities for them to practice language knowledge in the classroom. Opportunities for social interaction promote language development, and these include discussion, working with partners and small groups, and "reporting out" information orally and in writing. For example, it is appropriate, depending on students' language proficiency, to ask them to explain a process to a peer using newly learned vocabulary. Activities such as describing the results of an experiment, specifying why a character reacted in a particular way, and listing the steps in a process all help ELs produce and practice new language and vocabulary, as long as they are supported in a caring environment.

Whether to correct ELs' language errors during practice time is a topic of controversy (Crawford, 2003; Peregoy & Boyle, 1997). In general, consider students' stages of English language development when deciding to correct or not. For beginning English speakers, errors may be developmental and reflect students' native language use (e.g., not remembering to add past tense inflected endings to English verbs). Other errors may deal with placement of adjectives, sentence structure, plurals, and so forth. If errors impede communication, you can gently correct them by restating the sentence in correct form.

For example, Meeli, who recently emigrated from Estonia told her teacher, "My parents sends congratulations to you." She meant that her parents sent their greetings. In reply, Meeli's teacher responded, "Thank you. I think you mean 'greetings.' Please tell your parents I send them my greetings, too." Note that the confusion over the nouns, "congratulation" and "greetings" was corrected, but the teacher just modeled the appropriate usage of the verb "send" without making note of the correction. What is most important is that you be sensitive to errors that confuse communication; these usually can be corrected in a natural way.

Integration of Language Skills

Reading, writing, listening, and speaking are complex, cognitive language processes that are interrelated and integrated. As we go about our daily lives, we move through the processes in a natural way, reading what we write, talking about what we've read, and listening to others talk about what they've read and written. Most young children become grammatically competent in their home language by age five, and their continuing language development relates primarily to vocabulary, more sophisticated grammar usage (e.g., embedding subordinate clauses), and functional as well as sociocultural applications of language (e.g., using different language registers according to their audience, and developing rhetorical styles) (Peregoy & Boyle, 1997; TESOL, 1997). Proficiency in reading and writing is achieved much later and differences exist among individuals in levels of competence. Students in particular need to learn academic language for use in school settings (see Chapter 1 for a detailed discussion).

For English learners, students may achieve competence in written language earlier than oral language and ELs do not need to be proficient speakers before they start to read and write. In fact, the language processes—reading, writing, listening, and speaking—are mutually supportive. The ESL Standards (TESOL, 1997) specifically recommend developing these language skills in a holistic manner, recognizing their interdependent nature. Although the relationships among the processes are complex, practice in any one promotes development in the others.

Effective sheltered teachers understand the need to create many opportunities for English learners to practice and use all four language processes in an integrated manner. Throughout the day, ELs benefit from varied experiences that incorporate reading, promote interactions with others, provide the chance to listen to peers' ideas, and encourage writing about what is being learned. Because students have different preferred learning styles, when teachers teach through different modalities and encourage students to practice and apply new knowledge through multiple language processes, they have a better chance of meeting students' needs and furthering both their language and content development.

The Lesson

Unit: Ecosystems (11th grade)

The three eleventh-grade general biology classrooms described in the teaching vignettes in this chapter are in a large urban high school. Approximately 65 percent of the students in the classes are English learners and they are nearly all in the beginning and advanced-beginning stages of English language fluency. The other students in the classes are heterogeneously mixed.

The general biology standards for the eleventh grade require that teachers include the study of ecosystems, water and nutrient cycling, symbiosis, life cycles, and decomposition. Scientific processing skills include making observations, recording data, forming hypotheses, making models, project design, and experimentation. For the scenarios described in this chapter, the teachers have designed an extended unit on *ecosystems* (ecological communities that, together with their environment, form a unit) and *symbiosis* (a close relationship between two or more species that may or may not benefit each other). The lessons extend over several days.

Teaching Scenarios

Mr. Nguyen

Mr. Nguyen approached the subject of ecosystems by asking students to read the textbook chapter with a partner. He then provided photographs, illustrations, and procedural steps for creating an ecosystem that was essentially a covered terrarium—a container for plants and small animals. The materials he used to build the ecosystem included a glass tank, a variety of small plants, some sand, small rocks, soil, a turtle, a horned toad, and meal worms. He poured a small amount of water into the system and put the terrarium under a soft sunlamp. He presented a brief lecture on how the various species within the ecosystem might support each other within it.

Mr. Nguyen then showed a video on a variety of ecosystems that exist on earth. Students were given a study guide to use during the video that included two columns for structured note-taking. Over the next two weeks, each student was required to complete a standard lab observation report about the changes that occurred within the ecosystem. Throughout, students were encouraged to work in groups on writing up their observations and findings, and the most vocal students were enthusiastic participants during the shared discussions.

On the SIOP form in Figure 7.1, rate Mr. Nguyen on each of the Practice/Application indicators.

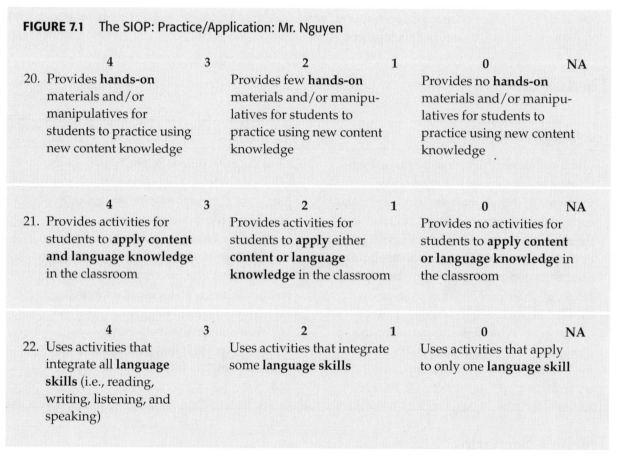

FIGURE 7.1 The SIOP: Practice/Application: Mr. Nguyen

4	3	2	1	0	NA
20. Provides **hands-on** materials and/or manipulatives for students to practice using new content knowledge		Provides few **hands-on** materials and/or manipulatives for students to practice using new content knowledge		Provides no **hands-on** materials and/or manipulatives for students to practice using new content knowledge	
4	**3**	**2**	**1**	**0**	**NA**
21. Provides activities for students to **apply content and language knowledge** in the classroom		Provides activities for students to **apply** either **content or language knowledge** in the classroom		Provides no activities for students to **apply content or language knowledge** in the classroom	
4	**3**	**2**	**1**	**0**	**NA**
22. Uses activities that integrate all **language skills** (i.e., reading, writing, listening, and speaking)		Uses activities that integrate some **language skills**		Uses activities that apply to only one **language skill**	

Ms. Dowden

Ms. Dowden decided that the best way for her students to understand and apply newly learned content about ecosystems was to have them read, discuss, write detailed observations about, and create their own models of ecosystems. After reading aloud the content and language objectives, she began the first lesson by introducing content vocabulary. Then students read the section of the biology textbook on ecosystems together in small groups. Ms. Dowden reviewed the key concepts by writing them on the board.

Because Ms. Dowden realized that many of the content concepts and key vocabulary in this unit were new and complex, she believed she could best meet everyone's needs, including ELs and English proficient students by dividing the class into two groups. As older adolescents, her students were able to work independently and most had experience with computers and the Internet, even though the amount of experience they had varied. Ms. Dowden directed students with higher levels of academic and English proficiency to some library references and Internet websites related to science and biology. These students were instructed to read and research the topic of ecosystems and symbiosis and design a method for creating an ecosystem using a variety of inexpensive and accessible materials they could find around their homes. Ms. Dowden pledged her assistance in helping them with the research and the project, but she urged them to work together as partners and in groups to create sustainable ecosystems. She explained how students were to write and submit their plans including materials, timeline, and so forth. Once they created their ecosystems, they were to monitor the changes that occurred within them, and eventually, they would include their findings on the districtwide general biology website.

While a third of the students were independently researching the library and the Internet, Ms. Dowden worked with the English learners and a few other students. She introduced them to a website on the classroom computer that included information about ecosystems. She had printed a few pages from the website and together students read these, comparing the information to what they learned in their textbooks. Ms. Dowden then introduced a project in which students were to create their own "ecocolumns"—stacked ecosystems made from plastic bottles (*Bottle Biology,* 1993). Simplified directions in the form of an illustrated sequence map provided steps for creating the ecocolumns along with a list of materials that were needed. The ELs volunteered to bring materials from home, including soil, water, plants, compost, spiders, fruit flies, snails, and two large plastic soda bottles for each ecocolumn.

The following day, while Ms. Dowden modeled the process, the ELs began creating their own ecocolumns from the soda bottles that were each cut into three sections. Chambers were created using the sections of the plastic bottles and an aquarium with water and rocks was prepared for the bottom section of the ecocolumn. Above it was a soil or decomposition unit, and above that was a plant or animal habitat. The top of the system included air holes and a precipitation funnel. Ms. Dowden modeled the creation of the ecocolumns, demonstrating each step of the process.

The students then created their own ecosystems; as they were doing so, Ms. Dowden encouraged them to discuss what was working and what wasn't, and why. Over the next two weeks, all students were expected to observe their ecosystems, including root and soil changes and the effects of light and water. Ms. Dowden provided models of data-recording sheets that showed what students might be observing and what they should record on the overhead. All students, including those who independently created their ecosystems, used the models as guides. The ELs used specially designed data sheets on which they recorded their data in a simplified format.

The students who designed their own ecosystems completed a "bioessay" to explain the effects of different substances on seed germination and plant development (*Bottle Biology,* 1993, p. 79). The ELs were encouraged to list the changes that occurred as a result of competition among the species in their ecosystems; that is, "Did one species do better than another, and if so, how do you know? Which appeared to be symbiotic? How do you know?" The ELs were also encouraged to contribute their findings to the general biology website.

Throughout this unit, Ms. Dowden emphasized to all students that there was no right or wrong way to build the ecosystem and/or the ecocolumn. Change was considered to be a natural part of the experience and students were encouraged to work together to determine what happened with their own systems and why.

On the SIOP form in Figure 7.2, rate Ms. Dowden on each of the Practice/Application indicators.

FIGURE 7.2 The SIOP: Practice/Application: Ms. Dowden

4	3	2	1	0	NA
20. Provides **hands-on** materials and/or manipulatives for students to practice using new content knowledge		Provides few **hands-on** materials and/or manipulatives for students to practice using new content knowledge		Provides no **hands-on** materials and/or manipulatives for students to practice using new content knowledge	

4	3	2	1	0	NA
21. Provides activities for students to **apply content and language knowledge** in the classroom		Provides activities for students to **apply** either **content or language knowledge** in the classroom		Provides no activities for students to **apply content or language knowledge** in the classroom	

4	3	2	1	0	NA
22. Uses activities that integrate all **language skills** (i.e., reading, writing, listening, and speaking)		Uses activities that integrate some **language skills**		Uses activities that apply to only one **language skill**	

Miss Delgado

Miss Delgado taught the lessons on ecosystems by having students work as partners to read the textbook chapter. She pointed out key vocabulary and orally reinforced the key concepts. To illustrate an ecosystem, she drew a layered ecosystem on the blackboard that included decaying plant matter, insects, and small animals. Students were directed to copy her illustration off the board and to label the various species within the ecosystem. Miss Delgado then showed a video on ecosystems and symbiosis. Each student was required to write a paragraph explaining how various species on the Earth support and contribute to each other's sustenance and viability.

On the SIOP form in Figure 7.3, rate Miss Delgado on each of the Practice/Application indicators.

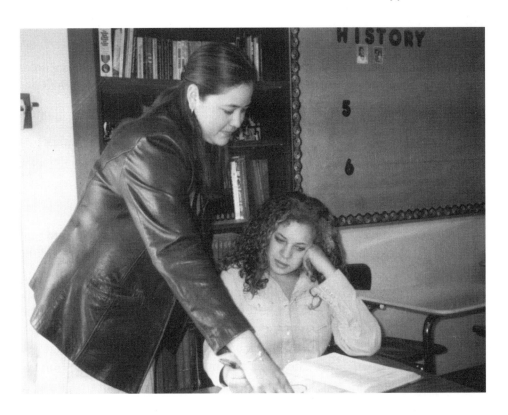

FIGURE 7.3   The SIOP: Practice/Application: Miss Delgado

4	3	2	1	0	NA
20. Provides **hands-on** materials and/or manipulatives for students to practice using new content knowledge		Provides few **hands-on** materials and/or manipulatives for students to practice using new content knowledge		Provides no **hands-on** materials and/or manipulatives for students to practice using new content knowledge	

4	3	2	1	0	NA
21. Provides activities for students to **apply content and language knowledge** in the classroom		Provides activities for students to **apply** either **content or language knowledge** in the classroom		Provides no activities for students to **apply content or language knowledge** in the classroom	

4	3	2	1	0	NA
22. Uses activities that integrate all **language skills** (i.e., reading, writing, listening, and speaking)		Uses activities that integrate some **language skills**		Uses activities that apply to only one **language skill**	

Discussion of Lessons

Mr. Nguyen, Ms. Dowden, and Miss Delgado differed substantially in how they taught their units on ecosystems. As you read our ratings, compare them to your own and those of colleagues.

20. *Provides Hands-On Materials and/or Manipulatives for Practice*

    Mr. Nguyen: 2

    Ms. Dowden: 4

    Miss Delgado: 1

Mr. Nguyen received a "2" for Hands-On Manipulatives and Practice. Although he modeled the creation of an ecosystem (the covered terrarium), he incorporated a "one-size-fits-all" approach by having everyone do the same thing. Because native English speakers represented one-third of his class, and the rest of the students were in the beginning to advanced-beginning stages of English proficiency, the most vocal and competent English speakers assumed primary responsibility for monitoring the changes in the ecosystem (terrarium). Therefore, ELs may have concluded the unit with few opportunities to participate in a hands-on manner, thus they most likely had limited mastery of the content and key vocabulary concepts.

Ms. Dowden received a "4" for Hands-On Manipulatives and Practice indicator. All students in her class, regardless of English proficiency, were expected to master the content concepts related to ecosystems and symbiosis. Also, all students were expected to create their own ecosystems; however, the ELs were provided with materials and clear directions, including modeling, to assist them in building their ecocolumns. The hands-on experimentation by all students reinforced the content concepts and key vocabulary, and the meaningful practice made concrete what could have been abstract for the English learners.

Miss Delgado received a "1" on the SIOP for Hands-On Manipulatives and Practice. Although she attempted to illustrate an ecosystem on the board, students were mostly passive while they copied her illustration and when they watched the video. Few of the students had the opportunity to practice using their newly learned content information or key vocabulary. It is therefore doubtful that ELs had a clear understanding of ecosystems or that students could apply what they had learned in any meaningful way.

21. *Provides Activities for Students to Apply Content and Language Knowledge*

    Mr. Nguyen: 3

    Ms. Dowden: 4

    Miss Delgado: 1

In his lesson on ecosystems, Mr. Nguyen provided his students with photographs, illustrations, and procedural steps for creating a terrarium. Even though he was the one who actually created the terrarium, his students noted changes within the ecosystem and reported on examples of symbiosis. Further, they completed data reports on their observations and Mr. Nguyen discussed what they were observing with students. They were encouraged to ask questions and to share their observations and hypotheses with other students.

Therefore, Mr. Nguyen received a "3" on the SIOP for Application of Content and Language Knowledge. Students were involved as observers in the creation of the ecosystem, and they applied what they learned through their data sheets and in their discussions. Language knowledge was applied through oral interactions and in the writing of the data reports; however, there were few opportunities for students to engage in student–student interactions, which provide language practice and develop language proficiency. The video reinforced the textbook content concepts and the demonstration provided another level of scaffolding.

Ms. Dowden received a "4" for the Application of Content and Language Knowledge indicator. Throughout the lessons, students were required to apply what they were learning, not only during the creation of their ecosystems, but also during discussion and through their submitted data sheets. ELs had multiple opportunities to apply what they were learning and to practice English (e.g., sharing observations of changes with partners and groups). While Ms. Dowden provided independent research opportunities for English-fluent students, she carefully scaffolded the learning for ELs; but note that she did not lessen her expectations that all her general biology students would master the content and language objectives.

After students read the textbook chapter, Miss Delgado drew an illustration of a layered ecosystem on the board. Students copied the drawing and labeled species. They watched the video on ecosystems and symbiosis and each wrote a paragraph about what they had learned.

Miss Delgado received a "1" for Application of Content and Language Knowledge. Although there was no opportunity for students to apply their content knowledge in a hands-on way, they could demonstrate what they knew through their written paragraph. There were very few opportunities for students to practice or apply their language knowledge orally.

22. *Integration of Language Skills*

   Mr. Nguyen: 3

   Ms. Dowden: 4

   Miss Delgado: 2

Mr. Nguyen received a "3" on the SIOP for Integration of Language Skills. Throughout their lesson on ecosystems, English learners were given the opportunity to read, write, listen, and discuss the content concepts. However, because he did not differentiate his instruction for ELs, his less vocal students may have felt reluctant to fully participate in class discussions. In addition, Mr. Nguyen's lessons were teacher-dominated so students' opportunities for language practice were somewhat limited.

For all of her students, Ms. Dowden facilitated the reading of the textbook chapter and the information on the website about ecosystems. The ELs followed her demonstration on how to build their ecocolumns, discussing their work throughout. Each student kept a data sheet on observed changes in the eco-columns and they were expected to talk about their findings with each other.

Therefore, Ms. Dowden received a "4" on the SIOP for Integration of Language Skills. Throughout the lessons in this unit, English learners were reading, discussing, and writing about the process of building their eco-systems. The language processes were well integrated into the delivery of the biology content because students were not only reading and writing about what they were learning, but they also had spoken interactions with the teacher and with each other.

Miss Delgado's lessons on ecosystems involved partner reading for the textbook chapter and a lecture with a blackboard illustration on the process of decomposition of plant material. Independently, students copied her illustration off the board and labeled the various species within the ecosystem. After she showed the video on ecosystems and symbiosis, students wrote paragraphs explaining how various species on the Earth support and contribute to each other's sustenance and viability.

Miss Delgado received a "2" on the Integration of Language Skills indicator. Her students read the textbook, listened to the mini-lecture, watched the video, and wrote paragraphs about their understandings. However, students had few chances to connect reading and writing activities with discussion, either with the teacher or each other. There were few opportunities for students to practice language and content concepts with each other.

Summary

With any type of new learning, practice and application of newly acquired skills are needed to ensure mastery of content concepts. Hands-on activities and materials, including manipulatives, enable students to forge connections between abstract and concrete concepts. Students make these connections most effectively when they use all language processes, including reading, writing, listening, and speaking, during practice and application.

Discussion Questions

1. Compare and contrast the following two teachers' approaches to teaching a lesson on nutrition.
   a. One teacher's approach involves a lecture, a diagram of the food pyramid, and a list of appropriate foods for each group. Students are then tested about their knowledge of the food pyramid.
   b. The other teacher's approach begins with students' maintaining a food diary for a week. Copies of the food pyramid are distributed and

explained, and all students must analyze their food consumption according to the recommendations on the pyramid. With a partner, students must design a nutritionally sound weekly menu for each day of the following week, and they must be prepared to defend their food choices to peer group members.

Which of the approaches to teaching this content concept is most appropriate for English learners? How do you know? Be as specific as you can.

2. In the preceding example, the second teacher might have included some hands-on manipulatives to enhance the lesson further. Why would this have helped English learners? What types of hands-on manipulatives might she have used? How could they have been incorporated into the lesson?

3. English learners benefit from the integration of reading, writing, listening, and speaking. For those with limited English language proficiency, tell what may be difficult. Is it performance of all four skills? What adjustments and techniques can a teacher use to provide ELs with successful experiences while they read, write, listen, and speak about new information they are learning? Include specific activities and examples in your answer.

4. With a large number of content standards in each subject area for which teachers and students are accountable, how is it possible to provide direct application and hands-on practice for lessons? What can teachers do to alleviate the conflict between "covering the content" and making it "accessible" for English learners?

8 Lesson Delivery

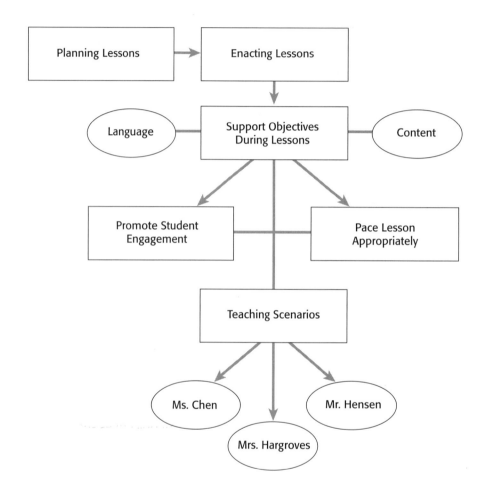

OBJECTIVES

After reading, discussing, and engaging in activities related to this chapter, you will be able to meet the following content and language objectives.

Content Objectives:

List suggestions for teachers to monitor if their lesson is supporting the content objectives

Describe strategies for improving student time-on-task throughout a lesson

Explain how a focus on a lesson's objectives can aid in pacing

Apply appropriate pacing strategies for English learners

Language Objectives:

Explore a situation where a great lesson plan is not enacted successfully and explain what might have gone wrong and what could be improved

Compare pacing considerations in classes that have only native English speakers with classes that have English learners

Discuss characteristics of an effective SIOP lesson

Background

This chapter addresses the way a lesson is delivered, how well the content and language objectives are supported during the lesson, to what extent students are engaged in the lesson, and how appropriate the pace of the lesson is to students' ability levels. You will see that this chapter parallels Chapter 2, Lesson Preparation, because the two are closely related. The effectiveness of a lesson's delivery—the level of student participation, how clearly information is communicated, students' level of understanding reflected in the quality of student work—often can be traced back to the preparation that took place before students entered the classroom. We will meet the teachers from Chapter 2 again and discuss how their level of preparation was executed in their lesson delivery.

Content Objectives

As we discussed in Chapter 2, content objectives should be stated orally and in writing for students and teachers alike to see. In this way, written objectives serve to remind us of the focus of the lesson, providing a structure to classroom procedures. Written objectives also allow students to know the direction of the lesson. Throughout the lesson and at its conclusion, the teacher and students can evaluate the extent to which the lesson delivery supported the content objectives.

Language Objectives

As you now know, language objectives are an important part of effective sheltered lessons. Teachers and students benefit from having a clear, simple language objective written for them to see and stated for them to hear during the lesson. The objective may be related to an ESL Standard such as, "Students will write to communicate with different people for different reasons;" or it may be related to teachers' scope and sequence of language skills that their own students need to develop such as, "Students will use punctuation and capitalization to make their writing readable." Whatever language objective the teacher chooses, it needs to be recognizable in the lesson's delivery.

Student Engagement

In observing sheltered classrooms, we have come to appreciate the importance of academic engaged time. English learners are the students who can least afford to have valuable time squandered through boredom, inattention, socializing, and other off-task behaviors. Time also is wasted when teachers are ill prepared; have poor classroom management skills; spend excessive amounts of time making announcements, passing out and handing in papers; and the like. The most effective teachers minimize these behaviors and maximize time spent actively engaged in instruction (Mastropieri & Scruggs, 1994). English learners who are working to achieve grade-level competence benefit from efficient use of class time. Further, many of these learners have had uneven schooling experiences, missing time in school due to circumstances beyond their control, and are then further disadvantaged by inefficient use of class time.

There are actually three aspects to student engagement that should be considered: (1) allocated time, (2) engaged time, and (3) academic learning time (Berliner, 1984). Allocated time reflects the decisions teachers make regarding the amount of time to spend studying a topic (e.g., math versus reading) and a given academic task (e.g., how much time to spend on reading comprehension versus decoding skills). As we have discussed throughout this book, effective sheltered instruction teachers plan for and deliver lessons that are balanced between teacher presentation of information and opportunities for students to apply the information in meaningful ways. Effective sheltered teachers use instructional time wisely.[1]

Engaged time refers to the time students are actively participating in instruction during the time allocated. The engaged time-on-task research has consistently concluded that the more actively students participate in the instructional process, the more they achieve. As Bickel and Bickel (1986) put it: "Students learn more when they are attending to the learning tasks that are the focus of instruction" (p. 493). Instruction that is understandable to ELs, that creates opportunities for students to talk about the lesson's concepts, and that provides hands-on activities to reinforce learning captures students' attention and keeps them more actively engaged.

---

[1] We believe that it is reasonable to deliver lessons that engage students 90 percent to 100 percent of the period. Lessons where students are engaged less than 50 percent of the time are unacceptable and warrant a "0" on the SIOP indicator for student engagement.

Academic learning time focuses on students' time-on-task, when the task is related to the materials they will be tested on. Creative, fun activities are not effective if they are unrelated to the content and language objectives of the lesson. According to Leinhardt et al. (1982):

> When teachers spend their time and energy teaching students the content the students need to learn, students learn the material. When students spend their time actively engaged in activities that relate strongly to the materials they will be tested on, they learn more of the material (p. 409).

Of course, sheltered teachers need to be explicit in their expectations and make certain that their English learners understand which materials relate to upcoming assessments.

In summary, effective SI teachers need to plan to use the entire class period efficiently, teach in ways that engage students, and make sure students are engaged in activities that specifically relate to the material on which they will be assessed.

Pacing

Pacing refers to the rate at which information is presented during a lesson. The pace of the lesson depends on the nature of the lesson's content, as well as the level of students' background knowledge. When working with ELs, it can be challenging to find a pace that doesn't present information too quickly yet is brisk enough to maintain students' interest, especially when a variety of English proficiency levels are represented in the same classroom. Finding an appropriate pace requires practice, but becomes easier as teachers develop familiarity with their students' skills.

The Lesson

Unit: The Gold Rush (4th grade)

The classrooms described in the teaching vignettes in this chapter are all in a suburban elementary school with heterogeneously mixed students. English language learners represent approximately 30 percent of the student population and the children speak a variety of languages. In the fourth-grade classrooms of teachers Ms. Chen, Mrs. Hargroves, and Mr. Hensen, the majority of the ELs are at the intermediate stage of English fluency.

As part of the fourth-grade social studies curriculum, Ms. Chen, Mrs. Hargroves, and Mr. Hensen have planned a unit on the California Gold Rush. The school district requires the use of the adopted social studies series although teachers are encouraged to supplement the text with primary source materials, literature, and realia. The content topics for the Gold Rush unit include: westward expansion, routes and trails to the West, the people who sought their fortunes, hardships, settlements, the discovery of gold, the life of miners, methods for extracting gold, the impact of the Gold Rush, and so forth.

Each of the teachers has created several lessons for this unit, beginning with a lesson plan (approximately 45 minutes per day) on routes and trails to the West. Specifically, the content of this lesson covers the Oregon Trail, the Overland Trail, and the route around Cape Horn.

Teaching Scenarios

To refresh your memory about the lessons on westward expansion and the Gold Rush taught by Ms. Chen, Mrs. Hargroves, and Mr. Hensen, we summarize them in the sections that follow. (See Chapter 2, Teaching Scenarios, for a complete description of the three lessons.)

Ms. Chen
Ms. Chen began the lesson on westward expansion by reading aloud the content and language objectives for the day.

Content Objectives

1. Find and label the three main routes to the west on a map.

2. Tell one or two facts about each of the three trails.

Language Objectives

1. Write sentences explaining how the three routes to the west were given their names.

2. Tell how the structure of some words gives clues to their meaning.

After a whole-class brainstorming and List-Group-Label activity about why people leave their homes and move to new locations, Ms. Chen assigned most of the class a quick-write on the Gold Rush. She then provided a "jump-start" for the English learners with very limited proficiency by introducing key vocabulary, passing around iron pyrite ("fool's gold"), looking together at a map of the trails west, and viewing several pictures of pioneers and Gold Rush characters.

Following this, Ms. Chen introduced the key vocabulary to the entire class, and discussed why roads, streets, and trails have particular names. She pointed out the three trails west on the wall map, discussed their names, and explained how the Overland Trail was a compound word that gave clues to its meaning (Over + Land = Overland).

Next, Ms. Chen distributed copies of maps and modeled on the overhead projector how to use colored pencils to color in the maps. Students worked together in small groups to complete their maps. Finally, with just a few minutes remaining in the period, Ms. Chen distributed a skeleton outline of the chapter

FIGURE 8.1   Lesson Delivery Section of the SIOP: Ms. Chen

	4	3	2	1	0	NA
23.	**Content objectives** clearly supported by lesson delivery		**Content objectives** supported somewhat by lesson delivery		**Content objectives** not supported by lesson delivery	
24.	**Language objectives** clearly supported by lesson delivery		**Language objectives** supported somewhat by lesson delivery		**Language objectives** not supported by lesson delivery	
25.	**Students engaged** approximately 90% to 100% of the period		**Students engaged** approximately 70% of the period		**Students engaged** less than 50% of the period	
26.	**Pacing** of the lesson appropriate to the students' ability level		**Pacing** generally appropriate, but at times too fast or too slow		**Pacing** inappropriate to the students' ability level	

that the students had read. The outline's headings (Locations, Characteristics, Challenges, and Advantages) provided an organizer for the information, and in groups, students began working together to fill in the outline. The lesson was concluded with a review of the content and language objectives. Then several students volunteered to report on a number of facts about each of the trails.

On the SIOP form in Figure 8.1, rate Ms. Chen's lesson for each of the indicators in Lesson Delivery indicators. Be able to defend your ratings and discuss them with others, if possible.

Mrs. Hargroves

Mrs. Hargroves began her lesson on the trails west by stating, "Today, you'll learn about the Oregon Trail, the Overland Trail, and the Route around Cape Horn. We'll also be working on maps, and I want you to color the Overland Trail a different color from the color you use for the Cape Horn route. When you learn about the Oregon Trail, you'll complete the map with a third color. By the time you're finished, you should have all three routes drawn on the map using different colors." She held up a completed map for the students to see as an example.

Following a brief lecture on westward expansion, Mrs. Hargroves directed students to the respective chapter in the text. Students looked at the illustrations and she responded to questions they had. She began reading the chapter and after a few minutes, she directed students to complete the reading independently. She circulated through the room, answering questions and helping with difficult words. After twenty minutes, Mrs. Hargroves stopped

FIGURE 8.2 Lesson Delivery Section of the SIOP: Mrs. Hargroves

4	3	2	1	0	NA
23. **Content objectives** clearly supported by lesson delivery		**Content objectives** supported somewhat by lesson delivery		**Content objectives** not supported by lesson delivery	
4	3	2	1	0	NA
24. **Language objectives** clearly supported by lesson delivery		**Language objectives** supported somewhat by lesson delivery		**Language objectives** not supported by lesson delivery	
4	3	2	1	0	NA
25. **Students engaged** approximately 90% to 100% of the period		**Students engaged** approximately 70% of the period		**Students engaged** less than 50% of the period	
4	3	2	1	0	NA
26. **Pacing** of the lesson appropriate to the students' ability level		**Pacing** generally appropriate, but at times too fast or too slow		**Pacing** inappropriate to the students' ability level	

the reading, distributed colored pencils and maps, and asked students to complete the maps with partners. When the maps were completed, she collected them and assigned a brief essay on the topic, "If you had been a pioneer, which trail would you have chosen? Why?"

On the SIOP form in Figure 8.2, rate Mrs. Hargroves's lesson for each of the Lesson Delivery indicators.

Mr. Hensen

Mr. Hensen began his lesson by asking how many of the students had traveled to California. They discussed the various modes of transportation used by students who had visited the state, and then Mr. Hensen linked their responses to the travel modes of the pioneers. Following a video on westward expansion, he introduced the key vocabulary for the day's lessons (Oregon Trail, Overland Trail, Route around Cape Horn).

Next, Mr. Hensen read aloud two paragraphs from the textbook chapter. He then numbered students off into six groups, assigned sections of the text to the newly formed groups, and engaged them in a Jigsaw reading activity for the remainder of the chapter. ELs were partnered with more proficient English readers for the Jigsaw activity. After the Jigsaw groups completed their reading, they returned to their home groups and shared what they had learned from the assigned text. Again, English learners were paired with students with greater English proficiency.

FIGURE 8.3 Lesson Delivery Section of the SIOP: Mr. Hensen

4	3	2	1	0	NA
23. **Content objectives** clearly supported by lesson delivery		**Content objectives** supported somewhat by lesson delivery		**Content objectives** not supported by lesson delivery	
4	3	2	1	0	NA
24. **Language objectives** clearly supported by lesson delivery		**Language objectives** supported somewhat by lesson delivery		**Language objectives** not supported by lesson delivery	
4	3	2	1	0	NA
25. **Students engaged** approximately 90% to 100% of the period		**Students engaged** approximately 70% of the period		**Students engaged** less than 50% of the period	
4	3	2	1	0	NA
26. **Pacing** of the lesson appropriate to the students' ability level		**Pacing** generally appropriate, but at times too fast or too slow		**Pacing** inappropriate to the students' ability level	

Mr. Hensen then directed the students in their home groups to divide up the three trails, with one to two students in each group. One group was asked to draw the Oregon Trail on a map, and the other students were to draw either the Overland or Cape Horn trails. Their next task was to tell the other students in their group how to color their maps, using the map in the text and their reading as a guide. Mr. Hensen circulated through the room, assisting as necessary, while the children completed the mapping activity. At the lesson's conclusion, students were directed to pass in their maps. Those maps that were not finished were assigned as homework.

On the SIOP form in Figure 8.3, rate Mr. Hensen's lesson for each of the Lesson Delivery indicators.

Discussion of Lessons

23. *Content Objectives Clearly Supported by Lesson Delivery*

    Ms. Chen: 4

    Mrs. Hargroves: 2

    Mr. Hensen: 3

Clearly, we believe (and our research supports it) that teachers must include content and language objectives in every lesson, not only for planning and teaching, but also for the students, especially English learners. They need to have a clear, explicit understanding of what the expectations are for a lesson. Recall that only Ms. Chen wrote her content and language objectives on the board, and read them aloud for her students. While Mrs. Hargroves had a content objective (but no language objective) written in her plan book, she stated her plans for the day orally to her students, without clearly defining their learning or language objectives. Mr. Hensen had neither content nor language objectives written in his plan book, yet he appeared to have a clear idea of where he was going with his lesson. However, at the outset of the lesson, his plans may not have been clear for some students.

In this section of the SIOP (Lesson Delivery), we move beyond having the content and lesson objectives written in plan books and on the board (or chart paper or transparency). Rather, the focus here is on whether the lesson delivery matches the stated (or unstated, in Mr. Hensen's case) objectives.

Ms. Chen received a "4" on Content Objectives. From the beginning of the lesson, she had a clearly defined content objective and her lesson delivery supported it. Her focus on the three routes to the west was supported by: 1) activating students' prior knowledge about why people leave their homes and move to a new location (brainstorming and List-Group-Label); 2) engaging some students in a quick-write about the Gold Rush, so that she could have a few minutes to preteach (jump-start) the English learners a topic about which they probably had little prior knowledge; 3) the shared reading of the textbook chapter; 4) the mapping activity; and 5) the skeleton outline that compared and contrasted the three trails.

In contrast, Mrs. Hargroves received a "1" on Content Objectives. As you may recall, she did not write an objective on the board and hurriedly stated what she wanted the students to do for the lesson. What is also problematic about her lesson is that the coloring of the maps seemed to be what was important to her, rather than her confirmation that each student understood the information about the trails west. Students were expected to read the chapter independently, which was most likely impossible for struggling readers and the English learners. Further, her lecture may have been difficult for her ELs to follow. The writing assignment, while a worthwhile topic ("If you had been a pioneer, which trail would you have chosen? Why?"), may or may not have been appropriate for her students, depending on their English proficiency and their ability to access the information in the text. Therefore, her lesson delivery did not support well her intended content objective.

Mr. Hensen was rated "3" on Content Objectives. Although he did not state the objectives, they were certainly implied and supported by his lesson. For example, at the end of the period, he asked several students to report on some differences in the trails; this initial feedback provided information about whether the students had met the day's objective. His constant monitoring, and the various grouping activities, provided additional information about who was meeting the objective and who was having difficulty. He might have added a quick group-response activity (pencils up/pencils down or whiteboard) to determine if all students understood the differences in the trails. Surely, the skeleton outline to be completed the following day would provide him with definitive information about his students' meeting of the content objectives. Had Mr. Hensen written his objectives on the board and gone over them with his students, he would have received a "4" for this indicator.

24. *Language Objectives Supported by Lesson Delivery*

    Ms. Chen: 4

    Mrs. Hargroves: 0

    Mr. Hensen: 1

Ms. Chen was rated "4" on the Language Objectives indicator. Objectives were clearly written and stated and students had several opportunities to meet them. During the discussion of the street names, students had a chance to discuss why and how streets and routes were named. Additionally, students were asked to use complete sentences.

Mrs. Hargroves received a "0" for Language Objectives. She did not write or state any language objectives, and although she did assign a reading and writing activity, for many of the students the text was inaccessible. Therefore, the writing activity would be difficult, if not impossible, for them to complete.

Mr. Hensen received a "1" for Language Objectives. He did not write or state his language objectives, but as with the content objectives, they were implied. He engaged students in a Jigsaw activity for reading the text, and then they returned to their home groups and explained what they had learned from the reading.

25. *Students Engaged Approximately 90%–100% of the Period*

   Ms. Chen: 4

   Mrs. Hargroves: 1

   Mr. Hensen: 4

Ms. Chen is an enthusiastic teacher who plans lessons that use each minute of class time to its fullest. As illustrated in the lesson, Ms. Chen spent time presenting materials and allowed students to work together. They eagerly participated in whole-group and small-group discussions and Ms. Chen made sure they were on-task as she walked around the room. In addition, the content of the lesson was directly related to the district's content standards on which the students will be assessed at the end of the unit.

   Ms. Chen received a "4" for this indicator because her lesson met all the criteria for active student engagement: She used the allocated time in an effective way, basing the lesson on the text, teaching outlining and mapping skills, providing opportunities for interaction and application of concepts, and so forth. Students were actively engaged throughout and the material was relevant to the assignment.

   Mrs. Hargroves received a "1" for Engagement. Recall that Mrs. Hargroves read part of the text chapter aloud which cut its substantial length. She then allotted twenty minutes for students to read the remaining portion of the text chapter. Most students completed the reading in about ten minutes. Some began talking amongst themselves, while others tried to finish the reading. Overall, students were engaged less than 50 percent of the period. During Mrs. Hargroves's lecture on westward expansion, many students were disengaged until she discussed the illustrations and the trails on the wall map.

   Mr. Hensen received a "4" for Engagement. His students were actively engaged throughout the lesson. From the opening question about trips to California, through the video, and the Jigsaw activity, all students were held accountable for learning the material. During the map activity, students not only colored a trail, but were also responsible for assisting each other in finding and coloring the additional trails.

26. *Pacing of Lesson Appropriate to Students' Ability Level*

   Ms. Chen: 4

   Mrs. Hargroves: 1

   Mr. Hensen: 3

Ms. Chen received a "4" for Pacing. She understood that the English learners in her class may have needed a slower pace than the native English speakers. Therefore, she provided them a jump-start that enabled them to be able to keep up with the whole-class activities. She also moved the pace along by reading aloud and doing a shared reading of the text. In this way, she scaffolded instruction for the ELs and all students were able to work at roughly the same pace. The groups for the map activity included four to five students with both native English speakers and ELs who assisted one another as needed.

The pacing of Mrs. Hargroves's lesson was slow and monotonous at times, especially when she lectured, yet she covered material too quickly at other times. Many students were off-task because of the problematic pace of the lesson. Mrs. Hargroves received a "1" for Pacing because it was inappropriate for the students' ability level—too slow to maintain interest and too quick for ELs to understand the information presented orally.

Mr. Hensen received a "3" for Pacing. With the discussions, videos, Jigsaw reading activity, group work, and map coloring, some students, especially the English learners, may have felt a bit rushed. However, he also provided substantial scaffolding, and did allow students to complete their maps at home.

Summary

The importance of setting and meeting objectives cannot be overemphasized. Many teachers may feel comfortable having a general objective in mind and moving along with a lesson's flow, but that approach is not helpful for English learners. Delivering a lesson geared to objectives that have been made clear to students benefits all. The teacher stays on-task and the students know what is important to focus on and remember. By incorporating a variety of techniques that engage students throughout the lesson, teachers not only give students opportunities to learn, practice, and apply information and language skills, but they also help to ensure meeting the lesson's objectives.

Pacing is another important aspect of lesson delivery and appropriate pace is critical for English learners. Information that is presented at a pace suitable for native English speakers may render that information meaningless, especially for beginning English speakers. Finding the right pace for a lesson depends in part on the content of the lesson and students' prior knowledge about the topic. As illustrated in the lessons here, effective sheltered teachers accommodate the language and learning needs of their students.

Discussion Questions

1. Effective sheltered teachers not only plan content objectives for their lessons but they also *teach to them*. What does this mean? Why is it important? If you were observing a classroom in which the teacher was clearly teaching to content objectives, how might it look? What problems might arise in a classroom in which a teacher had no specific content objectives for a lesson? Be specific.

2. Suppose three new middle school students, all with limited English proficiency, joined a social studies or history class during mid-year. The other students in the class include a few former ELs and native English speakers. What are some language objectives the teacher could write for each of the following content concepts?

   a. Economic trends during the Great Depression

    b. The relationship between the run on banks and the crash of the Stock Market

    c. Migration of people from the Dust Bowl of Oklahoma

3. How does a teacher or supervisor determine whether a majority of students, including English learners, are engaged during a lesson? What techniques could be used to sustain engagement throughout the period? What should the teacher do if he or she senses that students are off-task? Why is sustained engagement so critical to ELs' academic progress?

4. A sheltered teacher in a class with a mix of ELs and native English speakers finds that she is having difficulty pacing lessons so that her English learners complete tasks successfully. If she slows her pace too much, her native English speakers lose interest and are off-task. If she quickens her pace in order to keep those students engaged, her ELs have difficulty keeping up. What suggestions could you give her about how to determine a pace that would be appropriate for all students? How should she organize her classroom to accomplish this?

9 Indicators of Review/Assessment

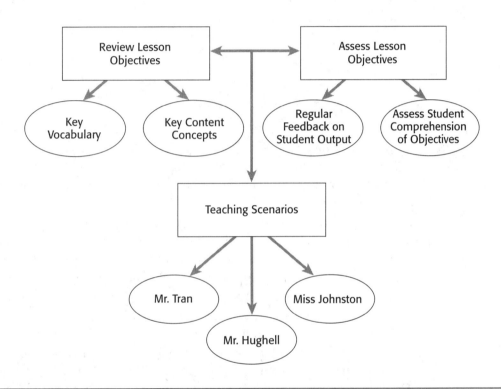

OBJECTIVES

After reading, discussing, and engaging in activities related to this chapter, you will be able to meet the following content and language objectives.

Content Objectives:

Select techniques for reviewing key content concepts

Incorporate a variety of assessment strategies into lessons

Recognize challenges in assessing the content learning of students with limited English proficiency

Language Objectives:

Select techniques for reviewing key vocabulary throughout a lesson and a unit

Design assessments to determine students' academic language learning

Explain how feedback can be valuable for student language development

Use oral, written, and physical means to provide specific feedback to students on their performance

In elementary and secondary classrooms, scheduling time for review and assessment is often difficult. However, effective teachers realize that throughout a lesson and particularly at the end, it is important to determine how well students have understood and retained key vocabulary and content concepts. Teachers must know who is ready to move on and who will benefit from additional instruction and support. This determination is at the heart of effective assessment and instruction, and it is essential for English learners' success.

This chapter describes how effective sheltered teachers incorporate review and assessment into their daily lessons. It also describes how the final section of the SIOP can be used to evaluate the effectiveness of these important elements of instruction.

Background

Teachers of English learners must realize how critically important review is for students. While they sit in class, they receive 40 minutes, 50 minutes, perhaps 75 minutes of input through a new language. Unless the teacher takes the time to highlight and review key information and explicitly indicate what students should focus on and learn, they may not know what is important. Students, especially those at the early stages of English proficiency, devote considerable energy to figuring out what the teacher is saying or the text is telling them at a basic level. They are much less able to evaluate which pieces of information among all the input they receive are important to remember. That is why the teacher must take the time to review and summarize throughout a lesson and particularly as a wrap-up at the end.

When working with English learners, teachers must also assess the students' knowledge level throughout the lesson, not just at the end of the period or the next day. In order to teach the students effectively, teachers need information about their learning from multiple indicators. One single assessment approach is insufficient for all students, but especially those who may have difficulty articulating their level of understanding through English, their new language. As teachers gather information about what students understand or do not understand, they can adjust their instructional plan accordingly. *Scenarios for ESL Standards-Based Assessment* (TESOL, 2001) is an excellent resource for classroom assessment ideas that are linked to standards and can measure student academic performance. Effective sheltered instruction involves reviewing important concepts, providing constructive feedback through clarification, and making instructional decisions based on student response. In the end, you must have enough information to evaluate the extent to which students have mastered your lesson's objectives. This teach, assess, review, and reteach process is cyclical and recursive (see Figure 9.1).

FIGURE 9.1   Effective Teaching Cycle for English Learners

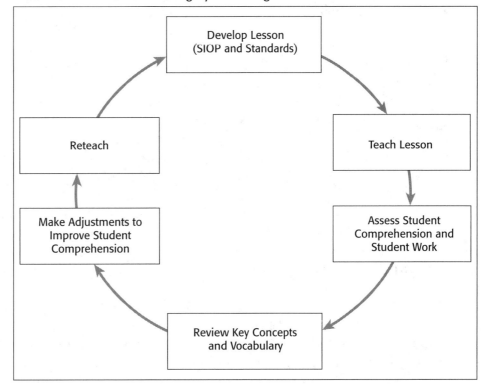

Review of Key Vocabulary

In Chapter 2, we stated that effective teachers incorporate in their lesson plans techniques that support ELs' language development. In Chapter 3, we discussed the importance of building background through teaching key content vocabulary as well as elements of language structure and functional language use. We suggested that language objectives should be identified in lesson plans, introduced to students at the beginning of a lesson, and reviewed throughout the lesson.

We can help develop key vocabulary by teaching and then reviewing terminology and concepts through *analogy*—the process of relating newly learned words to other words with the same structure or pattern. In Chapter 2, we gave the example of "photo" (meaning light) in a lesson on photosynthesis, and suggested referring students to other words with the same morpheme (e.g., photography). Reviewing key vocabulary also involves drawing students' attention to tense, parts of speech, and sentence structure. Repeating and reinforcing language patterns helps students become familiar with English structures.

Multiple exposures to new terminology also build familiarity, confidence, and English proficiency. Words and concepts may be reviewed through paraphrasing, such as "Remember to *share your ideas;* that is, if you have something you want to say, tell it to the others in your group." Another example of a paraphrase is, "The townspeople were *pacifists,* those who would not fight in a war." Paraphrasing as review provides an effective scaffold for ELs, especially after words and phrases have been previously defined and discussed in context.

Key vocabulary also can be reviewed more systematically. It is important to remember that it is ineffective to teach vocabulary through the "dreaded word list" on which students must write (or copy) dictionary definitions (Ruddell, 2001). Research findings are very clear—as stated previously, isolated word lists and dictionary definitions alone do not promote vocabulary and language development. We also know that students do not learn vocabulary words when the teacher just orally introduces and defines them and then expects students to remember the definitions. The more exposures students have to new words, especially if the vocabulary is reinforced through multiple modalities, the more likely they are to remember and use them.

An effective way to incorporate ongoing vocabulary study and review is through the use of individual Word Study Books (Bear et al., 2000). A Word Study Book is a student-made personal notebook that includes frequently used words and concepts. Bear et al. (1996) recommend that vocabulary in Word Study Books be organized by English language structure, such as listing together all the words studied so far that end in -tion, -sion, and -tation. This may be a useful framework. We also believe Word Study Books can be used for content study where words are grouped by topic (e.g., American Revolution words related to protest or government). Some students may benefit by creating semantic maps of the words, for example, linking events to related verbs, adjectives, adverbs, and so forth.

Helping students review and practice words in nonprint ways is beneficial as well. Students may draw a picture to depict a concept or to remember a word. They may demonstrate the meaning through physical gestures or act out several words within the context of a role play. Pictionary and charade-like games at the end of a lesson can stimulate an engaging review of vocabulary.

Remember that we also need to help students become comfortable with "school talk" by introducing and modeling academic tasks throughout lessons and units. For example, if you are planning to have ELs engage in literature discussion circles, it is important to review what "discussion" means, what "turn-taking" is, what it means to "share ideas," how questions are asked and answered, and so forth. Reviewing this terminology provides the necessary scaffolding so that students understand the expectations for their participation in routine activities. School talk also includes language that is found in test directions or question prompts. Increasingly, our English learners need exposure, practice, and review of those types of terms and phrasings (e.g., "Which of the following is *not* a herbivore?") to help prepare them better for the accountability measures they will be called upon to perform.

Review of Key Content Concepts

Just as it is important to review key vocabulary periodically throughout a lesson, and especially at its conclusion, it is also essential that English learners have key content concepts reviewed during and at the end of a lesson. Understandings are scaffolded when you stop and briefly summarize, along with students' help, the key content covered to that point. For example, in a lesson on Egyptian mummification, you might say something like the following: "Up to this point, we learned that little was known about Mummy No. 1770 until it was donated to the museum. After the scientists completed the autopsy, they discovered three important things. Who remembers what they were?" This type of review is usually informal and it can lead into the next section of the text or a discussion: "Let's read this next section to see what else the scientists learned." Or, if predictions about an upcoming section of a text have been made or hypotheses about an experiment developed, teachers should always refer to these afterwards, and assess their validity with the students.

One favorite wrap-up technique of several SIOP teachers is Outcome Sentences. A teacher can post sentence starters on the board, such as:

I wonder . . .

I discovered . . .

I still want to know . . .

I learned . . .

I still don't understand . . .

and students take turns selecting one and completing an outcome sentence orally. These prompts can also be used for journal writing.

A more structured review might involve students summarizing with partners, writing in a journal, or listing key points on the board. It is important to link the review to the content objectives so that you and the students stay focused on the essential content concepts. Toward the end of the lesson, a final review helps ELs assess their own understandings and clarify misconceptions. Students' responses to review should guide your decisions about what to do next, such as a summative evaluation or, if needed, additional re-teaching and assessing.

Providing Feedback on Student Output

Periodic review of language, vocabulary, and content enables teachers to provide feedback to students that clarifies and corrects misconceptions and misunderstandings. Feedback also helps develop students' proficiency in English when it is supportive and validating. For example, teachers can model correct English usage when restating a student's response: "Yes, you're correct, the scientists *were confused* by what they thought was a baby's skull lying next to the mummy." Paraphrasing also supports students' understandings and validates answers if we add after the paraphrase, "Is this what you're thinking (or saying)?" If students are only able to respond to questions in one or two words, you can validate their answers in complete sentences: "You're right! *Embalming* is the process of preserving bodies."

Feedback is generally given orally or in writing, but teachers can also provide it through facial expressions and body language. A nod, smile of support, pat on the shoulder or encouraging look can take away fear of speaking aloud, especially for students who are beginning to develop English proficiency. Additionally, students can provide feedback to each other. Partners or groups can discuss among themselves, giving feedback on both language production and content understanding, but then report to the whole class. The teacher can facilitate feedback by providing appropriate modeling.

Assessment of Lesson Objectives

Within the context of lesson delivery for English learners, we see review and assessment as an ongoing process, especially related to a lesson's language and content objectives. Historically, educators have blurred the line between assessment and evaluation, generally using the term "evaluation" for both formative and summative judgments. The teacher's role in evaluation was primarily as a judge, one who conveyed a value on the completion of a given task. This value was frequently determined from the results of periodic quizzes, reports, or tests that served as the basis for report card grades in elementary and secondary schools.

Today, however, many educators distinguish between assessment and evaluation (Wiggins, 1998). *Assessment* is defined as "the gathering and synthesizing of information concerning students' learning," while *evaluation* is defined as "making judgments about students' learning. The processes of assessment and evaluation can be viewed as progressive: first, assessment; then, evaluation" (McLaughlin & Vogt, 1996, pp. 104, 106).

Assessment occurs throughout a lesson, as evidenced in lesson plans and in periodic review to determine if students are understanding and applying content concepts. Assessment must be linked to the instruction and needs to target the lesson objectives. Just as students need to know what the objectives are, they need to be informed about how and what types of assessments they will have. Toward the end of the lesson, students' progress is assessed to see whether it is appropriate to move on or whether it is necessary to review and re-teach. This type of assessment is *informal, authentic, multidimensional,* and includes *multiple indicators* that reflect student learning, achievement, and attitudes (McLaughlin & Vogt, 1996; O'Malley & Pierce, 1996).

Informal assessment involves on-the-spot, ongoing opportunities for determining the extent to which students are learning content. These opportunities may include teacher observations, anecdotal reports, teacher-to-student and student-to-student conversations, quick-writes and brainstorming, or any number of tasks that occur within regular instruction and that are not intended to be graded or evaluated according to set criteria.

Authentic assessment is characterized by its application to real life, where students are engaged in meaningful tasks that take place in real-life contexts (McLaughlin & Kennedy, 1993). Authentic assessment is usually *multidimensional* because teachers use different ways of determining student performance. These may include written pieces, audiotapes, student and parent interviews, videotapes, observations, creative work and art, discussion, performance, oral group responses, and so forth.

These multidimensional student performances usually involve *multiple indicators,* specific evidences related to the language and content objectives or standards. For example, a student may indicate proficiency with an objective through a piece of writing, through active participation in a group activity, and through insightful questions he asks during discussion. The teacher thus has more than one piece of evidence indicating he is progressing toward mastery of the particular content or language objective.

Periodic assessments before and during lessons can eventually lead to evaluation of a student's demonstrated performance for an objective or standard. This evaluation, while summative, also may be informal and take a variety of forms. Often, rubrics are used to ascertain a developmental level of performance for the particular goal, objective, or standard. For example, on a developmental rubric student performance may be characterized as "emergent," "beginning," "developing," "competent," or "proficient." Other rubrics may communicate evaluative information, such as "inadequate," "adequate," "thorough," or "exceptional" (McLaughlin & Vogt, 1996). Whichever rubric is used, results of assessment and evaluation are often shared with other interested stakeholders, such as parents and administrators, and with the students themselves.

Assessments can be individual or group administered. Individual oral or written responses tell you how one student is performing, while group responses may quickly tell you how the entire group is progressing. Group response is especially sensitive to the needs of ELs, and there is a variety of methods for eliciting group responses, including some of our favorites:

- **Thumbs up/thumbs down:** Generally, this is used for questions that elicit "agree/disagree" responses. (If students agree, they raise their thumbs.) It can also be used for yes/no questions or true/false statements. Older students may be more comfortable responding with "pencils up/pencils down" (point of pencil up or down). Students can also indicate "I don't know" by making a fist, holding it in front of the chest, and wiggling it back and forth. The pencil used by older students can also be wiggled to indicate that the answer is unknown.
- **Number wheels:** A number wheel is made from tag board strips (5″ × 1″) held together with a round-head brass paper fastener. Each strip has a number printed on it, either 0 to 5 or 0 to 10, depending on your needs and students' ages. Students use their individual number wheels to indicate their answers to questions or statements that offer multiple-choice

responses. Possible answers are displayed on the board, overhead, or pocket chart and the teacher asks the questions or gives the statements orally.

For example, if you were teaching a lesson on possessives, you could write the following on the board:

1. boys
2. boy's
3. boys'

Each child has a number wheel and you say, "Show me the correct use of the word 'boys' in the following sentences. Remember that you can show me a "0" if you don't know the answer. Ready? 'The little boy's dog was hungry and was barking.' Show me!"

Students then find the number 2 strip and holding their number wheels in front of their chests, they display their answers. They repeat the process as you give the next sentence. Be sure to give plenty of "wait time" before giving the direction, "Show me!"

You may think that number wheels are only appropriate for younger students but middle school and high schools students enjoy working with them too, and they provide you with much needed information about students' understandings of language and content concepts.

■ **Response boards:** Either small chalkboards or dry erase boards can be used for group responses. Each student has a board and writing instrument. You ask a question, students respond on their boards, and then turn them to face you when you say, "Show me!" Older students seem to prefer working with the dry erase boards and will willingly use them in a classroom in which approximations are supported and errors are viewed as steps to effective learning. Dry erase boards (12″ × 12″) can be inexpensively cut from "bathroom tile board," which is available at home and building supply stores.

Group response activities are very effective for assessing, reviewing, and providing feedback. By looking around the room, teachers quickly gauge how many students understand what is being assessed. If students are having difficulty with language and content concepts, and this is obvious from individual answers given during a group response activity, review and re-teaching are necessary.

As teachers plan for formal and informal assessments, they should keep in mind that because language and content are intertwined in sheltered classes, separating one from the other in the assessment process is difficult. It is, however, necessary to do so. When students have difficulty, teachers need to determine if it is the content that has not been mastered, or if it is a lack of English proficiency that is interfering with their acquisition and application of information.

A general rule of thumb is to plan multiple assessments. Having the students perform a test on one day provides only limited information. Alternative assessment techniques balance the norm- and criterion-referenced tests teachers are required to give. These alternative techniques include performance-based tasks, portfolios, journals, and projects. All of these assessments allow students to demonstrate their knowledge more fully than would be possible on a multiple-choice test. Although all students can benefit from a wide range of assessment procedures, variety is particularly important for ELs because they: (1) are often unfamiliar with the type of standardized tests usually required in U.S. schools, and (2) may have different learning and testing styles.

Finally, to the extent possible, students should be evaluated on their personal progress to determine if learning has taken place. In sheltered classes in particular, where students may have different levels of language proficiency, the value of this approach becomes apparent. If teachers gather baseline data on what their students know and can do with the content information before instruction occurs and then what they know and can do afterwards, teachers can identify student growth.

The Lesson

Unit: Egyptian Mummies (8th grade)

The classrooms described in the teaching vignettes in this chapter are all in a large urban middle school with a heterogeneously mixed student population. English learners represent approximately 45 percent of the students who are in the teachers' eighth-grade classes and the majority are native Spanish speakers, most of whom are at an intermediate level of English proficiency.

The three eighth-grade language arts/social studies core teachers, Mr. Tran, Mr. Hughell, and Miss Johnston, are teaching an extended unit on Egypt. The lessons illustrated here are on the topic of Egyptian mummies. Each of the teachers has planned a three-day lesson using the chapter titled "Mummy No. 1770: A Teenager" (Cooper et al., 1999). This chapter tells of a mummy that was in the possession of the Manchester Museum in England. Because very little was known about this mummy, the museum made it available to a group of scientists who wanted to use modern techniques for determining its age, its mummification process, and how the person had lived. The chapter describes what the scientists learned, including when the thirteen-year-old lived (A.D. 260), what she had eaten, what her life was like, how she died, and how her body was preserved.

The described teaching vignettes represent the second day of the lessons taught by Mr. Tran, Mr. Hughell, and Miss Johnston.

Teaching Scenarios

The following vignettes illustrate how Mr. Tran, Mr. Hughell, and Miss Johnston reviewed the language and content objectives of their second day's lesson on the chapter, "Mummy No. 1770: A Teenager" and assessed student learning. As you read, think about the SIOP indicators for Review/Assessment: Review of Key Vocabulary, Review of Key Concepts, Feedback on Student Output, and Assessment of Student Understanding of Lesson Objectives.

Mr. Tran

In Mr. Tran's lesson plan, he listed the following language and content objectives for English learners: "The learner will be able to (1) describe how scientists learned about Mummy No. 1770, (2) identify major discoveries scientists made during the autopsy of the mummy, and (3) define and correctly use the following vocabulary words: mummy, autopsy, evidence, embalming, amputation, and tissue." Mr. Tran's lesson plan for the first day included the following activities:

1. Brainstorming words about mummies that students already knew
2. Creating a Word Wall with the brainstormed words
3. Group reading of the first five pages of the chapter
4. Adding of new words to the Word Wall, selected by students from the reading (Vocabulary Self-Collection Strategy—VSS)
5. Completing first section of a sequence chain (graphic organizer) listing initial steps used by the scientists
6. Including on the sequence chain words from the Word Wall (mummy, evidence, and autopsy)

On the second day of the lesson (the one observed for the SIOP evaluation), Mr. Tran began by referring back to the Word Wall. First, the whole class read the words aloud in sequence and again in random order. To assess student comprehension, Mr. Tran asked for volunteers to give informal definitions for a few of the words, focusing on the key vocabulary he had selected to emphasize (mummy, evidence, autopsy) and reminding them of the reading from the day before. When needed, he clarified definitions, assisted students with pronunciations, and gently corrected errors.

Mr. Tran then asked students to review the sequence chains they had begun the previous day with their partners. Feedback was provided by peers as they shared their graphic organizers with each other in order to make corrections or additions about the steps scientists took in analyzing Mummy No. 1770. Students were prompted to include words from the Word Wall, especially the key vocabulary (mummy, evidence, autopsy). Mr. Tran circulated and listened to the discussions of several pairs. After the partner sharing, the entire class discussed the information on their sequence chains and Mr. Tran informally assessed the students' knowledge.

Next, students reviewed the major discoveries of the scientists described to this point in the reading and two were listed on the board. The teacher referred to illustrations on pages five through seven of the chapter and asked students to predict what they think happened to the teenage girl and how scientists might have reached conclusions about her death. He wrote on the board, "What *evidence* did the scientists discover during the *autopsy* of the *mummy*?" as a focal question for the rest of the lesson.

Students were directed to look for additional scientific discoveries as they read the next four pages with partners. They were told to complete a T-chart with the following column headings: "Evidence scientists discovered about No. 1770's life" and "Evidence scientists discovered about No. 1770's death."

As a matter of practice, Mr. Tran walked around the room while students were working. He frequently smiled, voiced encouragement, answered questions, and provided support for his students' efforts. When this task was completed, Mr. Tran asked students to share their ideas as a class so he could determine what they had learned and make sure all students could complete their charts.

The lesson continued as students reviewed their papers and the text to find additional words for the Word Wall. Among the words added were "embalming," "amputation," and "tissue." (See Figure 9.2: Word Wall.) Mr. Tran wrote "embalm," "embalmer," and "embalming" on the board and discussed the differences in meaning. He also asked a volunteer to differentiate between the meaning of "tissue" in the text and the more common meaning—something one uses to blow one's nose.

Students then completed the second section of their sequence chains, indicating the subsequent steps the scientists had taken to gather evidence from the mummy. Mr. Tran encouraged students to include the new key vocabulary (embalming, amputation, and tissue) on the graphic organizer. He concluded the lesson by asking students to review with their partners the steps taken by the scientists and to determine two more major discoveries detailed

FIGURE 9.2   Use of Word Wall

Word Wall: Mummies

archaeologists	jewels	sarcophagus
amputation		spirits
artifacts		
autopay		
	linen	
		tissue
		tombs
coffin		Tutankhamen
	mummification	
	mummy	
drying-out-process		
		X-ray
	oils	
embalming		
evidence		
	perfumes	wrappings
	pharoahs	
	preservation	
	pyramids	
gold		

in the text. These were then discussed and added to those on the board from the previous day. Finally, Mr. Tran highlighted in yellow on the Word Wall the six key vocabulary words and these were reviewed one last time before the bell rang.

On the SIOP form in Figure 9.3, rate Mr. Tran for each of the Review/Assessment features.

FIGURE 9.3   Review/Assessment Section of the SIOP: Mr. Tran

4	3	2	1	0	NA
27. Comprehensive **review of key vocabulary**		Uneven **review of key vocabulary**		No **review of key vocabulary**	
28. Comprehensive **review of key content concepts**		Uneven **review of key content concepts**		No **review of key content concepts**	
29. Regularly provides **feedback** to students on their output (e.g., language, content, work)		Inconsistently provides **feedback** to students on their output		Provides no **feedback** to students on their output	
30. Conducts **assessment** of student comprehension and learning of all lesson objectives (e.g., spot checking, group response) throughout the lesson		Conducts **assessment** of student comprehension and learning of some lesson objectives		Conducts no **assessment** of student comprehension and learning of lesson objectives	

Mr. Hughell

Mr. Hughell's lesson plan noted the following objectives: "(1) Write a paragraph on what mummies teach scientists about how Egyptians lived, (2) explain how mummies were preserved, and (3) match twenty vocabulary words with their definitions."

The plan for the first day of the lesson included the following activities:

1. Distributing a list of twenty words and definitions related to mummies along with page numbers on which the words could be found in the chapter text

2. Reading aloud one-half of the chapter while students follow along
3. Having students find the first group of ten vocabulary words in the chapter
4. Having students work with a partner to write an original sentence related to the topic of mummies for each word

Mr. Hughell began the second day of the lesson by asking volunteers to read several of their vocabulary sentences written the previous day. As students read, Mr. Hughell corrected language errors when needed. He clarified content misconceptions, modeled appropriate pronunciation, and reminded students of the correct definitions for the vocabulary. Mr. Hughell then gave students five minutes to review what had been read the previous day. He asked volunteers to summarize what they had learned about Mummy No. 1770 and how mummies were prepared. Several students responded briefly and Mr. Hughell prompted others to elaborate. He highlighted key points by writing them on the board and made additions to the students' summaries.

He then asked for volunteers to read the next set of ten words and definitions from the vocabulary list. He informed students that they would have a

FIGURE 9.4   Review/Assessment Section of the SIOP: Mr. Hughell

4	3	2	1	0	NA
27. Comprehensive **review of key vocabulary**		Uneven **review of key vocabulary**		No **review of key vocabulary**	

4	3	2	1	0	NA
28. Comprehensive **review of key content concepts**		Uneven **review of key content concepts**		No **review of key content concepts**	

4	3	2	1	0	NA
29. Regularly provides **feedback** to students on their output (e.g., language, content, work)		Inconsistently provides **feedback** to students on their output		Provides no **feedback** to students on their output	

4	3	2	1	0	NA
30. Conducts **assessment** of student comprehension and learning of all lesson objectives (e.g., spot checking, group response) throughout the lesson		Conducts **assessment** of student comprehension and learning of some lesson objectives		Conducts no **assessment** of student comprehension and learning of lesson objectives	

vocabulary matching quiz on these words the following day. Students were then directed to read the rest of the chapter silently, and encouraged by Mr. Hughell to ask for help if they found words they did not understand. Following the reading, students worked with partners to write ten more sentences for the remaining words on the vocabulary list.

At the end of the period, Mr. Hughell called on a few volunteers to read their sentences aloud quickly, and asked if anyone had questions. Because not everyone had finished writing the sentences, he assigned the remaining ones for homework and reminded students of the vocabulary quiz planned for the next day. He suggested that students review the entire chapter at home because in addition to the vocabulary quiz, they were going to be writing a paragraph in class on what scientists have learned from mummies. He would evaluate the students' comprehension of the chapter with the written paragraph and quiz the following day.

On the SIOP form in Figure 9.4, rate Mr. Hughell for each of the Review/ Assessment indicators.

Miss Johnston

Miss Johnston's lesson plans revealed one objective for the three-day lesson on mummies: "The learner will understand how mummies were made." The plan included the following for all three days: "(1) Read chapter on Mummy No. 1770, and (2) complete the worksheet questions."

Miss Johnston began the second day of the lesson by calling on a student to summarize the chapter that had been read aloud the previous day. The student responded, "We took turns reading about how some guys in a museum unwrapped an old mummy." Another student added, "And scientists learned the mummy was a girl with no legs." Although the responses were brief and only related simple facts, Miss Johnston offered no further explanation or review.

Miss Johnston then distributed a worksheet to students that had multiple-choice and fill-in-the-blank questions covering information in the text chapter, along with two short essay questions. Students worked individually but were allowed to use their books while completing the worksheets. If they finished early, they were given a word search puzzle and asked to find ten words related to mummies. The teacher circulated through the room, answering questions and keeping students on task.

Toward the end of the period, to assess their learning, she asked them to exchange papers. She read the correct answers for the multiple-choice and fill-in-the-blank questions aloud and students marked their peers' papers. When she asked how many students only got one or two wrong answers, no one raised their hand. She did not pursue the discussion to see if some questions were problematic for most of the class. The lesson concluded with students turning in their essays so Miss Johnston could grade them. She told them to bring in shoe boxes and craft materials for dioramas that each student would make on the following day as a culminating activity.

On the SIOP form in Figure 9.5, rate Miss Johnston for each of the Review/ Assessment indicators.

FIGURE 9.5 Review/Assessment Section of the SIOP: Miss Johnston

4	3	2	1	0	NA
27. Comprehensive **review** of key vocabulary		Uneven **review of key** vocabulary		No **review of key** vocabulary	

4	3	2	1	0	NA
28. Comprehensive **review** of key content concepts		Uneven **review of key** content concepts		No **review of key content** concepts	

4	3	2	1	0	NA
29. Regularly provides **feedback** to students on their output (e.g., language, content, work)		Inconsistently provides **feedback** to students on their output		Provides no **feedback** to students on their output	

4	3	2	1	0	NA
30. Conducts **assessment** of student comprehension and learning of all lesson objectives (e.g., spot checking, group response) throughout the lesson		Conducts **assessment** of student comprehension and learning of some lesson objectives		Conducts no **assessment** of student comprehension and learning of lesson objectives	

Discussion of Lessons

27. *Review of Key Vocabulary*

Mr. Tran: 4

Mr. Hughell: 1

Miss Johnston: 0

The emphasis on vocabulary and content instruction, practice, review, and assessment varied across the three classrooms.

Mr. Tran had clearly defined language and vocabulary objectives, and throughout the lesson his instruction and activities were congruent with these objectives. He built upon what students already knew about mummies, incorporated student selection of important terms (Vocabulary Self-Collection Strategy), and ensured the key vocabulary words were included on the Word Wall. He pointed out similarities in word structure and differences in word meaning (e.g., embalm/embalming and tissue/tissue).

Mr. Tran's English learners were challenged to articulate orally and in writing the key vocabulary. However, even though many terms and phrases related to mummies were introduced, discussed in the text, and included on the Word Wall, sequence chain, and worksheet, Mr. Tran limited to six the number of words students were expected to master. It is important to note that he repeatedly reinforced these words, at the beginning, in the middle, and again at the end of the lesson. By using the vocabulary in context, repeating the words orally, and writing the question on the board ("What *evidence* did the scientists discover during the *autopsy* of the *mummy*?"), Mr. Tran reviewed the pronunciation, meanings, and usage of the words.

Finally, Mr. Tran expected students to use the new key vocabulary orally and in their writing during partner, small group, and whole class discussion. As he listened, he could readily determine who had met the vocabulary objectives, and who had not.

Mr. Hughell reviewed the vocabulary sentences from the first day, provided definitions and page numbers, and allowed students to write their sentences with partners. However, it is unrealistic to expect English learners, as well as struggling readers, to master such a large number of vocabulary words (i.e., twenty words) using the approaches he selected. He did not assist students in learning the words through analogy, pictorial representations, or exploration of language structure, and provided very few exposures to the words. The sentences that the partners were writing were not expected to result in connected text, thus the students only used the words in isolated instances. Moreover, many students did not complete the assignment in class so he was unable to review or assess student understanding of the words.

Mr. Hughell ran out of time at the end of the period and expected students to conduct their own review of the chapter at home. Obviously, this did not provide the type of scaffolding that English learners need and did not represent effective review of language, vocabulary, and content.

Miss Johnston had no language objectives for the lesson plan and did not introduce, teach, or review any key vocabulary to assist students in completing the worksheet. There may have been words in the multiple choice questions that students were unfamiliar with, reflecting "test language," but she gave them no opportunity to ask about them, nor did she explain the words to the students in advance. Some students (those who finished the worksheets early) practiced finding vocabulary on the word search. However, English learners and struggling readers were least likely to complete the word search because it was intended only for those who completed the worksheet quickly. It is important to note that word searches, while engaging, do not constitute effective review of vocabulary because students are expected to simply match spellings without knowing pronunciations or meanings, and do not receive any teacher support.

28. *Review of Key Concepts*

 Mr. Tran: 4

 Mr. Hughell: 1

 Miss Johnston: 1

Most teachers, if they review at the end of a lesson, focus on the content concepts. In these three scenarios, the teachers did so to varying degrees.

Throughout the lesson, Mr. Tran consciously and consistently reviewed content directly related to his objectives. Students reviewed the information they learned the previous day and the new information from this lesson as a class and with partners. Mr. Tran created opportunities for students to correct errors or add information to the sequence chains and T-charts so that he could clarify misunderstandings. At the conclusion of the lesson, Mr. Tran had students review the major discoveries.

Mr. Hughell provided a basic review of the previous day's reading. He gave students time to focus on their previous learnings and had volunteers summarize what had been read. He asked others to elaborate and wrote the information on the board so all students could follow along. Most important, he clarified points and added information to their summaries. But these efforts were primarily directed to the Building Background section of the SIOP. In terms of reviewing the day's key concepts, Mr. Hughell was less successful. He ran out of time at the end of the period, and consequently failed to review content concepts adequately before the lesson concluded. It was inappropriate for him to require English learners to review at home an entire text chapter that had specialized terminology. The *teacher* is the one to provide this review, or scaffold student efforts to review by themselves, prior to assessment and evaluation.

Miss Johnston took a different approach in reviewing content concepts with the students but it yielded little success with English learners. Initially, she asked students to summarize the chapter read. Although two students made an attempt, each stated only one sentence, which recalled a fact but did not summarize the information. Miss Johnston's major effort at concept review was through an individualized paper-and-pencil assignment. This was, however, an assessment of student knowledge or reading comprehension but not a true review of content concepts for her students. Students could peruse the textbook to find information, but neither the class as a whole nor students in groups had an opportunity to discuss and clarify understandings about the content material. Moreover, Miss Johnston's only objective was vague ("Students will understand how mummies were made") and did not provide clearly defined content concepts for the students.

29. *Feedback on Student Output*

Mr. Tran: 4

Mr. Hughell: 2

Miss Johnston: 1

Mr. Tran, Mr. Hughell, and Miss Johnston had some similar and some different techniques for providing feedback to the students during their lessons.

Mr. Tran scaffolded students' learning by clarifying, discussing, and correcting responses. He encouraged peer support and feedback when the graphic organizers were shared and he used explanation and discussion to help students understand how to evaluate the importance of the scientists' discoveries. He moved around the classroom during the lesson offering support and encouragement. Mr. Tran clearly used review, assessment, and feedback to develop his students' language proficiency and content knowledge.

Mr. Hughell frequently clarified misconceptions and gave clear corrections for students' errors. However, his feedback would have been more effective had it better scaffolded students' developing language proficiency and content knowledge. That is, Mr. Hughell's feedback was primarily corrective rather than supportive. He essentially told students their answers were incorrect and then gave them the correct ones, rather than assisting them in formulating the correct responses themselves. Mr. Hughell also directed students to read the text independently and ask for help if needed. Many students, English learners especially, may be reluctant to ask for help for fear of appearing incapable or because they don't know how to formulate the questions they need to ask.

Because Mr. Hughell's classroom was quite teacher-centered (he delivered instruction mostly by standing at the front of the room), students had little opportunity to work together to provide each other with helpful feedback. His teaching would be more effective for English learners if he created a more supportive classroom environment. He could begin by providing more sensitive feedback to his students' responses.

Miss Johnston attempted to help students by answering questions while they were completing their worksheets. She also corrected the papers in class, providing the answers for the questions. However, the amount of feedback she provided students was very limited, and not particularly supportive. When she gave the correct responses to the worksheet questions, she provided little or no explanation, and she did not consider student output on an individualized basis during the lesson. In all, English learners received very little supportive feedback during the observed lesson.

30. *Assessment of Student Understanding of Lesson Objectives*

   Mr. Tran: 4

   Mr. Hughell: 2

   Miss Johnston: 1

Assessing student learning is a critical step in the teaching and learning cycle. The three teachers in these vignettes all conducted some assessment but in different ways.

As his lesson unfolded, Mr. Tran's assessment opportunities included group response, partner, and whole class reporting, as well as individual written work. His assessments occurred throughout the lesson, and were authentic, multidimensional, and included multiple indicators. Most important, his assessment was directly linked to his language and content objectives.

Mr. Hughell did not assess student understanding well in the observed lesson. He called upon a few students to read their vocabulary sentences aloud, so for those students he was able to assess their sense of the words' meanings, but he had no way of knowing whether the rest of the students, particularly the English learners, understood the vocabulary terms. When students read the chapter silently, he did not assess their reading comprehension of the content. He planned some summative assessments, namely the vocabulary matching test and the written paragraph, and tried to match assessment to his objectives ("Write a paragraph on what mummies teach scientists about how Egyptians lived; Explain how mummies were preserved; Match twenty vocabulary words with their definitions"). However, these assessments were scheduled for the following day, too late to guide review, feedback, and re-teaching during instruction. By the time he discovered who had met the language and content objectives and who had not, the three-day lesson would be completed.

Miss Johnston was less successful on this SIOP item. The factual recall sentences elicited from the two students at the start of the lesson yielded no information about the understanding of the rest of the students. Although the worksheet constituted summative evaluation, there was no ongoing assessment throughout the lesson. Students responded to the worksheet individually and only after she collected the papers, looked at the scores, and graded their essays—after the class had ended—would she have a sense of what students had learned. As with Mr. Hughell, this information would arrive too late to guide review and re-teaching. There was no learning objective related to the creation of the dioramas, and students were not provided with a rubric or criteria upon which their projects would be assessed. It is doubtful the dioramas would tell Miss Johnston much about her students' understanding of key vocabulary and content concepts. Finally, her one objective ("The students will understand how mummies were made") was too general and not directly measurable.

Summary

Review and assessment are integrated processes, essential for all students, but they are critical to the success of English learners. Effective sheltered teachers carefully plan for periodic review and informal assessment throughout lessons. This informal assessment is authentic, multidimensional, and it includes multiple indicators of students' performance. Effective sheltered teachers also design appropriate evaluation of key vocabulary and content concept objectives at the conclusion of the lesson. Most important, review and assessment guide teaching and re-teaching, inform decision making, lead to supportive feedback, and provide for fair and comprehensive judgments about student performance.

Discussion Questions

1. Many sheltered teachers introduce key vocabulary at the beginning of the lesson, but often neglect to revisit the new terms systematically throughout the lesson and review them at its conclusion. How can you ensure that the lesson's key academic vocabulary is reviewed at the end of each lesson? Describe a variety of ways you would review the terms, as well as the mechanisms you could put in place to build a vocabulary review into each lesson.

2. Research has shown that gratuitous compliments to students (e.g., "Good job" or "Keep up the good work") do little to motivate them or assist with their learning. Instead, teachers should give regular, substantive feedback to students on their verbal contributions and on their work. What are some ways to provide constructive, specific feedback to students? Consider class size and English proficiency levels as you answer this question.

3. It is important for teachers to make sure their teaching is "connecting" with their students, particularly ELs. A well-planned lesson is ineffective if students do not understand the content due to limited language proficiency or unfamiliarity with the background of academic content being taught. Consistent assessment of students' comprehension is critical for effective sheltered lessons. How can teachers check for understanding? How would a teacher know that the students comprehend? Why is ongoing assessment critical when teaching English learners?

4. One of the features of quality sheltered instruction is that teachers carefully select key content concepts and teach in a way that will ensure students have a good understanding and knowledge of those concepts. What are some ways to conduct a comprehensive review of a lesson's concepts? Why is a final review important?

10 Issues of Reading Development and Special Education for English Learners

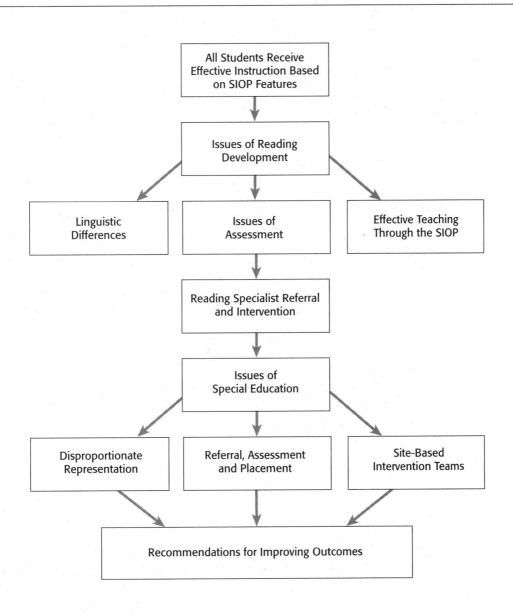

In our work with teachers and administrators throughout the United States, a persistent question concerns appropriate instruction for English learners who exhibit difficulties with reading and learning. Teachers often feel ill-prepared to provide content instruction for these students because they're not sure whether a student's difficulty is due to a reading problem, a learning disability, or a lack of English proficiency. Unfortunately, the result of this confusion has been both under- and over-representation of English learners in remedial and special education classes. In this chapter, we discuss issues of assessment, identification, and instruction for students who may be experiencing reading and/or learning problems. It is beyond the scope of this book to provide a comprehensive discussion of this topic. Instead, we hope to stimulate your thinking and discussion with colleagues about these issues, and to provide you with some ways to more appropriately evaluate your students' performance in class. We begin with a discussion of issues related to reading development for English learners, and then move on to issues related to special education.

Issues of Reading Development

Teachers face many challenges related to the literacy development of their English learners. The task of teaching ELs to read is made difficult in part due to the complexity of learning to read and write in a language one does not understand. However, it is not always possible for children to learn to read first in their primary language. Therefore, teachers must often find ways to help their students learn to read and write in English at the same time they are learning to speak and understand the language. Research suggests that English learners need systematic, high-quality literacy instruction from the start that includes opportunities to read, write about, discuss, and listen to literature and informational text. Students need a wide variety of materials from which to select, and they need to be encouraged to discuss and share what they have read on a regular basis. Dictated stories (the Language Experience Approach) are very effective for developing English fluency and confidence in reading English. However, English learners also need explicit instruction in the aspects of English that may differ from their native languages, including the phonology, morphology, and syntax of English (Au, Garcia, Goldenberg, & Vogt, 2002).

An additional challenge when teaching ELs to read in English is determining their reading proficiency. Students who arrive in the United States with well-developed reading skills in their native language have mastered many of the essentials of reading. They have learned that print carries meaning, and if their home language is alphabetic, they have learned that phonemes (sounds) are represented by graphemes (letters and letter combinations), and that when put together these graphemes create words and meaning (the alphabetic principle). They have also learned the syntax (structure) of their first language, and though they may be challenged by learning English syntax, they can use their knowledge of their first language's structure to make connections with English. English learners whose first language is nonalphabetic (such as Mandarin), will need to learn an alphabetic sound–symbol system in order to speak, read, and write English, but will carry over their understandings of the reading and writing processes to their new language.

Therefore, students who read satisfactorily in their primary language do not have to re-learn how to read or write. However, they do need to learn English. With comprehensible input and explicit instruction in the structure of English they have a better chance of transferring their existing reading skills to the reading of English. For example, for students whose primary language is Spanish, there are many cognates that link English vocabulary and spelling with Spanish (estudiar=study; excepción=exception). Using dictionaries in Spanish, English, French, and German as resources helps students make these connections as they explore similarities in the languages (Bear, Templeton, Helman, & Baren, 2003). It is also clear that English learners need to be immersed in print, with many opportunities to read appropriate books, stories, and informational texts, ideally in their home language as well as in English (Krashen, 2003).

In contrast to those ELs who have well-developed literacy skills in their primary language, there are other students who enter American schools who have had little or no reading instruction in their primary language, or for whom reading and writing are very difficult. These students are often referred to special education programs inappropriately, when other interventions, such as longer exposure to high quality, scaffolded instruction; more direct, small group, or individual instruction; or referral to a reading specialist may be more appropriate. It is important for teachers to know whether their English learners can read in their primary language, and to be able to ascertain whether difficulty in content subjects may be due to a reading problem or a lack of English proficiency.

Many teachers, rightly, want to know the "reading level" of their students. This information helps the teacher match texts to students. For example, if a seventh-grade student is reading at approximately the fourth-grade reading level, he is likely to have difficulty comprehending his seventh-grade social studies textbook. The too-difficult text will either need to be adapted, or the student will require considerable assistance in accessing the content information from the text. It is challenging enough to teach struggling readers who are native English speakers. With English learners, the problem of struggling readers is even more complex.

Classroom teachers and reading specialists use a variety of assessments to determine their students' reading proficiency. However, commonly used assessments that yield a particular reading level (such as fourth grade) may be inappropriate for English learners. For example, a common diagnostic instrument for assessing students' fluency and comprehension is an informal reading inventory (IRI). During this assessment, a student reads silently or orally a series of increasingly difficult, leveled passages. The teacher or reading specialist marks reading errors, asks comprehension questions, and based on a student's reading proficiency determines approximate *independent, instructional,* and *frustration* reading levels.

Think of your own reading. If you read for pleasure and enjoy lying in a hammock with a favorite book during the summer, you'll most likely select an independent-level text that doesn't require you to look up the meaning of words, take notes, or work very hard while reading. However, if you're taking a graduate course, your textbook should be at your instructional level. You expect to have assistance from your professor, and after a lecture or class discussion on the topic, the text is more accessible for you. You may experience frustration-level reading when you read detailed and complex directions that accompany a new computer, confusing income tax forms, or a text on a subject for which you have very little knowledge or experience.

What we know is that it is futile to assign any students, native English speakers and English learners alike, text that is written at their frustration level. Instead, we need to select texts that are written at the student's instructional level, if possible, and then provide additional assistance so that the text becomes accessible. If this level of text isn't available, then we must adapt the grade-level text through rewriting, providing a detailed study guide, highlighting the key concepts, or providing detailed marginal notes. Without these, the instructional- and frustration-level texts will be largely inaccessible, especially for English learners.

It's important to remember that successful reading of any text is also dependent on a number of other variables, including familiarity with the topic being read; vocabulary knowledge; the flexible use of a variety of reading skills and strategies; motivation; and purpose-setting. For students who are reading in their native language, these variables are relatively easy to assess, and the selection of appropriate text materials can be made with a reasonable amount of confidence. However, our usual battery of reading assessments may not yield reliable results for English learners, and selection of appropriate texts is considerably more difficult. A student who is assessed at grade level in his native language may be assessed as reading at a considerably lower level in English. Using results from an IRI (or worse, a standardized achievement test) in English might suggest that the student has a serious reading problem. However, if the student doesn't have difficulty reading in his native language, it's unlikely he'll have a reading problem in his new language. Likewise, if the student has a reading problem in his first language, he may very well have difficulty reading in English.

So, how do we determine whether a student's academic difficulties are due to a reading problem or English proficiency if our usual battery of reading assessments, such as phonemic awareness and phonics tests, IRIs, and vocabulary tests, may be unreliable for use with English learners? First, we need to recognize that the phonology of a student's native language may differ substantially from that of English. Although we may teach phonics explicitly and effectively, some ELs may not hear or be able to reproduce the sounds of English because these sounds do not exist in their primary language. The consonant sounds may be considerably different, the number of vowels may vary, and such things as vowel combinations, commonly found in English (*ea, ie, oa*) may be nonexistent in the students' home languages.

As an example, consider Tables 10.1 and 10.2 (Au, Garcia, Goldenberg, & Vogt, 2002). These represent just a few of the differences in consonants and vowels in English that may give speakers of other languages difficulty.

TABLE 10.1 Table of Selected Consonant Sounds

Key:
1 = Often a problem
2 = May be a problem at beginning of words
3 = May be a problem at the end of words

Consonant Sound:	Arabic	Chinese	Hmong	Khmer	Russian	Spanish	Vietnamese
/b/		2	1		3	3	3
/ch/							1
/d/		2			3	3	3
/g/	1	2	1	1	3	3	3
/j/			1	1		1	1
/k/					2	2	2
/p/	1				2	2	2
/sh/				1		1	1
/t/					2	2	2
/th/	1			1	1		1
/th/	1	1		1	1	1	1
/v/	1	1				1	3
/z/		1		1		1	1

Adapted from Au, Garcia, Goldenberg, & Vogt, 2002, p. R5–R6

TABLE 10.2 Vowel Sounds

Key: Language	Features
Arabic	8 vowels and diphthongs (compared to 20 in English) Possible confusion: Short vowels
Chinese	Fewer vowel sounds in Chinese than English Chinese is a tonal language. Each syllable pronounced with a particular tone that gives it its meaning.
Hmong	6 pure vowels and 7 diphthongs Hmong is a tonal language. Each syllable pronounced with a particular tone that gives it its meaning.
Khmer	16 vowels and 11 diphthongs Possible confusion: Short vowels that don't exist in Khmer (as in *b*at, *b*et, *b*it)
Russian	No diphthongs in Russian Possible confusion: Difficulty with /ûr/ after /w/ as in *work, word;* short vowels, such as short ă and ĕ
Spanish	5 pure vowel sounds and 5 diphthongs Possible confusion: Sounds of long ē, long ō (as in *pool*); short *oo* (as in *pull*)
Vietnamese	Complex vowel system with 11 pure vowels and many more diphthongs and triphthongs Possible confusion: May simplify long vowels in English; variations in the length of vowels in English may be confusing because in English they don't carry a difference in meaning

Adapted from Au, Garcia, Goldenberg, & Vogt, 2002, p. R12

It's not just the sound system (the phonemes) that can cause difficulty for English learners. Because of English orthography (the spelling system), some ELs may have difficulty learning to read and write the language. Orthographies of various languages are described in terms of whether they are *transparent* with highly regular words that are easy to decode (such as Spanish and Italian), or they are *deep or opaque,* with correspondences between letters and sounds that are much less direct (such as French and English). A language like German is considered to be *semitransparent* because its orthography lies somewhere between deep and transparent (Bear, Templeton, Helman, & Baren, 2003). The point is that some students who have a primary language that is transparent (such as Spanish) may have a difficult time learning a language that is deep (such as English). However, in some studies that compare orthographic knowledge, bilingual learners have been found to negotiate satisfactorily between their languages and literacies (Tolchinsky & Teberosky, 1998).

Rather than being confused by orthographic differences, these students can apply what they know about the structure of their primary language to the language they are learning.

So, what do we do about those who *are* confused, and despite appropriate instruction in English, reading, and language arts, are not making satisfactory progress? First, it's important to examine the students' present instructional context. The following questions might guide this inquiry:

1. What evidence do you have that a particular student is having difficulty with reading?
2. Do you have any evidence that this student has difficulty reading in his or her home language? If not, how might you gather some? If you are not fluent in the student's language, is there another student who is? Is there a community liaison or family member who could provide information about the student's L1 literacy development?
3. If your evidence points to a reading problem, what have you and other teachers done to accommodate the student's needs?
   a. Are the student's teachers incorporating cognitive and metacognitive strategy instruction (see Chapter 5) in the language arts and content subjects?
   b. Are the student's teachers adapting content and texts to provide greater accessibility (see Chapter 2)?
   c. Are the student's teachers scaffolding instruction (see Chapter 5) through flexible grouping (see Chapter 6)?
   d. Are the student's teachers providing multiple opportunities for practice and application of key content and language concepts (see Chapter 7)?

At this point, we hope you're getting the idea that appropriate instruction for this student involves all of the elements of the SIOP model: those listed above as well as comprehensible input, appropriate pacing, meaningful activities, sufficient wait time, and so forth. Certainly, a student with reading problems will benefit from the effective practices advocated in the SIOP model.

Will this type of instruction overcome a serious reading problem? Probably not. But, here's the key: If you (and your colleagues) have done all you can to provide effective English language development and content instruction using the SIOP model, and a student is still struggling with reading, it is appropriate and important that the student be referred to a reading specialist. The reading specialist can do a thorough, diagnostic assessment, and implement an intervention designed for the student's literacy needs. If after the intensive intervention, the student is still struggling with school, then further intervention and referral to special education might be warranted.

In 2003, the International Reading Association published a position paper titled, "The Role of Reading Instruction in Addressing the Overrepresentation of Minority Children in Special Education in the United States." It is available on the IRA website, *http://www.reading.org*.

Issues Related to Special Education

The previous discussion of reading is closely related to any discussion of special education because approximately 80 percent of referrals to special education are for reading problems. It is critically important that school personnel provide the support and assistance necessary when English learners exhibit learning difficulties and exhaust every option before considering referral to special education. There has been a long history of disproportionate representation of minority students in special education, especially those from low socioeconomic backgrounds (Artiles, 1998; Dunn, 1968). There are a number of factors that may contribute to the disproportionate number of minority students referred to and placed in special education.

One factor is that teachers and administrators in general education often fail to provide effective instruction in reading and math—content areas basic to learning in other areas—and also fail to manage their classrooms effectively (Orfield, Losen, & Edley, 2001). This is more often the case in urban schools where students have the greatest needs. When teachers feel unprepared to work with students who struggle academically or who exhibit inappropriate classroom behaviors, referral to special education is often the first option to which they turn.

Another factor may be a mismatch between minority-learner characteristics and the materials and teaching methods presented in school, which contributes to underachievement among this group of students (Powers, 2001; Vogt & Shearer, 2003). Much of what students understand and are able to do in school is based on their background, and most academic tasks and curricula reflect middle class values and experiences (See Chapter 3 for more discussion). Reliance on paper-and-pencil tasks, independent reading of dense text, and information presented orally are only some of the types of academic tasks that create difficulties for English learners. Also, students who are culturally and linguistically diverse may not have the requisite background knowledge and experience to perform well academically, nor do they have behaviors that are consistent with the values of school. In general, students achieve better educational outcomes if they have been reared in a culture that has expectations and patterns of behaviors that are consistent with those of the school (Comer, 1984). If that is not the case, then instruction such as that characterized in the SIOP provides the best opportunity for English learners to participate successfully in the academic program of school.

Underachievement among minority youth, which often leads to special education referral and placement, may also be explained by outside factors such as the effects of poverty (Smith, 2001), poor study habits and poor time management (Ford, 1998), cultural differences in students' and teachers' behavioral expectations (Patton & Townsend, 1999), and language differences (Cummins, 1984; Echevarria & Graves, 2003; Genesee, 1994). Obviously, all the complexities of underachievement cannot be ameliorated with good instruction alone; however, quality of instruction is a variable that makes a difference, and it is something that is under the control of school personnel.

It should be mentioned that English learners are also sometimes under-referred for special education services for many of these same reasons. Either teachers are unsure whether to refer ELs to special education or ELs are allowed to languish without services because of low expectations or lack of understanding of the critical relationship between quality of instruction and student performance.

Special Education Referral, Assessment, and Placement

Disproportionate representation of minority students in special education is most pronounced among the mild and moderate disability categories, such as learning disabilities and speech and language disorders. The characteristics of

FIGURE 10.1 Causes of Confusion in Assessing Students with Language Differences and/or Language Learning Disabilities

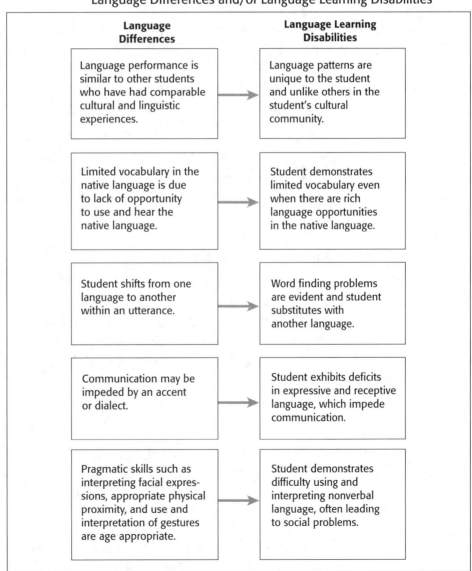

Language Differences	Language Learning Disabilities
Language performance is similar to other students who have had comparable cultural and linguistic experiences.	Language patterns are unique to the student and unlike others in the student's cultural community.
Limited vocabulary in the native language is due to lack of opportunity to use and hear the native language.	Student demonstrates limited vocabulary even when there are rich language opportunities in the native language.
Student shifts from one language to another within an utterance.	Word finding problems are evident and student substitutes with another language.
Communication may be impeded by an accent or dialect.	Student exhibits deficits in expressive and receptive language, which impede communication.
Pragmatic skills such as interpreting facial expressions, appropriate physical proximity, and use and interpretation of gestures are age appropriate.	Student demonstrates difficulty using and interpreting nonverbal language, often leading to social problems.

students in these categories are not as easily identifiable as they are in students with more significant disabilities and therefore require subjective judgment. For English learners, behaviors associated with the normal second-language acquisition process may be confused with language and/or learning disabilities (See Figure 10.1). The subjectivity of identification is exacerbated because mild to moderate disabilities do not have a clear biological cause, prompting some to argue that the disabilities themselves are socially constructed (Barnes, Mercer, & Shakespeare, 1999). What is considered "normal" is influenced by a number of factors including culture, age, community practice, point in history, and school expectations. The labels associated with mild disabilities are assigned arbitrarily and are subject to extreme variability in identification rates. For example, three times as many children are served as learning disabled in Massachusetts as in Georgia, and ten times as many children are labeled mentally retarded in Alabama as in New Jersey (MacMillan & Reschly, 1998).

All students placed in special education programs have gone through a referral, assessment, and placement process. The special education process is initiated once a student is experiencing considerable difficulties in the general education program—academic, behavioral, or both. For English learners, low English language proficiency, gaps in educational experience, and cultural differences influence the referral process. The reality is that teachers have a tremendous impact on who is referred and who is not. Research indicates that there are two factors that influence referral: (1) teacher tolerance and (2) the interaction of perceived student ability or behavior with the teacher's own expectations and approach to instruction and classroom management (Podell & Soodak, 1993). So, if teachers have an appreciation of cultural and linguistic differences and the modifications those differences require, intervention in the general education classroom is more likely.

Site-Based Intervention Teams

Typically, when a student is experiencing difficulties, she or he is first referred to a site-based team that examines the reason for the referral and makes recommendations for interventions to be implemented within the general education program. Site-based intervention teams have been shown to decrease referral and special education placement (Fuchs, Fuchs, & Bahr, 1990; Ysseldyke & Marston, 1999), and even reduce disproportionate referrals of minority students to special education (Powers, 2001). The kinds of interventions typically recommended by site based teams are listed below:

- Small group or individualized instruction
- Match methods, materials, and tasks to learner needs
- Contextualize instruction
- Provide more modeling and practice
- Parent conference and involvement
- Assessment of medical needs (hearing, vision, nutrition)
- Primary language support

- Explicit teaching of learning strategies for students who need assistance in "learning how to learn"
- More intensive English language development
- Counseling services
- Modification of assignments

There are a number of recommendations for improving outcomes for students who are experiencing learning difficulties (Echevarria, Powers, & Elliott, in press).

Earlier Intervention

Students who are experiencing difficulties require systematic interventions to enable them to participate fully in the academic and social opportunities offered by school. Currently, before students are eligible for specialized support services they must exhibit significant academic or behavior problems. Why should students have to establish a pattern of failure before assistance is provided?

All students should be screened for potential reading problems because early identification and intervention reduces problems that are exacerbated by time and continued failure. Screening tools that identify gaps in pre-reading skills provide the kind of early identification and intervention students need.

Better Training

All school personnel training programs should address effective instruction for English learners—general education, special education, reading specialists, and administrators. Preparing general education and special education personnel to work effectively with English learners begins at the pre-service level. Teacher preparation programs (general and special education) that address issues of diversity, second language acquisition, culturally relevant instruction methods, and empirically supported interventions contribute to a teaching force that implements meaningful and appropriate instruction for students with differing abilities (Echevarria & Graves, 2003). Students' interactions with their teacher can be either disabling or empowering and the quality of teacher–student interaction has a significant impact on academic performance and classroom behavior (Kea & Utely, 1998). Further, instruction that takes into consideration students' English language development needs has a positive impact on achievement (Short & Echevarria, 1999).

Effective teachers reflect on their practice and are mindful of the interaction between the learner and the instructional setting, materials, and teaching methods, and make adjustments as needed to facilitate learning. The importance of context to learning cannot be overstated; characteristics of the classroom and school can increase the risk for academic and behavioral problems. Teachers need training in understanding the interaction between learning and context, avoiding the deficit model which views academic and behavior problems as a within-child problem. We have empirical and anecdotal evidence that many academic and behavioral difficulties can be attributed to the impact of the instructional setting (teacher, materials, methods) on the student, rather than some inherent problem of the learner.

Search for Interventions Rather Than Disabilities

School-based intervention teams have the potential to provide appropriate, effective instructional programs for English learners, especially when such teams have a diverse membership of individuals, including parents, who are most knowledgeable about the issues related to diverse learners (Harry, 1992). Together, the team brainstorms ideas and suggests strategies to implement within the general education program. The emphasis is on resolving the problem within the general education program by identifying interventions rather than labeling a student with a disability.

In too many instances, when students experience difficulties, school personnel begin by viewing the difficulty as residing *within* the student. Rather, we need to adopt an "All, Some, Few" model of instructional services (Kukic, 2002), seen in Figure 10.2. This instructional service pyramid illustrates that all students should receive high quality, appropriate instruction. For English learners, that would be the type of instructional practices featured in the SIOP. A subset of students will require more intensive interventions to meet their learning needs (specific interventions). Finally, if the student is receiving effective instruction and repeated interventions fail to produce the desired results, special education may be considered by the team (specialized services). Few students would be in this category and this consideration is based on a student's insufficient response to general education interventions and the team's determination that an additional level of support is needed to increase achievement.

The benefits of focusing on the pyramid model of intervention and the student's responsiveness to interventions rather than disability are twofold: (1) more students' needs are met in the least restrictive environment; and (2) useful information is gathered for designing individualized programs for the student. The first point suggests that fewer minority students will be

FIGURE 10.2   Instructional Service Pyramid

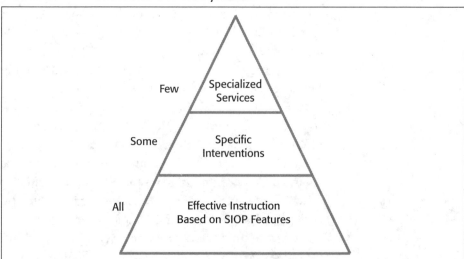

identified as disabled, and the second point promises that for those who are in need of special education, their programs will be improved by identifying instructional strategies and curriculum modifications that are effective for an individual child (Echevarria, Powers, & Elliott, in press).

Students with Special Needs

Many of the features of the SIOP are effective for students with learning differences. However, it is also important to keep in mind the unique characteristics of students with special needs.

- Focus students' attention by limiting the clutter and excessive visual stimuli in the classroom. While we advocate Word Walls and other visuals to assist students in information recall and vocabulary development, they must be used with discretion. Students with special needs are often distracted by artwork and projects hanging around the room.
- Repetition is essential. Students will retain more information if it is repeated and reviewed frequently. Poor memory is often a characteristic of students with special needs, especially memory that is associated with symbols, (e.g., letters and numbers).
- Allow extra time for students to process information. Students with learning differences are often just processing a question by the time the answer is given. Teachers may use strategies such as asking a question, letting the student know he or she will be asked for the answer, then coming back to the student.
- Assessment should be scaffolded to measure understanding. Students' disabilities can interfere with their demonstration of knowledge and understanding. These students may have difficulty with vocabulary, expressing their ideas, or using language adequately. Rather than asking a student to write an explanation of a concept, have him list the features of the concept or label a graphic organizer that is provided; ask the student to complete an outline rather than generate a summary or essay; or select examples from a list provided rather than producing examples.
- Be sensitive to frustration levels. Students with special needs often have a lower frustration threshold than typical learners, which may result in outbursts or giving up easily. A structured learning environment, scaffolded instruction, and opportunities to experience success help alleviate frustration.

Summary

One of the most critical issues facing educators is delivering an instructional program appropriate for *all* students in their classes: those with limited English proficiency, those who excel academically, those who are performing at grade level, those with low academic levels, those who find reading difficult, those who have experienced persistent failure, those who work hard but continue to struggle academically, and those with problematic behaviors.

This chapter provided an overview of issues related to reading and special education, including how linguistic differences in home languages and English may cause English learners difficulty with reading and writing. When classroom teachers implement the features of the SIOP model, many students with reading and learning difficulties find success. Very often, students' academic difficulties have more to do with the curriculum, teaching methods, and classroom setting than with any deficit in the child. That said, some students will still struggle with reading and learning, despite best practices in teaching. We recommend referral to a reading specialist, if warranted. If this or other interventions do not alleviate the problem, then referral to special education may be necessary. What is most important is to avoid labeling students with reading problems or disabilities, and instead provide them with the most appropriate and effective instructional context possible.

Discussion Questions

1. Analyze your school and/or district's assessment program in reading and language arts. Are reading specialists available to help with the assessment and instruction of students with reading problems? If not, who has the expertise for helping teachers and administrators design an effective assessment program in literacy? What happens to teachers' district-required literacy assessment results? Are they used for designing appropriate instruction for students, including English learners? Are professional development programs in place to assist teachers and administrators in increasing their knowledge and skills in teaching reading? These are critical questions to consider when planning literacy instruction for English learners (and all students, for that matter), and they should be asked when designing school-wide and district inservice and professional development.

2. In this chapter we have discussed some of the reasons why minority children, including many English learners, are over- and under-represented in special education. For your own school or district, determine the number of English learners who are designated as receiving special education services (this information should be available at your district office). Compare this number (as a percentage of the total) to the number of native English speakers designated as special education students. If there appears to be a disproportionate number of ELs in special education, what can you do to make sure students have been appropriately placed? How can you, as a teacher, specialist, or administrator, ensure that English learners receive adequate and suitable assessment and referral?

3. How would you respond to a teacher who says, "Well, if I follow the SIOP model and make sure my ELs are able to access content using these

activities, techniques, and approaches, my on-level kids and native English speakers will be bored." Do you agree with this statement? Why or why not? How can teachers with only a few English learners in their classrooms organize instruction so that all students' needs are met? Which, if any, of the activities, methods, or approaches in this book are inappropriate for some students, such as accelerated learners? Or, are all of these instructional approaches appropriate for all students? Obviously, we believe that all students benefit from the instruction that is integral to the SIOP model. But, from our experience, some teachers think otherwise. Prepare a response to these teachers' concerns.

11 Scoring and Interpretation of the SIOP

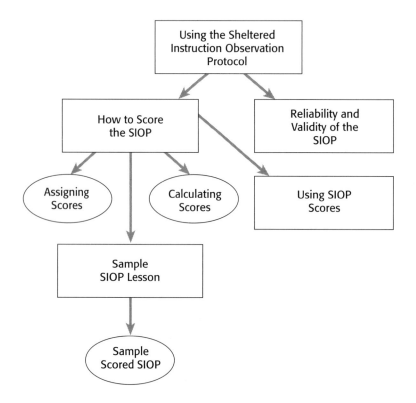

OBJECTIVES

After reading, discussing, and engaging in activities related to this chapter, you will be able to meet the following content and language objectives.

Content Objectives:

Examine how all the SIOP features fit into one lesson plan

Use the Sheltered Instruction Observation Protocol to score and assess a teacher's lesson

Language Objectives:

Use SIOP scores for post-observation discussions with teachers

Explain the value of observing and rating teachers over time on the SIOP

Since its inception, the Sheltered Instruction Observation Protocol (SIOP) has been used by educators in a number of ways. Initially, we designed the SIOP because we found that school personnel and researchers wanted and needed an objective measure of high-quality sheltered lessons, and the SIOP provided an explicit model of sheltered instruction. Over time, the ways that the SIOP is used have expanded. As schools respond to the No Child Left Behind Act of 2001, administrators must demonstrate that their teachers are "highly qualified." The SIOP provides a tool for gauging the quality of teaching. The quantitative and qualitative information the instrument provides, documents teacher effectiveness and improvement. Further, school-wide knowledge about, and implementation of, the SIOP provides a common language and conceptual framework from which to work. School site administrators have reported that the features of the SIOP bring together in one place many of the ideas and techniques staff have learned through district professional development efforts. For example, a school staff may have received inservice training in cooperative learning, multiple intelligences, or differentiated instruction, but teachers struggle with how to incorporate these varied ideas into their teaching practice. The SIOP provides a framework for systematically addressing and incorporating a variety of strategies into one's teaching practice.

Further, the reality is that many administrators have not had the opportunity to learn about effective instruction for English learners to the same extent as have teachers on their staff. Yet the administrator is responsible for observing and providing feedback to teaching personnel. The SIOP provides school site administrators with a means for providing clear, concrete feedback to the teachers they observe. The format of the SIOP allows for rating of lessons, but more importantly has space for writing comments that will be constructive for improving instruction for English learners.

University faculty have also found the SIOP to be useful in courses that specifically address sheltered instruction, as well as in other courses where meeting the needs of English learners is addressed. Faculty who supervise field experience find that the SIOP assists in providing concrete examples of techniques necessary for making instruction comprehensible for English learners. Feedback on the rating and comments sections of the instrument assist student teachers in their professional growth.

For a number of years, teachers have been using the SIOP as a planning and teaching guide. Sample lesson plan formats can be found in Chapter 2, Appendix B, and at *http://www.siopinstitute.net.*

Teachers also find the SIOP useful for self-assessment by videotaping lessons and scoring themselves on the various SIOP components. Teachers report that the objectivity provided by the camera is valuable in recognizing areas of strength and areas that need attention.

Finally, the SIOP is a tool researchers can use to determine the extent to which sheltered instruction is implemented in a given classroom. It also can be used to measure consistency and fidelity of implementation.

FIGURE 11.1 SIOP Heading

The Sheltered Instruction Observation Protocol (SIOP)
(Echevarria, Vogt, & Short, 2000, 2004)

Observer(s):_____ Teacher:_____

Date:_____ School:_____

Grade:_____ Class/Topic:_____

ESL Level:_____ Lesson: Multi-day Single-day *(circle one)*

Total Points Possible: 120 (Subtract 4 points for each NA given)_____

Total Points Earned: _____ Percentage Score: _____

Directions: Circle the number that best reflects what you observe in a sheltered lesson. You may give a score from 0–4 (or NA on selected items). Cite under "Comments" specific examples of the behaviors observed.

The heading on the first page of the SIOP form is fairly self-explanatory (see Figure 11.1). It is intended to provide a context for the lesson being observed. There is space for the observer's name and the date of the observation. Other information, such as the teacher's name, school, grade of the class being observed, ESL level of the students, and the academic content area, is also included. We recognize that an observation at one point in time does not always accurately represent the teacher's implementation of sheltered instruction strategies and techniques. Therefore, there is a place for the observer to indicate if the lesson is part of a multi-day unit, or is a single-day lesson.

In using the SIOP over the past several years, we have found that it is useful to videotape a lesson and analyze it later. Teachers, supervisors, and researchers alike have found this to be an effective way of recording and measuring teachers' growth over time. The heading has a place for the observer to indicate the tape number for a given lesson.

Finally, there is a box for the total score the teacher received on the SIOP. It is most useful to represent a teacher's score as a percent since NA affects a total score number (see next section for an explanation of scoring).

How to Score the SIOP

Scores may be assigned in a number of ways: (1) during the observation itself, as individual features are recognized; (2) after the observation, as the observer reflects on the entire lesson, referring to observational field notes; or (3) after the observation while watching a videotape of the lesson. The third option is often useful so that the teacher and observer are able to share the same point of reference when discussing the lesson.

It is important to stress that not all items on the SIOP will be present in every lesson. However, some items, such as items under Preparation, Comprehensible Input, Interaction, and Review/Assessment, are essential for each lesson. Over the course of time (several lessons, a week), all items should be represented in one's teaching.

Assigning Scores

The observer determines the level of implementation, guided by the scenario descriptions in this book. There are myriad ways that a teacher can implement an item, but the chapters were designed to show a graphic example for each item for scores ranging from 4 to 0. The SIOP provides a 5-point scale as well as space for qualitative data. It is recommended that the observer use the "Comments" section to record examples of the presence or absence of each feature. That way, both the observer and the teacher have specific information, besides a score, to use in their post-lesson discussion. More information may be added to the Comments section during review of the SIOP, documenting the content of the discussion for future reference, which is particularly useful as subsequent lessons are planned.

Naturally, there is an element of subjectivity to interpreting the items and assigning scores. Observers must be consistent in their scoring. For example, one person may think that for Item #3 (Content concepts appropriate for age and educational background level of students) only grade-level materials are appropriate while another observer may feel that the same content found in materials for lower grade levels can be used because of the students' low reading levels or because students have interrupted educational backgrounds. In either case, observers must be consistent in their interpretation and scoring across settings.

We suggest that, to assist in more accurate scoring, the observer ask the teacher for a copy of the lesson plan in advance of observing the class. That way, the observer is better able to score the Preparation section, as well as recognize NA items.

Not Applicable (NA) Category

The Not Applicable (NA) scoring option is important because it distinguishes a feature that is "not applicable" to the observed lesson from a score of "0," which indicates that the feature should have been present but was not. For example, Mr. Leung taught a five-day unit on the solar system. During the first few lessons of the unit, Mr. Leung concentrated on making the rather dense information accessible to his students. He adapted the text to make it understandable for them and provided ample opportunities for students to use strategies. On the final day of the unit, an observer was present. Mr. Leung wrapped up the unit by having the students complete an enjoyable hands-on activity wherein they applied the concepts they had learned. It was obvious that the students had learned the content and were able to use it in the activity.

However, because of the nature of that particular lesson, there was no observed adaptation of content (Item #5). Mr. Leung was not penalized by receiving a score of "0" because the lesson did not lend itself to that item and Mr. Leung had covered that item on another day. A score of NA would be correct in this case.

In the case of Mrs. Nash, however, it would be appropriate to score this feature as "0." Mrs. Nash also taught a unit on the solar system. On the first day of the unit, she showed a video about the solar system and had a brief oral discussion following the movie. The next day an observer was present as she read from the text and then had students answer chapter questions. There was no evidence that any of the content had been adapted to the variety of student proficiency levels in her class. In fact, many students appeared to be confused as they tried to answer questions based on readings from the grade-level textbook.

The distinction between a "0" and "NA" is an important one since a score of "0" adversely affects the overall score for the lesson, while an "NA" does not because a percent is to be used.

Calculating Scores

There are thirty items on the SIOP, each with a range of possible scores from "0" to "4," or NA. After scoring each item, the observer then tallies all numeric scores. The score is written over the total possible score, usually 120 (30 items × a score of "4"). So, an example of a total score would be written, 115/120. Because of the NA, adding the individual scores for a grand total is meaningless. It is more informative to know the total score based on the total possible score.

Let's take a step-by-step look at how a teacher's total score is calculated.

Mr. Leung received a score of "4" on 20 items, a score of "3" on 5 items, a score of "2" on 4 items, and 1 NA. The sum of those scores is 103.

$$
\begin{aligned}
20 \times 4 &= 80 \\
5 \times 3 &= 15 \\
2 \times 4 &= 8 \\
\textbf{Total score} &= \overline{\textbf{103/116}}
\end{aligned}
$$

The score of 116 was derived in this way: If Mr. Leung had received a "4" on each item of the SIOP (a perfect score), he would have had a total score of 116.

$$29 \times 4 = 116$$

The number of items is 29 instead of 30 because one item was not applicable (NA); he was only rated on 29 items.

For the lesson observed, Mr. Leung received a total score of 103/116. The total score can be converted to a percentage, if that form is more useful. Simply divide the numerator by the denominator: $103 \div 116$. In this case, Mr. Leung imple-

FIGURE 11.2 The Step-by-Step Process for Tallying Scores

1. Add the teacher's scores from all items.
2. Count the number of NAs, multiply by 4, then subtract this number from 120.
3. Divide the number from step 2 into the number from step 1 (the adjusted possible score into the teacher's score).

mented the SIOP at a level of 88 percent. You can see the importance of distinguishing between a score of "0" and NA. For Mr. Leung, a "0" score would have changed his total score from 88 percent to 85 percent. Let's see how.

$$
\begin{aligned}
20 \times 4 &= 80 \\
5 \times 3 &= 15 \\
2 \times 4 &= 8 \\
1 \times 0 &= 0 \\
\text{Total score} &= \overline{103/120}^{[1]}
\end{aligned}
$$

The step-by-step process for tallying scores is shown in Figure 11.2.

Sample Lesson

In this section of the chapter, we will describe an entire science lesson conducted by a sixth-grade teacher and show how she was scored on the SIOP. Ms. Clark received training and has been using the SIOP for lesson planning and delivery for about 16 months. This lesson took place at the end of the first quarter of the school year. The class consisted of beginning ESL students from varying language and country backgrounds. The class has been studying a unit on minerals and visited a local natural history museum. The students have examined rocks in class as well. Ms. Clark provided us with a lesson plan before we conducted the observation.

In the classroom, the desks were arranged in three circular groups. Some students had to turn around to see the board and overhead screen at the front of the room. The class objectives and agenda were written on a whiteboard at the side. Two bulletin boards in the back of the room displayed the students' work for a language arts project and a science project. A Spanish-speaking bilingual aide assisted the teacher and also helped newly arrived Spanish-speaking students. The class period was 45 minutes long.

[1]The highest possible score on the SIOP for all 30 items is 120 (30 items × a score of "4"). If Mr. Leung were rated on all 30 items, his total score would be 103/120 or 85 percent.

The teacher began the class by complimenting the students for their performance on a test they had taken on minerals and singled out one student who received the highest "A" in the class. She then asked the students to read the objectives and activities for the day silently while she read them aloud:

Content Objective: Today we will develop an understanding of what volcanoes are and why they erupt.

- First, I will demonstrate how rocks could move and what happens when they move.
- Second, you will use a semantic web worksheet to recall what you know about volcanoes.
- Third, I will use a model to show how a volcano erupts.
- Fourth, you will make predictions about the story, "Pompeii . . . Buried Alive," and then read pages 4 to 9 silently.
- Fifth, you will refer to information on page 6 in the book to write on a worksheet the steps that happen before a volcano erupts.
- Your homework is to draw a volcano and label the parts. The vocabulary words for the day are: melts, blast, mixture, rumbles, straw, pipe shepherd, giant, peddler, crater, lava, magma, magma chamber.

The teacher then demonstrated for the class what happens when rocks move against each other, using two stacks of books. After placing the stacks side by side on a desk, she pushed against one stack so the other stack slid off the desk and scattered onto the floor. She asked the students what happens when one set of rocks moves another set of rocks. The students responded that the rocks break.

The aide distributed semantic web worksheets to the students and asked them to write "Volcano" in the center circle. Then, in the other spaces, they were to write everything they already knew about volcanoes. While the students worked, the teacher and aide circulated to monitor the students' understanding of the task and to see how they were progressing.

After the students filled in their webs, the teacher led them in a discussion of what they had written and wrote some of their comments on the whiteboard:

- Lava melts and explodes
- When it erupts, all that force comes from the middle of the earth
- Volcanoes are formed deep inside the earth
- When a volcano is under water, the lava comes out and makes an island

The teacher repeated that she was going to make a model volcano and asked the class what a "model" is. One student answered that it is an example, not a real volcano. All of the students were watching as the teacher showed them a bottle and explained it would be like the magma chamber that is inside a volcano. She poured a cup of warm water inside the bottle. While it cooled slightly, she showed the class a diagram of the model for the experiment, with the corresponding volcano parts labeled. They discussed each part of the volcano and in doing so emphasized some of the key vocabulary words: crater, magma pipe, lava, magma, magma chamber, basin.

The teacher returned to the model and placed a few drops of liquid dish detergent in the warm water. Next, she picked up an object and asked the students to identify it. One student said it was a measuring spoon. The teacher measured a teaspoon of baking soda and put it into the water and detergent mixture. She asked the students to identify where she was putting it. The students responded, "magma chamber." She put in a second teaspoon of baking soda, then held up the bottle for the students to observe, and then they reviewed the ingredients. To speed up the process, she added vinegar to the bottle. She asked them, "When was the last time we used vinegar?" The students said they had used it on the previous day. The "volcano" began to erupt and the teacher displayed the bottle so that the students could see the foam overflowing.

The class reviewed the process and the ingredients for the model volcano. Individual students were called to the front to participate in a second volcano demonstration, each one completing one of the steps to produce another "eruption." The second "lava" flow was a bit larger than the first.

The teacher asked the whole class to think about "What causes a volcano to erupt?" and added, "We used warm water. What will happen to heat in a chamber?" One student answered, "Heat rises." The teacher explained that it was not just the heat that caused the eruption and asked them to think of the other ingredients and what happened when they were mixed. The teacher went on to explain, "The mixture of gases produces carbon monoxide," and wrote "carbon monoxide" and its chemical symbol on the board. She also asked them what they knew about plants and said, "They breathe in carbon monoxide. We breathe out carbon monoxide; we breathe in oxygen." [This part was an error, but the teacher did not realize her mistake in calling carbon dioxide (for plants and humans), carbon monoxide.]

One student wanted to know why rocks come out of volcanoes and another student offered an explanation, "The volcano is inside of a mountain of rocks." The teacher commented that whatever is inside the chamber when it erupts will come out with the lava, and if they had put small bits of material inside their model, those bits also would have come out when it erupted.

The teacher and aide handed out the story books, "Pompeii . . . Buried Alive," to the students, and they began pre-reading activities. The teacher focused their attention on the title and asked them to predict what they thought the book would be about. One student said, "Volcanoes erupting." The teacher asked, "Where do you think it takes place?" Students guessed various places: Nicaragua, Rome, Greece, England. The teacher commented on the togas in the cover's picture. She then directed their attention to the back cover and read the summary aloud, stating the story took place 2000 years ago in Italy. She asked, "Is it a true story?" Some students guessed yes; others no. "How do you know it's true?" They discussed that the term "took place" and the use of a specific time in history meant that it was true. The teacher then asked for a student volunteer to point out Italy on the wall map and the class discussed the location of Italy in southern Europe.

The teacher asked how many of the students came from countries with volcanoes. Students from Ethiopia, El Salvador, and Guatemala said they knew about volcanoes in their countries. One student asked if it had to be a hot country to have a volcano. The teacher asked if they knew where the most recent eruption had occurred. She told them it was Montserrat in the Caribbean and that volcanoes often occur in warm countries but not all are in warm countries. She asked if they knew about a volcano in the United States and told them about Mt. St. Helens in Washington, a state that is cold in winter. She showed them Washington on the map. One student commented on the way precipitation forms and tried to compare it with what happens in the formation of a volcano.

The teacher directed the students to read pages 4 to 9 silently for two minutes. While they were reading, she distributed worksheets with a sequencing exercise to describe what happens before a volcano erupts. The instructions told students to put the sentences in order according to what they read on page 6. They could refer back to the reading.

The teacher began to read the passage aloud slowly about three minutes later, although some students indicated that they had not yet finished reading it silently. As she read, she again displayed the transparency with the model volcano diagram on the overhead and referred to it and to the key vocabulary as she read. She also paused from time to time to ask comprehension questions. Students were able to answer questions orally, using the model and naming the parts of a volcano. They discussed unknown words in the reading, such as peddler, rumbled, and shepherd, as they went along.

As the period drew to a close, the teacher told the students they would complete the sequencing worksheet the next day. She reminded them of the homework—draw a volcano in their journal and label the parts. They were also told to place the webs they had completed in their journals. The teacher then led a brief wrap-up of the lesson, asking questions about a volcano, which students answered.

On the following pages you will see how Ms. Clark was scored on the SIOP items and the Comments that provide evidence for her score (see Figure 11.3).

Using SIOP Scores

Scores can be used "as is" to serve as a starting point for a collaborative discussion between a teacher and a supervisor or among a group of teachers. We have found that videotaping a lesson, rating it, and discussing it with the teacher provides an effective forum for professional growth. We also get valuable information from teachers explaining a student's behavior or why something may not have taken place despite the lesson plan that included it, for example. The discussion may take place between the teacher and the observer,

FIGURE 11.3   The Sheltered Instruction Observation Protocol (SIOP)

The Sheltered Instruction Observation Protocol (SIOP)
(Echevarria, Vogt, & Short, 2000, 2004)

Teacher: __Ms. Clark__
School: __Cloverleaf__
Class/Topic: __Science__
Lesson: Multi-day / (Single-day) *(circle one)*

Observer(s): __J. Cruz__
Date: __4/3__
Grade: __6__
ESL Level: __6__

Total Points Possible: 120 (Subtract 4 points for each NA given) __120__
Total Points Earned: __94__   Percentage Score: __78%__

Directions: Circle the number that best reflects what you observe in a sheltered lesson. You may give a score from 0–4 (or NA on selected items). Cite under "Comments" specific examples of the behaviors observed.

Preparation

	4	3	2	1	0
1. Clearly defined **content objectives** for students	④	3	**Content objectives** for students implied	1	No clearly defined **content objectives** for students

Comments: Content objectives were written and stated at the beginning of the lesson.

	4	3	2	1	0
2. Clearly defined **language objectives** for students	4	③	**Language objectives** for students implied	1	No clearly defined **language objectives** for students

Comments: Key vocabulary was listed, but the language skills to be targeted were listed and stated as activities and not written as objectives.

	4	3	2	1	0
3. **Content concepts** appropriate for age and educational background level of students	4	3	② **Content concepts** somewhat appropriate for age and educational background level of students	1	**Content concepts** inappropriate for age and educational background level of students

Copyright © 2004 Pearson Education, Inc. Reproduction of this material is restricted to use with Echevarria, Vogt, and Short, *Making Content Comprehensible for English Learners.*

187

4. Supplementary materials used to a high degree, making the lesson clear and meaningful (e.g., computer programs, graphs, models, visuals)

4	3	2	1	0
		Some use of **supplementary materials**		No use of **supplementary materials**

Comments: Good use of supplementary materials to enhance students' understanding of volcanoes such as copies of semantic maps, pull-down maps, a book, Pompeii . . . Buried Alive, a transparency indicating the parts of a volcano, stacks of books to demonstrate rocks pushing against each other, household items to illustrate a volcanic eruption.

5. Adaptation of content (e.g., text, assignment) to all levels of student proficiency

4	3	2	1	0	NA
		Some **adaptation of content** to all levels of student proficiency		No significant **adaption of content** to all levels of student proficiency	

Comments: All students were given the same text with which to work. There were no specific adaptations made to the text itself to address the varying levels of language proficiency. However, the teacher had prepared a sequencing activity for students to complete where she identified sentences that explained the process of a volcanic eruption and students were required to put the steps in order. In addition, she began reading the text aloud to the students and paused frequently to ask questions and to check for clarification.

6. Meaningful activities that integrate lesson concepts (e.g., surveys, letter writing, simulations, constructing models) with language practice opportunities for reading, writing, listening, and/or speaking

4	3	2	1	0
		Meaningful activities that integrate lesson concepts, but provide little opportunity for language practice with opportunities for reading, writing, listening, and/or speaking		No **meaningful activities** that integrate lesson concepts with language practice

Comments: There were a lot of meaningful and interesting activities that provided students with language practice (e.g., participation in building the model volcano, discussing information from their semantic maps about volcanoes, and reading authentic text).

Building Background

7. Concepts explicitly linked to students' background experiences

4	3	2	1	0	NA
		Concepts loosely linked to students' background experiences		Concepts not explicitly linked to students' background experiences	

Comments: The teacher tapped into students' understanding of volcanoes by asking them to complete a semantic mapping exercise writing everything they knew about volcanoes.

	4	3	②	1	0
8.	**Links explicitly made** between past learning and new concepts		**Few links made** between past learning and new concepts		**No links made** between past learning and new concepts

Comments: There were few links made between past learning and its connection to new concepts. The teacher initiated the class by reminding the students of the visit to the Museum of Natural History and also reminded them of the rocks they had brought in. However, she did not explain how the visit or the collection of rocks related to that day's lesson about volcanoes.

	④	3	2	1	0
9.	**Key vocabulary empha-sized** (e.g., introduced, written, repeated, and highlighted for students to see)		**Key vocabulary** introduced, but not emphasized		**Key vocabulary** not emphasized

Comments: The key vocabulary words used for this lesson were written on the board, stated to the students at the beginning of the lesson, and reiterated throughout the lesson particularly when the teacher and students constructed the model volcano.

Comprehensible Input

	④	3	2	1	0
10.	**Speech** appropriate for students' proficiency level (e.g., slower rate, enunciation, and simple sentence structure for beginners)		**Speech** sometimes inappropriate for students' proficiency level		**Speech** inappropriate for students' proficiency level

Comments: The teacher explained tasks well and modeled the demonstrations first before the students participated.

11. **Explanation of academic tasks clear**
(4) 3 **Explanation of academic tasks somewhat clear** 2 1 **Explanation of academic tasks unclear** 0

Comments: The teacher explained tasks well and modeled the demonstrations first before the students participated.

12. **Uses a variety of techniques** to make content concepts clear (e.g., modeling, visuals, hands-on activities, demonstrations, gestures, body language)
(4) 3 Uses some **techniques** to make content concepts clear 2 1 Uses few or no **techniques** to make content concepts clear 0

Comments: A variety of techniques were used in this lesson: the use of the OHT with a diagram of a volcano and the labeled parts, brainstorming in the semantic mapping activity, demonstrating a model of a volcanic eruption, and reading about the topic after exploring it orally and visually. Used sequencing steps to check reading comprehension.

Strategies

13. Provides ample opportunities for students to use **strategies**
4 (3) Provides students with inadequate opportunities to use **strategies** 2 1 No opportunity for students to use **strategies** 0

Comments: The teacher used various strategies with students such as accessing prior knowledge and having them make predictions. Students, however, used these strategies with the teacher, not with other students.

14. Consistent use of **scaffolding** techniques throughout lesson, assisting and supporting student understanding (e.g., think-alouds)
(4) 3 Occasional use of **scaffolding** techniques 2 1 No use of **scaffolding** techniques 0

Comments: The teacher used various scaffolding techniques throughout the lesson to promote and assess students' comprehension of content concepts by means of questions, visuals, models, graphic organizers, prereading predictions, and demonstrations.

4	3	2	1	0
15. Teacher uses a variety of question types, including those that promote higher-order thinking skills (e.g., literal, analytical, and interpretive questions)	③	Teacher infrequently poses questions that promote higher-order thinking skills		Teacher does not pose questions that promote higher-order thinking skills

Comments: Most of the questions for this beginning level consisted of more factual/identification questions. In some cases, more elaborated responses were required of students; for example, "What happens when one set of rocks moves against another?" "Can you think of other places in the world where eruptions have occurred?" "Tell me about volcanoes in your country?" "How do you know this is a true story?"

Interaction

4	3	2	1	0
16. Frequent opportunities for interaction and discussion between teacher/student and among students, which encourage elaborated responses about lesson concepts	③	Interaction mostly teacher-dominated with some opportunities for students to talk about or question lesson concepts		Interaction primarily teacher-dominated with no opportunities for students to discuss lesson concepts

Comments: The teacher engaged the students in discussions about volcanoes throughout the class period. The semantic mapping exercise, the demonstration, and the prereading activity were all means that facilitated student interaction. The majority of interactions were teacher-student.

4	3	2	1	0
17. Grouping configurations support language and content objectives of the lesson	3	Grouping configurations unevenly support the language and content objectives	②	Grouping configurations do not support the language and content objectives

Comments: Although students were seated in groups, there was little opportunity for them to interact to practice their language skills. The whole-class setting supported the demonstration about volcanic eruption.

18. Consistently provides sufficient wait time for student responses

4	③	2	1	0
Consistently provides **sufficient wait time for student responses**		Occasionally provides **sufficient wait time for student responses**		Never provides sufficient **wait time for student responses**

Comments: At times there were students who wanted to respond, but were overlooked, perhaps because the period was running out of time. For those students selected to respond, the teacher allowed them time to articulate their thoughts.

19. Ample opportunities for students to clarify key concepts in L1 as needed with aide, peer, or L1 text

④	3	2	1	0	NA
		Some opportunity for students to **clarify key concepts in L1**		No opportunity for students to **clarify key concepts in L1**	

Comments: Only a few students could be identified as using their L1 during the lesson and they were seated in the far left corner of the classroom where the bilingual aide assisted them. The other students in the classroom did not seem to need to use their L1 text.

Practice/Application

20. Provides hands-on materials and/or manipulatives for students to practice using new content knowledge

4	③	2	1	0	NA
Provides **hands-on** materials and/or manipulatives for students to practice using new content knowledge		Provides few **hands-on** materials and/or manipulatives for students to practice using new content knowledge		Provides no **hands-on** materials and/or manipulatives for students to practice using new content knowledge	

Comments: The lesson involved manipulatives. During the experiment/demonstration for the volcanic eruption, for example, the teacher used materials such as a bottle, liquid detergent, warm water, measuring spoons, baking soda, and vinegar. Only a few students, though, used these materials themselves.

4   ③   2   1   0   NA

21. **Provides activities for students to apply content and language knowledge** in the classroom   Provides activities for students to **apply either content or language knowledge** in the classroom   Provides no activities for students to **apply content or language knowledge** in the classroom

Comments: For the most part, students applied content and language. More student-student interactions would have been beneficial and provided better opportunities for assessment.

4   ③   2   1   0

22. **Uses activities that integrate all language skills** (i.e., reading, writing, listening, and speaking)   Uses activities that integrate **some language skills**   Uses activities that apply only one **language skill**

Comments: The lesson allowed students an opportunity to use all language skills (some more than others) such as listening, speaking, and reading. Writing was evident mostly in the semantic mapping activity. Some predicting and scanning for information was part of the reading skills practiced.

Effectiveness of Lesson Delivery

4   ③   2   1   0

23. **Content objectives clearly supported by lesson delivery**   **Content objectives** supported somewhat by lesson delivery   **Content objectives** not supported by lesson delivery

Comments: The demonstration and discussion along with the constant repetition of key vocabulary served to accomplish most of the content objectives for the lesson. While students seemed to indicate an understanding of what volcanoes are, it is not certain that they fully understand what causes them to erupt.

4   3   ②   1   0

24. **Language objectives clearly supported by lesson delivery**   **Language objectives** supported somewhat by lesson delivery   **Language objectives** not supported by lesson delivery

Comments: Most of the language objectives were supported by the delivery. Students did not have a chance to complete the sequencing activity based on the reading in order to assess their reading comprehension.

25. Students engaged

(4) — Students engaged approximately 90% to 100% of the period

3

2 — Students engaged approximately 70% of the period

1

0 — Students engaged less than 50% of the period

Comments: Students were on-task throughout the lesson activity.

26. Pacing of the lesson appropriate to the students' ability level

4

3

(2) — Pacing generally appropriate, but at times too fast or too slow

1

0 — Pacing inappropriate to the students' ability level

Comments: The pacing seemed fine, but was a little rushed at times which prevented students from completing some activities such as the individual silent reading and sequencing activity.

Lesson Review/Evaluation

27. Comprehensive review of key vocabulary

4

3

(2) — Uneven review of key vocabulary

1

0 — No review of key vocabulary

Comments: Teacher reviewed key vocabulary at the beginning of the lesson and reinforced it throughout. No final review took place at the end of the lesson.

28. Comprehensive review of key content concepts

4

(3)

2 — Uneven review of key content concepts

1

0 — No review of key content concepts

Comments: The key content concepts were reviewed throughout the lesson, but there was no comprehensive review to wrap up the lesson, other than the final question posed to students at the end of the class, "What is a volcano?"

4

3⃝

2

1

0

29. Regularly provides **feedback** to students on their output (e.g., language, content, work)

Inconsistently provides **feedback** to students on their output

Provides no **feedback** to students on their output

Comments: The teacher gave positive feedback to students' responses in most cases. In some instances, when time was short, she did not always respond to students whose hands were raised. She guided the brainstorming and prereading discussions.

4

3

2⃝

1

0

30. Conducts **assessment** of student comprehension and learning of all lesson objectives (e.g., spot checking, group response) throughout the lesson.

Conducts **assessment** of student comprehension and learning of some lesson objectives

Conducts no **assessment** of student comprehension and learning of lesson objectives

Comments: Throughout the lesson, the teacher checked students' understanding of some concepts and of the instructional tasks. She monitored the classroom to answer questions and to provide assistance. During the reading activity, however, students were not allotted sufficient time to read individually and the sequencing activity was moved to the following day. Therefore, it is unclear how she was able to assess individual student comprehension before she began reading the text to students.

FIGURE 11.4 SIOP Teacher Rating Form

SIOP Teacher Rating Form

Teacher	Observation 1 Score/Date	Observation 2 Score/Date	Observation 3 Score/Date

or a group of teachers may meet on a regular basis to provide feedback to one another and assist in refining their teaching.

Scores also can be documented on an SIOP Teacher Rating Form over time to show growth (see Figure 11.4). Using percentages, teachers can see how their implementation of the SIOP features improves. This type of documentation is also useful for research purposes to document systematic implementation of the SIOP and fidelity of implementation.

Further, plotting scores on a graph, as seen in Figure 11.5, is a very effective way to illustrate strong areas as well as areas that require attention, or areas teachers have highlighted as important for their own growth. If a teacher consistently shows low scores on certain items, that provides the teacher with clear feedback for areas on which to focus. Staff developers and teacher educators can use the scores to determine areas for further discussion and practice in workshops and course sessions if several teachers are having difficulty with the same feature or component.

Finally, while the SIOP is a useful tool for professional development, scores should be used with caution. Many variables impact the success or

FIGURE 11.5 Ms. Clark's Scores

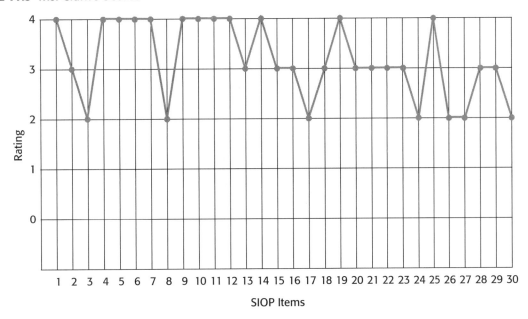

failure of a given lesson such as time of day, time of year, dynamics between students, and the like. Rather than just doing one observation and scoring of a teacher, several lessons should be rated over time for a fuller picture of the teacher's implementation of sheltered instruction.

Reliability and Validity of the SIOP

After several years of field-testing and refining the SIOP, a study was conducted (Guarino, Echevarria, Short, Schick, Forbes, & Rueda, 2001) to establish the validity and reliability of the instrument. The findings of the study indicated that the SIOP is a highly reliable and valid measure of sheltered instruction (see Appendix C for a discussion of the study).

Summary

This book has been developed for teachers, supervisors, administrators, teacher trainers, and researchers as a resource for increasing the effectiveness of instruction for English learners. We have presented a research-based, professional development model of sheltered instruction, operationalized in the SIOP, that can be used as an observation instrument, as well as a lesson planning guide.

The SIOP provides concrete examples of the features of sheltered instruction, and the book has been written as a way to illustrate and elucidate those features by describing how real teachers might actually teach sheltered lessons. The use of vignettes allows readers to "see" what each feature might look like in a classroom setting. The features of the SIOP represent best practice for teaching English learners.

Discussion Questions

1. The SIOP has a number of uses by different constituencies (e.g., teachers, supervisors, administrators, and researchers). How can you begin using the SIOP? What additional uses might it have for you or other constituencies?

2. Reread the sample lesson on pages 183–186. Would you score this lesson differently from the sample SIOP scores? On what items would you differ? What was the basis of your disagreement?

3. Look at the sample SIOP and change any two scores to 1. What would be the total score and percentage score on the revised and recalculated SIOP?

4. Imagine that you and a supervisor have just watched a videotape of your sheltered lesson. You are discussing the SIOP rating sheet that each of you scored independently. What would be the most collaborative way to approach the discussion of your teaching? What would yield the most useful information for improving your teaching?

The Sheltered Instruction Observation Protocol (SIOP) and Abbreviated SIOP

The Sheltered Instruction Observation Protocol (SIOP)
(Echevarria, Vogt, & Short, 2000, 2004)

Observer(s): _____
Date: _____
Grade: _____
ESL Level: _____

Teacher: _____
School: _____
Class/Topic: _____
Lesson: Multi-day   Single-day   *(circle one)*

Total Points Possible: 120 (Subtract 4 points for each NA given) _____
Total Points Earned: _____   Percentage Score: _____

Directions: Circle the number that best reflects what you observe in a sheltered lesson. You may give a score from 0–4 (or NA on selected items). Cite under "Comments" specific examples of the behaviors observed.

Preparation

4	3	2	1	0
1. Clearly defined **content objectives** for students		**Content objectives** for students implied		No clearly defined **content objectives** for students

Comments:

4	3	2	1	0
2. Clearly defined **language objectives** for students		**Language objectives** for students implied		No clearly defined **language objectives** for students

Comments:

4	3	2	1	0
3. **Content concepts** appropriate for age and educational background level of students		**Content concepts** somewhat appropriate for age and educational background level of students		**Content concepts** inappropriate for age and educational background level of students

Comments:

4. Supplementary materials used to a high degree, making the lesson clear and meaningful (e.g., computer programs, graphs, models, visuals)

4	3	2	1	0
		Some use of **supplementary materials**		No use of **supplementary materials**

Comments:

5. Adaptation of content (e.g., text, assignment) to all levels of student proficiency

4	3	2	1	0	NA
		Some **adaptation of content** to all levels of student proficiency		No significant **adaption of content** to all levels of student proficiency	

Comments:

6. Meaningful activities that integrate lesson concepts (e.g., surveys, letter writing, simulations, constructing models) with language practice opportunities for reading, writing, listening, and/or speaking

4	3	2	1	0
		Meaningful activities that integrate lesson concepts, but provide little opportunity for language practice with opportunities for reading, writing, listening, and/or speaking		No **meaningful activities** that integrate lesson concepts with language practice

Comments:

Building Background

7. Concepts explicitly linked to students' background experiences

4	3	2	1	0	NA
		Concepts loosely linked to students' background experiences		**Concepts not explicitly linked** to students' background experiences	

Comments:

8. Links explicitly made between past learning and new concepts

4	3	2	1	0
Links explicitly made between past learning and new concepts		**Few links made** between past learning and new concepts		**No links made** between past learning and new concepts

Comments:

9. Key vocabulary emphasized (e.g., introduced, written, repeated, and highlighted for students to see)

4	3	2	1	0
Key vocabulary emphasized (e.g., introduced, written, repeated, and highlighted for students to see)		**Key vocabulary** introduced, but not emphasized		**Key vocabulary** not emphasized

Comments:

Comprehensible Input

10. Speech appropriate for students' proficiency level (e.g., slower rate, enunciation, and simple sentence structure for beginners)

4	3	2	1	0
Speech appropriate for students' proficiency level (e.g., slower rate, enunciation, and simple sentence structure for beginners)		**Speech** sometimes inappropriate for students' proficiency level		**Speech** inappropriate for students' proficiency level

Comments:

11. Explanation of academic tasks clear

4	3	2	1	0
Explanation of academic tasks clear		**Explanation of academic tasks** somewhat clear		**Explanation of academic tasks** unclear

Comments:

4	3	2	1	0
12. Uses a variety of **techniques** to make content concepts clear (e.g., modeling, visuals, hands-on activities, demonstrations, gestures, body language)		Uses some **techniques** to make content concepts clear		Uses few or no **techniques** to make content concepts clear

Comments:

Strategies

4	3	2	1	0
13. Provides ample opportunities for students to use **strategies**		Provides students with inadequate opportunities to use **strategies**		No opportunity for students to use **strategies**

Comments:

4	3	2	1	0
14. Consistent use of **scaffolding** techniques throughout lesson, assisting and supporting student understanding (e.g., think-alouds)		Occasional use of **scaffolding** techniques		No use of **scaffolding** techniques

Comments:

4	3	2	1	0
15. Teacher uses a variety of **question types, including those that promote higher-order thinking skills** (e.g., literal, analytical, and interpretive questions)		Teacher infrequently poses **questions that promote higher-order thinking skills**		Teacher does not pose **questions that promote higher-order thinking skills**

Comments:

Interaction

	4	3	2	1	0	
16.	Frequent opportunities for **interaction** and discussion between teacher/student and among students, which encourage elaborated responses about lesson concepts		**Interaction** mostly teacher-dominated with some opportunities for students to talk about or question lesson concepts		**Interaction** primarily teacher-dominated with no opportunities for students to discuss lesson concepts	

Comments:

	4	3	2	1	0	
17.	**Grouping configurations** support language and content objectives of the lesson		**Grouping configurations** unevenly support the language and content objectives		**Grouping configurations** do not support the language and content objectives	

Comments:

	4	3	2	1	0	
18.	Consistently provides sufficient **wait time for student responses**		Occasionally provides sufficient **wait time for student responses**		Never provides sufficient **wait time for student responses**	

Comments:

	4	3	2	1	0	NA
19.	Ample opportunities for students to **clarify key concepts in L1** as needed with aide, peer, or L1 text		Some opportunity for students to **clarify key concepts in L1**		No opportunity for students to **clarify key concepts in L1**	NA

Comments:

Practice/Application

	4	3	2	1	0	NA
20.	Provides **hands-on** materials and/or manipulatives for students to practice using new content knowledge		Provides few **hands-on** materials and/or manipulatives for students to practice using new content knowledge		Provides no **hands-on** materials and/or manipulatives for students to practice using new content knowledge	NA

Comments:

	4	3	2	1	0	NA
21.	Provides activities for students to **apply content and language knowledge** in the classroom		Provides activities for students to **apply either content or language knowledge** in the classroom		Provides no activities for students to **apply content or language knowledge** in the classroom	NA

Comments:

	4	3	2	1	0
22.	Uses activities that integrate all **language skills** (i.e., reading, writing, listening, and speaking)		Uses activities that integrate some **language skills**		Uses activities that apply only one **language skill**

Comments:

Effectiveness of Lesson Delivery

	4	3	2	1	0
23.	**Content objectives** clearly supported by lesson delivery		**Content objectives** supported somewhat by lesson delivery		**Content objectives** not supported by lesson delivery

Comments:

	4	3	2	1	0
24. Language objectives	Language objectives clearly supported by lesson delivery		Language objectives supported somewhat by lesson delivery		Language objectives not supported by lesson delivery

Comments:

	4	3	2	1	0
25. Students engaged	Students engaged approximately 90% to 100% of the period		Students engaged approximately 70% of the period		Students engaged less than 50% of the period

Comments:

	4	3	2	1	0
26. Pacing of the lesson	Pacing of the lesson appropriate to the students' ability level		Pacing generally appropriate, but at times too fast or too slow		Pacing inappropriate to the students' ability level

Comments:

Lesson Review/Evaluation

	4	3	2	1	0
27.	Comprehensive review of key vocabulary		Uneven review of key vocabulary		No review of key vocabulary

Comments:

	4	3	2	1	0
28.	Comprehensive review of key content concepts		Uneven review of key content concepts		No review of key content concepts

Comments:

	4	3	2	1	0
29.	Regularly provides **feedback** to students on their output (e.g., language, content, work)		Inconsistently provides **feedback** to students on their output		Provides no **feedback** to students on their output

Comments:

	4	3	2	1	0
30.	Conducts **assessment** of student comprehension and learning of all lesson objectives (e.g., spot checking, group response) throughout the lesson.		Conducts **assessment** of student comprehension and learning of some lesson objectives		Conducts no **assessment** of student comprehension and learning of lesson objectives

Comments:

The Sheltered Instruction Observation Protocol: Abbreviated Version

On the following two pages, you will see an abbreviated version of the SIOP. Once you become familiar with the complete SIOP, you may find it easier to use this version. Note that the *descriptors* for the rubric (0–4) are absent here. Use instead "Highly Evident," "Somewhat Evident," "Not Evident," and NA when rating.

The Sheltered Instruction Observation Protocol (SIOP)
(Echevarria, Vogt, & Short, 2000, 2004)

Observer(s):_____ Teacher:_____
Date:_____ School:_____
Grade:_____ Class/Topic:_____
ESL Level:_____ Lesson: Multi-day Single-day *(circle one)*

Total Points Possible: 120 (Subtract 4 points for each NA given)_____
Total Points Earned: _____ Percentage Score: _____

Directions: Circle the number that best reflects what you observe in a sheltered lesson. You may give a score from 0–4 (or NA on selected items). Cite under "Comments" specific examples of the behaviors observed.

	Highly Evident		Somewhat Evident		Not Evident	
I. Preparation	**4**	**3**	**2**	**1**	**0**	**NA**
1. Clearly defined **content objectives** for students	❑	❑	❑	❑	❑	
2. Clearly defined **language objectives** for students	❑	❑	❑	❑	❑	
3. **Content concepts** appropriate for age and educational background level of students	❑	❑	❑	❑	❑	
4. **Supplementary materials** used to a high degree, making the lesson clear and meaningful (e.g., computer programs, graphs, models, visuals)	❑	❑	❑	❑	❑	
5. **Adaptation of content** (e.g., text, assignment) to all levels of student proficiency	❑	❑	❑	❑	❑	❑
6. **Meaningful activities** that integrate lesson concepts (e.g., surveys, letter writing, simulations, constructing models) with language practice opportunities for reading, writing, listening, and/or speaking *Comments:*	❑	❑	❑	❑	❑	
II. Instruction						
•1) Building Background	**4**	**3**	**2**	**1**	**0**	**NA**
7. **Concepts explicitly linked** to students' background experiences	❑	❑	❑	❑	❑	❑
8. **Links explicitly made** between past learning and new concepts	❑	❑	❑	❑	❑	
9. **Key vocabulary emphasized** (e.g., introduced, written, repeated, and highlighted for students to see) *Comments:*	❑	❑	❑	❑	❑	
•2) Comprehensible Input	**4**	**3**	**2**	**1**	**0**	**NA**
10. **Speech** appropriate for students' proficiency level (e.g., slower rate and enunciation, and simple sentence structure for beginners)	❑	❑	❑	❑	❑	
11. **Explanation of academic tasks** clear	❑	❑	❑	❑	❑	
12. Uses a variety of **techniques** to make content concepts clear (e.g., modeling, visuals, hands-on activities, demonstrations, gestures, body language) *Comments:*	❑	❑	❑	❑	❑	
•3) Strategies	**4**	**3**	**2**	**1**	**0**	**NA**
13. Provides ample opportunities for students to use **strategies**	❑	❑	❑	❑	❑	

	Highly Evident		Somewhat Evident		Not Evident	
	4	**3**	**2**	**1**	**0**	**NA**
14. Consistent use of **scaffolding** techniques throughout lesson, assisting and supporting student understanding, such as think-alouds	❏	❏	❏	❏	❏	
15. Teacher uses a variety of **question types, including those that promote higher-order thinking skills** throughout the lesson (e.g., literal, analytical, and interpretive questions) *Comments:*	❏	❏	❏	❏	❏	

•4) Interaction	**4**	**3**	**2**	**1**	**0**	**NA**
16. Frequent opportunities for **interaction** and discussion between teacher/student and among students, which encourage elaborated responses about lesson concepts	❏	❏	❏	❏	❏	
17. **Grouping configurations** support language and content objectives of the lesson	❏	❏	❏	❏	❏	
18. Consistently provides sufficient **wait time for student response**	❏	❏	❏	❏	❏	
19. Ample opportunities for students to **clarify key concepts in L1** *Comments:*	❏	❏	❏	❏	❏	❏

•5) Practice/Application	**4**	**3**	**2**	**1**	**0**	**NA**
20. Provides **hands-on** materials and/or manipulatives for students to practice using new content knowledge	❏	❏	❏	❏	❏	❏
21. Provides activities for students to **apply content and language knowledge** in the classroom	❏	❏	❏	❏	❏	
22. Uses activities that integrate all **language skills** (i.e., reading, writing, listening, and speaking) *Comments:*	❏	❏	❏	❏	❏	

•6) Lesson Delivery	**4**	**3**	**2**	**1**	**0**	**NA**
23. **Content objectives** clearly supported by lesson delivery	❏	❏	❏	❏	❏	
24. **Language objectives** clearly supported by lesson delivery	❏	❏	❏	❏	❏	
25. **Students engaged** approximately 90% to 100% of the period	❏	❏	❏	❏	❏	
26. **Pacing** of the lesson appropriate to the students' ability level *Comments:*	❏	❏	❏	❏	❏	

III. Review/Assessment	**4**	**3**	**2**	**1**	**0**	**NA**
27. Comprehensive **review of key vocabulary**	❏	❏	❏	❏	❏	
28. Comprehensive **review of key content concepts**	❏	❏	❏	❏	❏	
29. Regularly provides **feedback** to students on their output (e.g., language, content, work)	❏	❏	❏	❏	❏	
30. Conducts **assessment** of student comprehension and learning of all lesson objectives (e.g., spot checking, group response) throughout the lesson *Comments:*	❏	❏	❏	❏	❏	

Lesson Plans

On the following pages, you will find two lesson plan formats that teachers have found helpful in their planning and teaching. The first is designed to be used by teachers who are very familiar with the SIOP and who like the feature of the checklist reminders for many of the SIOP indicators. Because the Lesson Sequence area is somewhat small, some teachers may wish to duplicate the form and use the back side for additional planning information. For an example of a completed lesson plan using this format, see Ms. Chen's lesson in Chapter 2.

The second lesson plan provided in this Appendix includes an outline format with all of the eight SIOP categories. It provides a daily reminder of the effective instructional elements to include when teaching English learners.

For additional lesson planning ideas, please see teachers' lessons at our website: *http://www.siopinstitute.net*.

SIOP Lesson Plan

Date: _____   Grade/Class/Subject: _____

Unit/Theme: _____   Standards: _____

Content Objective(s): _____

_____

Language Objective(s): _____

_____

Key Vocabulary	Supplementary Materials

SIOP Features

Preparation	Scaffolding	Grouping Options
___ Adaptation of Content	___ Modeling	___ Whole class
___ Links to Background	___ Guided practice	___ Small groups
___ Links to Past Learning	___ Independent practice	___ Partners
___ Strategies incorporated	___ Comprehensible input	___ Independent

Integration of Processes	Application	Assessment
___ Reading	___ Hands-on	___ Individual
___ Writing	___ Meaningful	___ Group
___ Speaking	___ Linked to objectives	___ Written
___ Listening	___ Promotes engagement	___ Oral

Lesson Sequence

Reflections:

FIGURE B-1 SIOP Lesson Plan Outline

STANDARDS:

THEME:

LESSON TOPIC:

OBJECTIVES:

Language

Content

LEARNING STRATEGIES:

KEY VOCABULARY:

MATERIALS:

MOTIVATION:
(Building background)

PRESENTATION:
(Language and content objectives, comprehensible input, strategies, interaction, feedback)

PRACTICE/APPLICATION:
(Meaningful activities, interaction, strategies, practice/application, feedback)

REVIEW/ASSESSMENT:
(Review objectives and vocabulary, assess learning)

EXTENSION:

SIOP Research: The Effects of Sheltered Instruction on the Achievement of Limited English Proficient Students

"The Effects of Sheltered Instruction on the Achievement of Limited English Proficient Students" was a seven-year research project (1996-2003) conducted for the Center for Research on Education, Diversity & Excellence (CREDE), a national research center funded by the U.S. Department of Education, Office of Educational Research and Improvement (now known as the Institute of Education Sciences). This project worked with middle school teachers in four large metropolitan school districts—two on the East Coast and two on the West Coast—to identify key practices for sheltered instruction and develop a professional development model to enable more teachers to use sheltered instruction effectively in their classrooms. Dr. Jana Echevarria of California State University, Long Beach and Dr. Deborah Short of the Center for Applied Linguistics in Washington, DC were co-project investigators.

Although sheltered instruction has been widely advocated as an effective instructional strategy for language minority students, when this study began there had been little agreement among practitioners as to what sheltered instruction should look like in the classroom and few research investigations measuring what constituted an effective sheltered lesson. This project therefore set the following goals: (1) develop an explicit model of sheltered instruction, (2) use that model to train teachers in effective sheltered strategies, and (3) conduct field experiments and collect data to evaluate teacher change and the effects of sheltered instruction on LEP students' English language development and content knowledge.

The specific research questions posed by this project follow:

1. What are the characteristics of sheltered instruction, and how does it differ from high-quality non-sheltered instruction?
2. What are the characteristics of an effective professional development program for implementing quality sheltered instruction to a high degree?
3. Does sheltered instruction improve the achievement of LEP students in content areas such as social studies?
4. Are there significant differences in achievement data (reading scores, writing samples, attendance) for students of project teachers versus students in sheltered classes whose teachers have not received CREDE training?

This research project involved the active collaboration of practicing middle school teachers both in refining the model of sheltered instruction and in implementing it in their classrooms. In the first two years of the project we identified, based on literature review and classroom research, effective teaching strategies involved in sheltered instruction. The model began as a research observation instrument, the Sheltered Instruction Observation Protocol (SIOP), so that researchers could determine how well teachers were including these features of effective sheltered instruction in their lessons. Drawing from the literature on best practices, the SIOP incorporates topics such as scaffolding, learning strategies, literacy techniques, and use of meaningful curricula and materials. With feedback from the teachers, the protocol evolved into a lesson planning and delivery approach, the SIOP model (Echevarria, Vogt, & Short, 2000; Short & Echevarria, 1999). It is composed of 30 items grouped into eight components essential for making content comprehensible for English learners—Preparation, Building Background, Comprehensible Input, Strategies, Interaction, Practice/Application, Lesson Delivery, and Review/Assessment. The SIOP model shares many features recommended for high quality instruction for all students, but adds key features for the academic success of students learning through a second language, such as the inclusion of language objectives in every content lesson. This model can be applied in ESL classes as well as all content area classes because it offers a framework for instruction that incorporates best practices for teaching both language and content.

After several years of field-testing the SIOP, a study was conducted to establish the validity and reliability of the observation instrument. It was found to be a highly reliable and valid measure of sheltered instruction (Guarino, Echevarria, Short, Schick, Forbes, & Rueda, 2001). Experienced observers of classroom instruction (e.g., teacher education faculty who supervise student teachers) who were *not* specifically trained in the SIOP model were able to use the protocol to distinguish between high and low implementers of the model. A statistical analysis revealed an interrater of correlation .99.

As part of the research design, student data in the form of a writing assessment based on the IMAGE (Illinois Measure of Annual Growth in English) Test were gathered and analyzed. The IMAGE is the standardized test of reading and writing used by the state of Illinois to measure annual growth of these skills in their limited English proficient students in Grades 3 and higher. It has been correlated to and a predictor of scores on the IGAP (the state standardized test of achievement) given to all students in Illinois, except those exempted for linguistic development reasons or learning disabilities. The IMAGE Writing Test provides separate scores for five features of writing: Language Production, Focus, Support/Elaboration, Organization, and Mechanics, as well as an overall score.

During the 1998–99 school year, researchers gave prompts to middle school English language learning students that required expository writing, once in the fall (pre-test) and then again in the spring (post-test). Two distinct cohorts of English learners in sheltered classes participated: students whose teachers were trained in implementing the SIOP Model (the treatment group), and students whose teachers had no exposure to the SIOP Model (the control group). The students in both groups were in Grades 6–8 and represented mixed proficiency levels.

Results showed English learners in sheltered classes with teachers who had been trained in implementing the SIOP to a high degree improved their writing and out-performed the students in control classes by receiving overall higher scores for the spring assessment. They also made greater gains from the fall to spring administrations of the test. These findings were statistically significant. The results indicated that students whose teachers implemented the SIOP model of sheltered instruction improved significantly in all areas of writing over students in sheltered classes whose teachers were not familiar with the SIOP model. These results match the findings from the 1997–98 school year when a similar administration of a writing assessment requiring narrative writing was given. Secondary analyses of the data revealed that special education students who constituted a subset of the English learners made significant improvement overall in their writing as well, with both the narrative and expository assessments.

Specifically, with the 1998–99 assessment, comparisons between treatment and control on total scores (i.e., aggregated across the 5 scales) found the participants whose teachers were trained in the SIOP model made significantly better gains than the control group in writing ($F(1,312) = 10.79$; $p<.05$). Follow-up analyses on student performance on the various subtests of the writing assessment found that the treatment group performed at a significantly higher level in language production ($F(1,314) = 5.00$; $p<.05$), organization ($F (1,315) = 5.65$; $p<.05$) and mechanics ($F (1,315) = 4.10$; $p<.05$) than those in the control group, whose teachers had not received the study-developed training and support in delivering sheltered instruction (see Table 1 and Table 2). The treatment group did not make significant gains over the comparison group in their performance on the writing focus and elaboration subtests.

The project also developed and field-tested a professional development program for the SIOP model that incorporates key features of effective teacher development as recommended by Darling-Hammond (1998) and Garet, Porter, Desimone, Birman, & Yoon (2001). In this project, it has been found that through sustained, intensive interaction and coaching among staff developers and teachers—for at least one year—teachers can modify their pedagogy to promote both language and content learning among English learners. Two professional development videos (Hudec & Short, 2002a; 2002b), a training manual (Short, Hudec & Echevarria, 2002), and other materials have been developed to support this program, and institutes to prepare staff developers and teacher educators to coach others in the SIOP model have been held across the U.S. (See *http://www.siopinstitute.net* for more details.)

Since the SIOP model was finalized in 2000, the following uses for the observation tool and professional development program have been realized:

- Teacher lesson plan checklist
- Classroom observation tool by administrators

- Supervision and observation tool of student teachers
- Research observation tool for fidelity of model implementation
- Program of professional development

Summary: Selected Findings from the SIOP Research Project

- After 5 years of collaboration with practicing teachers, CREDE researchers developed a model of high quality sheltered instruction, known as the SIOP model. This model takes into account the special language development needs of English language learners which distinguishes it from high quality non-sheltered teaching.
- A study conducted to establish the validity and reliability of the Sheltered Instruction Observation Protocol found that the instrument is a highly reliable and valid measure of sheltered instruction (Guarino, Echevarria, Short, Schick, Forbes, & Rueda, 2001).
- 1997–98: Researchers compared English language learning students in classes whose teachers had been trained in implementing the SIOP to a high degree to a control group (taught by teachers not trained in the SIOP Model) using a prompt that required narrative writing. They scored the prompt using the writing rubric of the Illinois Measure of Annual Growth in English (IMAGE) Test. The English learners in classes whose teachers had been trained in implementing the SIOP to a high degree demonstrated significantly higher writing scores than the control group.
- 1998–99: Researchers compared English learners in classes whose teachers had been trained in implementing the SIOP to a high degree to a control group (taught by teachers not trained in the SIOP Model) using a prompt that required expository writing. They scored the prompt using the writing rubric of the Illinois Measure of Annual Growth in English (IMAGE) Test. The English learners in classes whose teachers had been trained in implementing the SIOP to a high degree demonstrated significantly higher writing scores than the control group and made greater gains from the pre-test to the post-test. See results in Tables 1 and 2.

TABLE 1 Mean Scores, Standard Deviations, and Sample Size for Treatment and Control Groups

	SIOP (Treatment)		Control	
	Pretest	Posttest	Pretest	Posttest
Total Score				
M	13.55	16.36	14.61	15.81
SD	3.42	3.33	3.36	3.45
N	238	238	77	77
Language Production				
M	2.65	3.22	2.77	3.09
SD	.78	.79	.78	.73
N	240	240	77	77
Focus				
M	2.81	3.30	3.01	3.17
SD	.87	.98	.88	.94
N	239	239	77	77
Support/Elaboration				
M	2.65	3.26	2.83	3.18
SD	.78	.72	.70	.81
N	241	241	77	77
Organization				
M	2.77	3.31	3.16	3.21
SD	.96	.78	.92	.71
N	241	241	77	77
Mechanics				
M	2.72	3.28	2.84	3.17
SD	.88	.87	.86	.94
N	241	241	77	77

TABLE 2 Analysis of Covariance of Posttest Writing Results by Treatment Condition

Variable	df	M Square	F-ratio	p
Total	1	78.276	10.785	.001*
Language Production	1	2.133	5.004	.026*
Focus	1	2.904	3.706	.055
Support & Elaboration	1	1.247	2.680	1.03
Organization	1	2.842	5.651	.018*
Mechanics	1	2.065	4.101	.044*

Note pretest scores for each measure served as the covariate for posttest dependent measures. $p < .05$*

References

Darling-Hammond, L. (1998). Teacher learning that supports student learning. *Educational Leadership, 55,* 6–11.

Echevarria, J., Vogt, M.E., & Short, D. (2000). *Making content comprehensible for English language learners: The SIOP model.* Needham Heights, MA: Allyn & Bacon.

Garet, M.S., Porter, A.C., Desimone, L., Birman, B.F., & Yoon, K.S. (2001). What makes professional development effective? Results from a national sample of teachers. *American Educational Research Journal, 38*(4), 915–945.

Guarino, A.J., Echevarria, J., Short, D., Schick, J. E., Forbes, S., & Rueda, R. (2001). The sheltered instruction observation protocol. *Journal of Research in Education, 11*(1), 138–140.

Hudec, J., & Short, D. (Prods). (2002a). *Helping English learners succeed: An overview of the SIOP model.* [Video]. Washington, DC: Center for Applied Linguistics.

Hudec, J., & Short, D. (Prods). (2002b). *The SIOP model: Sheltered instruction for academic achievement.* [Video]. Washington, DC: Center for Applied Linguistics.

Short, D., & Echevarria, J. (1999). *The sheltered instruction observation protocol: A tool for teacher-researcher collaboration and professional development* (Educational Practice Rep. No. 3). Santa Cruz, CA and Washington, DC: Center for Research on Education, Diversity & Excellence.

Short, D., Hudec, J, & Echevarria, J. (2002). *Using the SIOP model: Professional development manual for sheltered instruction.* Washington, DC: Center for Applied Linguistics.

Glossary

Academic language: Language used in formal contexts for academic subjects. The aspect of language connected with literacy and academic achievement. This includes technical and academic terms (*see* Cognitive/Academic Language Proficiency—CALP).

Additive bilingualism: Rather than neglecting or rejecting students' language and culture, additive bilingualism promotes building on what the child brings to the classroom and adding to it.

Alignment: Match among the ESL and content standards, instruction, curriculum, and assessment.

Alternative assessment: Analysis and reporting of student performances using sources that differ from traditional objective responses such as standardized and norm-referenced tests. Alternative assessments include portfolios, performance-based tasks, checklists, and so forth.

Assessment: The orderly process of gathering, analyzing, interpreting, and reporting student performance, ideally from multiple sources over a period of time.

Basic Interpersonal Communication Skills (BICS): Face-to-face conversational fluency, including mastery of pronunciation, vocabulary, and grammar. English language learners typically acquire conversational language used in everyday activities before they develop more complex, conceptual language proficiency.

Bilingual instruction: School instruction using two languages, generally a native language of the student and a second language. The amount of time that each language is used depends on the type of bilingual program, its specific objectives, and students' level of language proficiency.

Cognitive Academic Language Learning Approach (CALLA): An instructional model developed by Chamot and O'Malley (1987, 1994) for content and language learning that incorporates student development of learning strategies, specifically metacognitive, cognitive, and socio-affective strategies (*see* Learning Strategies).

Cognitive/Academic Language Proficiency (CALP): Language proficiency associated with schooling, and the abstract language abilities required for academic work. A more complex, conceptual, linguistic ability that includes analysis, synthesis and evaluation.

Communicative Competence: The combination of grammatical, discourse, strategic and sociolinguistic competence that allows the recognition and production of fluent and appropriate language in all communicative settings.

Constructivism: A theoretical perspective in which an individual's prior experiences, knowledge, and beliefs influence how understanding is developed and experiences are interpreted. In teaching, the focus is more on how knowledge is constructed rather than on products, with richly contextualized opportunities for students to engage in inquiry and discovery.

Content-based ESL: An instructional approach in which content topics are used as the vehicle for second language learning. A system of instruction in which teachers use a variety of instructional techniques as a way of developing second language, content, cognitive, and study skills, often delivered through thematic units.

Content objectives: Statements that identify what students should know and be able to do in particular

Note: The following sources were used for definitions in this glossary: Harris and Hodges, 1995; McLaughlin and Vogt, 1996; and the national ESL Standards (TESOL, 1997).

content areas. They support school district and state content standards and learning outcomes, and they guide teaching and learning in the classroom.

Content standards: Definitions of what students are expected to know and be capable of doing for a given content area. The knowledge and skills that need to be taught in order for students to reach competency. What students are expected to learn and what schools are expected to teach. May be national, state, or local-level standards.

Cross-cultural competence: The ability to understand and follow the cultural rules and norms of more than one system. The ability to respond to the demands of a given situation in a culturally acceptable way.

Culture: The customs, lifestyle, traditions, behavior, attitudes, and artifacts of a given people. Culture also encompasses the ways people organize and interpret the world, and the way events are perceived based on established social norms. A system of standards for understanding the world.

Dialect: The form of a language peculiar to a specific region. Features a variation in vocabulary, grammar, and pronunciation.

Engagement: When students are fully taking part in a lesson, they are said to be engaged. This is a holistic term that encompasses listening, reading, writing, responding, and discussing. The level of students' engagement during a lesson may be assessed to a greater or lesser degree. A low SIOP score for engagement would imply frequent chatting, daydreaming, nonattention, and other off-task behaviors.

English language learners (ELLs): Children and adults who are learning English as a second or additional language. This term may apply to learners across various levels of proficiency in English. ELLs may also be referred to as non-English speaking (NES), limited English proficient (LEP), and a non-native speaker (NNS).

ESL: English as a second language. Used to refer to programs and classes to teach students English as a second (additional) language.

ESOL: English speakers of other languages. Students whose first language is not English and who do not write, speak, and understand the language as well as their classmates.

Evaluation: Judgments about students' learning made by interpretation and analysis of assessment data; the process of judging achievement, growth, product, processes, or changes in these; judgments of education programs. The processes of assessment and evaluation can be viewed as progressive: first, assessment; then, evaluation.

Formative evaluation: Ongoing collection, analysis, and reporting of information about student performance for purposes of instruction and learning.

Grouping: The division of students into classes for instruction, such as by age, ability, or achievement; or within classes, such as by reading ability, proficiency, language background, or interests.

Holistic score: An integrated analysis of a student's performance based on specified criteria; results in a score on a rubric or rating scale (*see* Rubric and Rating scale).

Home language: The language, or languages, spoken in the student's home by people who live there. Also referred to as first language (L1), primary language, or native language.

Informal assessment: Appraisal of student performance through unstructured observation; characterized as frequent, ongoing, continuous, and involving simple but important techniques such as verbal checks for understanding, teacher-created assessments, and other nonstandardized procedures. This type of assessment provides teachers with immediate feedback.

Inter-rater reliability: Measures of the degree of agreement between two different raters on separate ratings of one assessment indicator using the same scale and criteria.

L1: First language. A widely used abbreviation for the primary, home, or native language.

Language minority: In the United States, a student whose primary language is not English. The individual student's ability to speak English will vary.

Language objectives: Statements that identify what students should know and be able to do while using English (or another language). They support students' language development, often focusing on vocabulary, functional language, questioning, articulating predictions or hypotheses, reading, writing, and so forth.

Language proficiency: An individual's competence in using a language for basic communication and for academic purposes. May be categorized as stages of language acquisition (*see* Stages of language proficiency).

Language competence: An individual's total language ability. The underlying language system as indicated by the individual's language performance.

Limited English Proficient (LEP): A term used to refer to a student with restricted understanding or use of written and spoken English; a learner who is still developing competence in using English.

Mnemonics: From the Greek *mnemon*, meaning "mindful." Mnemonics are devices to jog the memory. For example, steps of a learning strategy are often abbreviated to form an acronym or word that enables the learner to remember the steps. An example of a strategy would be teaching students to use mnemonics to write a complete sentence, such as in the use of PENS (Deshler, Ellis, and Lenz, 1996). The student is taught to *Preview* ideas, *Explore* words, *Note* words in a complete sentence, and *See* if the sentence is okay (*see* Learning strategy).

Multilingualism: The ability to speak more than two languages; proficiency in more than two languages.

Native language: An individual's first, primary, or home language (L1).

Native English speaker: An individual whose first language is English.

Non-English speaking (NES): Individuals who are in an English-speaking environment (such as U.S. schools) but who have not acquired any English proficiency.

Nonverbal communication: Paralinguistic messages such as intonation, stress, pauses and rate of speech, and nonlinguistic messages such as gestures, facial expressions, and body language that can accompany speech or be conveyed without the aid of speech.

Performance assessment: A measure of educational achievement where students produce a response, create a product, or apply knowledge in ways similar to tasks required in the instructional environment. The performance measures are analyzed and interpreted according to preset criteria.

Performance standards: A performance level stated in terms of specific criteria to be achieved, including ways in which students must demonstrate knowledge and skills; indicators of how well students are meeting a content standard or benchmark.

Portfolio assessment: A type of performance assessment that involves gathering multiple indicators of student progress to support course goals in a dynamic, ongoing process. Portfolios are purposeful collections of student performance that evince students' efforts, progress, and achievement over time.

Primary language: An individual's first, home, or native language (L1).

Pull-out instruction: Students are "pulled-out" from their regular classes for special classes of ESL instruction, remediation, or acceleration.

Rating scale: A way to record student performance on a continuum that indicates the range in which a given skill or competency has been achieved; often a Likert-scale continuum is used.

Realia: Real-life objects and artifacts used to supplement teaching; can provide effective visual scaffolds for English language learners.

Reliability: Statistical consistency in measurements and tests, such as the extent to which two assessments measure student performance in the same way.

Rubrics: Statements that describe indicators of performance, which include scoring criteria, on a continuum; may be described as "developmental" (e.g., emergent, beginning, developing, proficient) or "evaluative" (e.g., exceptional, thorough, adequate, inadequate).

Scaffolding: Adult (e.g., teacher) support for learning and student performance of the tasks through instruction, modeling, questioning, feedback, graphic organizers, and more, across successive engagements. These supports are gradually withdrawn, thus transferring more and more autonomy to the child. Scaffolding activities provide support for learning that can be removed as learners are able to demonstrate strategic behaviors in their own learning activities.

SDAIE (Specially Designed Academic Instruction in English): The State of California requires that all limited English proficient students receive content instruction in the core curriculum. SDAIE, another term for sheltered instruction, is the instructional methodology used to achieve this. Strategies employed are intended to help English language learners access content information while developing their English language skills (*see* Sheltered instruction).

Self-contained ESL class: A class consisting solely of English speakers of other languages for the purpose of learning English; content may also be taught. An effective alternative to pull-out instruction.

Sheltered instruction (SI): An approach to teaching that extends the time students have for receiving English language support while they learn content subjects. SI classrooms, which may include a mix of native English speakers and English language learners or only ELLs, integrate language and content while infusing sociocultural awareness. Teachers scaffold instruction to aid student comprehension of content topics and objectives by adjusting their speech and instructional tasks, and by providing appropriate background information and experiences. The ultimate goal is accessibility for ELLs to grade-level content standards and concepts while they continue to improve their English language proficiency (*see* SDAIE).

Sheltered teachers: Teachers who teach content subject matter to English language learners using sheltered instruction (SI) techniques.

Social language: Basic language proficiency associated with fluency in day-to-day situations, including the classroom (*see* Basic Interpersonal Communication Skills).

Sociolinguistic competence: The degree to which a language is used and understood in a given situation. The use of appropriate comments and responses in conversation (*see* Communicative competence).

Sociocultural competence: The ability to function effectively by following the rules and behavioral expectations held by members of a given social or cultural group.

Stages of language proficiency: (From Krashen and Terrell, 1983, 1984.)

Preproduction: Students at this stage are not ready to produce much language, so they primarily communicate with gestures and actions. They are absorbing the new language and developing receptive vocabulary.

Early production: Students at this level speak using one or two words or short phrases. Their receptive vocabulary is developing; they understand approximately one thousand words. Students can answer "who, what, and where" questions with limited expression.

Speech emergence: Students speak in longer phrases and complete sentences. However, they may experience frustration at not being able to express completely what they know. Although the number of errors they make increases, they can communicate ideas and the quantity of speech they produce increases.

Intermediate fluency: Students may appear to be fluent; they engage in conversation and produce connected narrative. Errors are usually of style or usage. Lessons continue to expand receptive vocabulary, and activities develop higher levels of language use in content areas. Students at this level are able to communicate effectively.

Advanced fluency: Students communicate very effectively, orally and in writing, in social and academic settings.

Standard American English: "That variety of American English in which most educational texts, government, and media publications are written in the United States; English as it is spoken and written by those groups with social, economic, and political power in the United States. Standard American English is a relative concept, varying widely in pronunciation and in idiomatic use but maintaining a fairly uniform grammatical structure" (Harris and Hodges, 1995, p. 241).

Standards-based assessment: Assessment involving the planning, gathering, analyzing, and reporting of a student's performance according to the ESL and/or district content standards.

Strategies: Mental processes and plans that people use to help them comprehend, learn, and retain new information. There are three types of strategies—cognitive, metacognitive, and social/affective—and these are consciously adapted and monitored during reading, writing, and learning.

Subtractive bilingualism: The learning of a new language at the expense of the primary language. Learners often lose their native language and culture because they don't have opportunities to continue learning or using it, or they perceive that language to be of lower status. Loss of the primary language often leads to cultural ambivalence.

Summative evaluation: The final collection, analysis, and reporting of information about student achievement or program effectiveness at the end of a given time frame.

Task: An activity that calls for a response to a question, issue, or problem.

Validity: A statistical measure of an assessment's match between the information collected and its stated purpose; evidence that inferences from evaluation are trustworthy.

Vignette: A short sketch that gives a description of an instructional process drawn from real-life classroom experiences.

References

Alvarez, M.C. (1990). Knowledge Activation and Schema Construction. Paper presented at the Annual Meeting of the American Educational Research Association, Boston, MA, 1990, 25p. [ED 317 988]

Anderson, R.C. (1984). Role of the reader's schema in comprehension, learning, and memory. In R.C. Anderson, J. Osborn, & R.J. Tierney (Eds.), *Learning to read in American schools: Basal readers and content texts.* Hillsdale, NJ: Erlbaum.

Anderson, R.C. (1994). Role of the reader's scheme in comprehension, learning, and memory. In R. Ruddell, M. Ruddell, & H. Singer (Eds.), *Theoretical models and processes of reading* (4th ed.). Newark, DE: International Reading Association.

Artiles, A. (1998). Overrepresentation of minority students: The case for greater specificity or reconsideration of the variables examined. *The Journal of Special Education, 32*(1) 32–36.

Au, K., Garcia, G.G., Goldenberg, C., & Vogt, M.E. (2002). *Handbook for English language learners.* Boston: Houghton Mifflin.

August, D., & Hakuta, K. (Eds.). (1997). *Improving schooling for language minority children: A research agenda.* Washington, DC: National Academy Press.

Baker, L., & Brown, A.L. (1984). Metacognitive skills and reading. In P.D. Pearson (Ed.), *Handbook of reading research.* New York: Longman.

Barnes, C., Mercer, G., & Shakespeare, T. (1999). *Exploring disability: A sociological introduction.* Cambridge: Polity Press.

Barnhardt, S. (1997). Effective memory strategies. *NCLRC Language Resource, 1* (6).

Bartolome, L.I. (1994). Beyond the methods fetish: Toward a humanizing pedagogy. *Harvard Educational Review, 64*(2), 173–194.

Barton, M.L., Heidama, C., & Jordan, D. (2002). Teaching reading in mathematics and science. *Educational Leadership, 60* (3), 24–28.

Baumann, J., Jones, L., & Seifert-Kessell, N. (1993). Using think-alouds to enhance children's comprehension monitoring abilities. *The Reading Teacher, 47*(3), 184–193.

Bean, T.W. (2000). Reading in the content areas: Social constructivist dimensions. In M.L. Kamil, P.B. Mosenthal, P.D. Pearson, & R. Barr (Eds.), *Handbook of reading research (Vol. III).* Mahwah, NJ: Lawrence Erlbaum Associates, pp. 629–644.

Bear, D.R., Invernizzi, M., Templeton, S., & Johnston, F. (2000). *Words their way: Word study for phonics, vocabulary, and spelling instruction* (2nd ed.). Upper Saddle River, NJ: Merrill-Prentice-Hall.

Bear, D.R., Templeton, S., Helman, L.A., & Baren, T. (2003). *Orthographic development and learning to read in different languages.* In G. Garcia (Ed.), English learners: Reaching the highest level of English literacy. Newark, DE: International Reading Association.

Beck, I.L., & McKeown, M.G. (2002). Questioning the author: Making sense of social studies. *Educational Leadership, 60* (3), 44–47.

Beck, I.L., Perfetti, C., & McKeown, M.G. (1982). Effects of long-term vocabulary instruction on lexical access and reading comprehension. *Journal of Educational Psychology, 74,* 506–521.

Berliner, D.C. (1984). The half-full glass: A review of research on teaching. In P.L. Hosford (Ed.), *Using what we know about teaching* (pp. 51–77). Alexandria,

VA: Association for Supervision and Curriculum Development.

Berman, P., McLaughlin, B., Minicucci, C., Nelson, B., & Woodworth, K. (1995). *School reform and student diversity: Case studies of exemplary practices for LEP students.* Washington, DC: National Clearinghouse for Bilingual Education.

Bickel, W.E., & Bickel, D.D. (1986). Effective schools, classrooms and instruction: Implications for special education. *Exceptional Children, 52* (6) 489–500.

Blachowicz, L.Z., & Fisher, P. (2000). *Vocabulary instruction.* In R.L. Kamil, P.B. Mosenthal, P.D. Pearson, & R. Barr (Eds.) Handbook of Reading Research, Vol. 3. (pp. 503–523) Mahwah, NJ: Lawrence Erlbaum Inc.

Bloom, B., Engelhart, M., Furst, E., Hill, W., & Krathworl, D. (Eds.). (1956). *Taxonomy of educational objectives: The classification of educational goals. Handbook I: Cognitive domain.* New York: David McKay Co.

Bottle biology: An idea book for exploring the world through plastic bottles and other recyclable materials. (1993). Dubuque, IA: Kendall/Hunt Publishing Company.

Bransford, J. (1994). Schema activation and schema acquisition: Comments on Richard C. Anderson's remarks. In R. Ruddell, M. Ruddell, & H. Singer (Eds.), *Theoretical models and processes of reading* (4th ed.). Newark, DE: International Reading Association.

Bruner, J. (1978). The role of dialogue in language acquisition. In A. Sinclair, R. Javella, & W. Levelt (Eds.), *The child's conception of language* (pp. 241–256). New York: Springer-Verlag.

Buehl, D. (1995). *Classroom strategies for interactive learning.* Madison: Wisconsin State Reading Association.

Buehl, D. (2001). *Classroom strategies for interactive learning* (2nd ed.). Newark, DE: International Reading Association.

Burke, J. (2002). The Internet reader. *Educational Leadership, 60* (3), 38–42.

Cantoni-Harvey, G. (1987). *Content-area language instruction: Approaches and strategies.* Reading, MA: Addison-Wesley.

Carrell, P. (1987). Content and formal schemata in ESL reading. *TESOL Quarterly, 21* (3), 461–481.

Chamot, A.U., & O'Malley, J.M. (1987). The cognitive academic language learning approach: A bridge to the mainstream. *TESOL Quarterly, 21*(2), 227–249.

Chamot, A.U., & O'Malley, J.M. (1994). *The CALLA handbook: Implementing the cognitive academic language learning approach.* Reading, MA: Addison-Wesley.

Chiesi, H., Spilich, G., & Voss, J. (1979). Acquisition of domain-related information in relation to high- and low-domain knowledge. *Journal of Verbal Learning and Verbal Behavior 18,* 257–274.

Christen, W.L., and Murphy, T.J. (1991). Increasing Comprehension by Activating Prior Knowledge. *ERIC Digest.* Bloomington, IN: ERIC Clearinghouse on Reading, English, and Communication. [ED 328 885]

Colburn, A., & Echevarria, J. (1999). Meaningful lessons. *The Science Teacher, 66*(2) 36–39.

Coltrane, B. (2002). English language learners and high-stakes tests: An overview of the issues. *ERIC Digest.* Washington, DC: ERIC Clearinghouse on Languages and Linguistics, Center for Applied Linguistics.

Comer, J.P. (1984). Home-school relationships as they affect the academic success of children. *Education and Urban Society, 16*(3), 323–337.

Crauford, A.N. (2003). Communicative approaches to second language acquisition: The bridge to second-language literacy. In G.G. Garcia (Ed.), *English learners: Reaching the highest level of English literacy.* Newark, DE: International Reading Association.

Cooper, J.D., Pikulski, J.J., Au, K., Calderon, M., Comas, J., Lipson, M., Mims, S., Page, S., Valencia, S., & Vogt, M.E. (1999). *Invitations to literacy.* Boston: Houghton Mifflin Company.

Crandall, J.A. (1993). Content-centered learning in the United States. *Annual Review of Applied Linguistics, 13,* 111–126.

Crawford, L.W. (1993). *Language and literacy learning in multicultural classrooms.* Boston: Allyn and Bacon.

Cummins, J. (1981). The role of primary language development in promoting educational success for language minority students. In *Schooling and language minority students: A theoretical framework* (pp. 3–49). Los Angeles: Evaluation, Dissemination, and Assessment Center, California State University, Los Angeles.

Cummins, J. (1984). *Bilingualism and special education: Issues in assessment and pedagogy.* Clevedon, England: Multilingual Matters.

Cunningham, P.M. (1995). *Phonics they use: Words for reading and writing.* New York: Harper-Collins College Press.

Darling-Hammond, L. (1998). Teacher learning that supports student learning. *Educational Leadership, 55*(5), 6–11.

Darling-Hammond, L., & McLaughlin, M.W. (1995). Policies that support professional development in an era of reform. *Phi Delta Kappan, 76*(8), 597–604.

Davis, S.J., & Winek, J. "Improving Expository Writing by Increasing Background Knowledge." *Journal of Reading 33*(3) December 1989, 178–181. [EJ 402 129]

Dermody, M., & Speaker, R. (1995). Effects of reciprocal strategy training in prediction, clarification, question generation, and summarization on fourth graders' reading comprehension. In K.A. Hinchman, D. Leu, & C.K. Kinzer (Eds.), *Perspectives on literacy research and practice*. Chicago: National Reading Conference.

Deshler, D., Ellis, E., & Lenz, B.K. (1996). *Teaching adolescents with learning disabilities,* 2nd Edition. Denver, CO: Love Publishing Company.

Diaz, D. (1989). *Language across the curriculum and ESL students: Composition research and 'sheltered' course.* (ERIC Document Reproduction Service No. ED326 057).

Dole, J., Duffy, G., Roehler, L., & Pearson, P.D. (1991). Moving from the old to the new: Research in reading comprehension instruction. *Review of Educational Research, 61*, pp. 239–264.

Duffy, G.G. (2002). The case for direct explanation of strategies. In C.C. Block & M. Pressley (Eds.), *Comprehension instruction: Research-based best practices*. New York: Guilford Press.

Dunn, L. (1968). Special education for the mildly retarded: Is much of it justifiable? *Exceptional Children, 34,* 5–22.

Echevarria, J. (1995a). Sheltered instruction for students with learning disabilities who have limited English proficiency. *Intervention in School and Clinic, 30* (5), 302–305.

Echevarria, J. (1995b). Interactive reading instruction: A comparison of proximal and distal effects of instructional conversations. *Exceptional Children, 61* (6) 536–552.

Echevarria, J. (1998). *A model of sheltered instruction for English language learners.* Paper presented at the conference for the Division on Diversity of the Council for Exceptional Children, Washington, DC.

Echevarria, J., & Graves, A. (2003). *Sheltered content instruction: Teaching English language learners with diverse abilities.* 2nd Ed. Boston: Allyn & Bacon.

Echevarria, J., Greene, G., & Goldenberg, C. (1996). *A comparison of sheltered instruction and effective non-sheltered instruction on the achievement of LEP students.* Pilot study.

Echevarria, J., Powers, K., & Elliott, J. (in press). Promising Practices for Curbing Disproportionate Representation of Minority Students in Special Education. *Issues in Teacher Education,* California Council for Teacher Education. Theme Issue on Special Needs Education. (no volume number yet, scheduled for publication Spring, 04).

Echevarria, J., Vogt, M.E., & Short, D. (2000). *Making content comprehensible for English language learners: The SIOP model.* Boston: Allyn & Bacon.

Erickson, F., & Shultz, J. (1991). Students' experience of the curriculum. In P. W. Jackson (Ed.), *Handbook of research on curriculum.* New York: Macmillan.

Fisher, D., Frey, N., & Williams, D. (2002). Seven literacy strategies that work. *Educational Leadership, 60* (3), 70–73.

Flood, J., Lapp, D., Flood, S., & Nagel, G. (1992). Am I allowed to group? Using flexible patterns for effective instruction. *The Reading Teacher, 45,* 608–616.

Ford, D. (1998). The underrepresentation of minority students in gifted education: Problems and promises in recruitment and retention. *Journal of Special Education, 32*(1), 4–14.

Fuchs, D., Fuchs, L.S., & Bahr, M.W. (1990). Mainstream assistance teams: A scientific basis for the art of consultation. *Exceptional Children, 57,* 128–139.

Gall, M. (November, 1984). Synthesis of research on teacher's questioning. *Educational Leadership, 40–47.*

Gardner, H. (1993). *Multiple intelligences: The theory in practice.* New York: Basic Books.

Genesee, F. (1994). *Educating second language children: The whole child, the whole curriculum, the whole community.* New York: Cambridge University Press.

Genesee, F. (Ed.). (1999). *Program alternatives for linguistically diverse students.* Educational Practice Report No. 1. Santa Cruz and Washington, DC: Center for Research on Education, Diversity & Excellence.

Goldenberg, C. (1992–93). Instructional conversations: Promoting comprehension through discussion. *The Reading Teacher, 46* (4), 316–326.

González, J.M., & Darling-Hammond, L. (1997). *New concepts for new challenges: Professional development for teachers of immigrant youth.* McHenry, IL: Delta Systems and CAL.

Goodlad, J. (1984). *A place called school: Prospects for the future.* New York: McGraw-Hill.

Gray, W.S., & Leary, B.E. (1935). *What makes a book readable?* Chicago: The University of Chicago Press.

Guarino, A.J., Echevarria, J., Short, D., Schick, J.E., Forbes, S., & Rueda, R. (2001). The Sheltered Instruction Observation Protocol. *Journal of Research in Education, 11,* (1), 138–140.

Gunderson, L. (1991). *ESL literacy instruction: A guidebook to theory and practice.* Englewood Cliffs, NJ: Regents/Prentice Hall.

Guthrie, J.T., & Ozgungor, S. (2002). In C.C. Block & M. Pressley (Eds.). *Comprehension Instruction: Research-Based Best Practices.* New York: Guilford Press.

Harris, T.L., & Hodges, R.E. Eds. (1995). *The literacy dictionary: The vocabulary of reading and writing.* Newark, DE: International Reading Association.

Harry, B. (1992). Restructuring the participation of African-American parents in special education. *Exceptional Children, 59*(2), 123–131.

Hayes, D.A., & Tierney, R.J. "Developing Readers Knowledge through Analogy." *Reading Research Quarterly 17*(2), 1982, 256–80.

Hiebert, E.H. (1983). An examination of ability grouping for reading instruction. *Reading Research Quarterly, 18,* 231–255.

Hudec, J., & Short, D. (Prods.) (2002a). *Helping English learners succeed: An overview of the SIOP model.* (Video). Washington, DC: Center for Applied Linguistics.

Hudec, J., & Short, D. (Prods.) (2002b). *The SIOP model: Sheltered instruction for academic achievement.* (Video). Washington, DC: Center for Applied Linguistics.

Hunter, M. (1982). *Mastery teaching: Increasing instructional effectiveness in secondary schools, college, and universities.* El Segundo, CA: TIP Publications.

Jamieson, A., Curry, A., & Martinez, G. (2001). School enrollment in the United States—Social and economic characteristics of students. *Current Population Reports,* P20-533. Washington, DC: U.S. Government Printing Office.

Jimenez, R.T., Garcia, G.E., & Pearson, P.D. (1996). The reading strategies of bilingual Latina/o students who are successful English readers: Opportunities and obstacles. *Reading Research Quarterly, 31*(1), 90–112.

Kauffman, D., Burkart, G., Crandall, J., Johnson, D., Peyton, J., Sheppard, K., & Short, D. (1994). *Content-ESL across the USA.* Washington, DC: ERIC Clearinghouse on Languages and Linguistics.

Kea, C., & Utley, C. (1998). To teach me is to know me. *Journal of Special Education 32*(1), 44–48.

Keene, E.O., & Zimmerman, S. (1997). *Mosaic of thought: Teaching comprehension in a reader's workshop.* Portsmouth, NH: Heinemann.

Krashen, S. (1985). *The input hypothesis: Issues and implications.* New York: Longman.

Krashen, S. (2003). Three roles for reading for minority-language children. In G. Garcia (Ed.), *English learners: Reaching the highest level of literacy learning.* Newark, DE: International Reading Association.

Krashen, S., & Terrell, T. (1983). *The natural approach: Language acquisition in the classroom.* Englewood Cliffs, NJ: Alemany/Prentice Hall.

Kukic, S.J. (2002). The complete school for all. Keynote presentation at the 2nd annual Pacific Northwest Behavior Symposium, Seattle, WA.

Latinos in education: Early childhood, elementary, undergraduate, graduate. (1999). Washington, DC: White House Initiative on Educational Excellence for Hispanic Americans. Retrieved on May 21, 2001 from http://www.ed.gov/offices/OIIA/Hispanic/rr/ech.html.

Leinhardt, G., Bickel, W., & Pallay, A. (1982). Unlabeled but still entitled: Toward more effective remediation. *Teachers College Record, 84* (2) 391–422.

Lemke, J. (1988). Genres, semantics, and classroom education. *Linguistics and Education 1,* 81–99.

Lipson, M., & Wixson, K. (2003). *Assessment and instruction of reading and writing difficulties: An interactive approach* (2nd ed.). New York: Longman.

MacMillan, D., & Reschly, D. (1998). Overrepresentation of minority students: The case for greater specificity or reconsideration of the variables examined. *Journal of Special Education, 32* (1), 15–2.

Macon, J., Buell, D., & Vogt, M.E. (1991). *Responses to literature: Grades K–8.* Newark, DE: International Reading Association.

Marshall, J. (2000). Research on response to literature. In R.L. Kamil, P.B. Mosenthal, P.D. Pearson, & R. Barr (Eds.). *Handbook of Reading Research, Vol. 3.* (pp. 381–402) Mahwah, N.J.: Lawrence Erlbaum, Inc.

Mastropieri, M.A., & Scruggs, T.E. (1994). *Effective instruction for special education.* Austin, TX: ProEd.

McCormick, C.B., & Pressley, M. (1997). *Educational psychology: Learning, instruction, assessment.* New York: Longman.

McDonnell, L.M., & Hill, P. (1993). *Newcomers in American schools: Meeting the educational needs of immigrant youth.* Santa Monica: Rand.

McLaughlin, M., & Allen, M.B. (2002b). *Guided comprehension: A teaching model for grades 3–8.* Newark, DE: International Reading Association.

McLaughlin, M., & Allen, M.B. (2002a). *Guided comprehension in action: Lessons for grades 3–8.* Newark, DE: International Reading Association.

McLaughlin, M., & Kennedy, A. (1993). *A classroom guide to performance-based assessment.* Princeton, NJ: Houghton Mifflin.

McLaughlin, M., & Vogt, M.E. (1996). *Portfolios in teacher education.* Newark, DE: International Reading Association.

McLaughlin, M., & Vogt, M.E. (2000). *Creativity and innovation in content area teaching: A resource for intermediate, middle, and high school teachers.* Norwood, MA: Christopher-Gordon Publishers.

Menken, K. (2000). *What are the critical issues in wide-scale assessment of English language learners?* (Issue Brief No. 6). Washington, DC: National Clearinghouse for Bilingual Education.

Miholic, V. "Constructing a Semantic Map for Textbooks." *Journal of Reading 33*(6) March 1990, 464–65. [EJ 405 094]

Mohan, B.A. (1986). *Language and content.* Reading, MA: Addison-Wesley.

Mohan, B.A. (1990). Integration of language and content. In *Proceedings of the first research symposium on limited English proficient students' issues* (pp. 113–160). Washington, DC: U.S. Department of Education, Office of Bilingual Education and Minority Languages Affairs.

Moss, M., & Puma, M. (1995). *Prospects: The congressionally mandated study of educational growth and opportunity.* (First year report on language minority and limited English proficient students). Washington, DC: U.S. Department of Education.

Muth, K.D., & Alvermann, D.E. (1999). *Teaching and learning in the middle grades.* Needham Heights, MA: Allyn & Bacon.

Nagel, G. (2001). *Effective grouping for literacy instruction.* Boston: Allyn & Bacon.

Nagel, G., Vogt, M.E., & Kaye, C. (1998). *Examining levels of thinking in the reflective discourse of teaching portfolios.* Paper presented at the Annual Meeting of the National Reading Conference. Austin, TX.

National Center for Education Statistics (NCES). (1997). *A profile of policies and practices for limited English proficient students: Screening methods, program support, and teacher training* (The 1993–94 Schools and Staffing Survey). Washington, DC: U.S. Department of Education, OERI.

National Center for Education Statistics. (2002). *Schools and staffing survey, 1999–2000: Overview of the data for public, private, public charter, and Bureau of Indian Affairs elementary and secondary schools.* (NCES 2002-313). Washington, DC: U.S. Department of Education, National Center for Educational Statistics.

National Clearinghouse for English Language Acquisition. (2002). *The growing numbers of limited English proficient students.* Retrieved December 1, 2002, from http://www.ncela.gwu.edu/states/stateposter.pdf.

National Commission on Teaching and America's Future (NCTAF). (1996). *What matters most: Teaching for America's future.* New York: Columbia University, Teachers College.

National Commission on Teaching and America's Future (NCTAF). (1997). *Doing what matters most: Investing in quality teaching.* New York: Columbia University, Teachers College.

National Council of Teachers of Mathematics. (1989). *Curriculum and evaluation of standards for school mathematics.* Reston, VA: NCTM.

No Child Left Behind Act of 2001. 107th Congress of the United States of America. Retrieved December 1, 2002, from http://www.ed.gov/legislation/ESEA02/107-110.pdf.

O'Malley, J.J., & Chamot, A.U. (1990). *Learning strategies in second language acquisition.* Cambridge: Cambridge University Press.

O'Malley, J.M., & Pierce, L.V. (1996). *Authentic assessment for English language learners: Practical approaches for teachers.* Reading, MA: Addison-Wesley.

Orfield, G., Losen, D., & Edley, Jr., C. (2001). The Civil Rights Project, Harvard University.

Palinscar, A.C., & Brown, A.L. (1984). Reciprocal teaching of comprehension-fostering and comprehension monitoring activities. *Cognition and Instruction, 1,* 117–175.

Paris, S. (2001). Classroom applications of research on self-regulated learning. *Educational Psychologist 36* (3), 89–102.

Paris, S.G., Lipson., M.Y., & Wixson, K. (1983). Becoming a strategic reader. *Contemporary Educational Psychology, 8,* 293–316.

Patton, J., & Townsend, B. (1999). Ethics, power and privilege: Neglected considerations in the education of African American learners with special needs. *Teacher Education and Special Education.* 22(4), 276–286.

Peregoy, S.F., & Boyle, O.F. (1997). *Reading, writing, and learning in ESL: A resource book for K–12 teachers* (2nd ed.). New York: Longman.

Podell, D.M. & Soodak, L.C. (1993). Teacher efficacy and bias in special education referrals. *Journal of Educational Researcher, 86* (4), 247–253.

Powers, K., (2001). Problem solving student support teams. *The California School Psychologist, 6,* 19–30.

Pressley, M. (2000). What should comprehension instruction be instruction of? In M.L. Kamil, P.B. Mosenthal, P.D. Pearson, & R. Barr (Eds.), *Handbook of reading research (Vol. III).* Mahwah, NJ: Lawrence Erlbaum Associates, pp. 545–561.

Pressley, M., Johnson, C., Symons, S., McGoldrick, J.A., & Kurita, J.A. (1989). Strategies that improve children's memory and comprehension of text. *The Elementary School Journal, 90,* 3–32.

Pressley, M., & Woloshyn, V. (Eds.) (1995). *Cognitive strategy instruction that really improves children's academic performance.* Cambridge, MA: Brookline Books.

Ramirez, J., Yuen, S., Ramey, D., & Pasta, D. (1991). *Executive summary: Final Report: Longitudinal study of structure English immersion strategy, early-exit and late-exit transitional bilingual education programs for language-minority children.* (Contract No. 300087-0156). Submitted to the U.S. Department of Education. San Mateo: Aguirre International.

Raphael, T.E. (1984). Teaching learners about sources of information for answering comprehension questions. *Journal of Reading 27,* 303–311.

Readence, J.E., Bean, T.W., & Baldwin, R.S. (2001). *Content area literacy: An integrated approach,* 8th ed. Dubuque, IA: Kendall/Hunt.

Readance, J., Bean, T., & Baldwin. (2001). *Teaching reading in the content areas.* 8th Ed. Dubuque, IA: Kendall Hunt.

Reutzel, D.R., & Morgan, B.C. (1990). "Effects of Prior Knowledge, Explicitness, and Clause Order on Children's Comprehension of Causal Relationships." *Reading Psychology 11*(2), 93–109. [EJ 408 397]

Rodriguez-Brown, Ed., *National Reading Conference Yearbook, 50:* National Reading Conference.

Rosenblatt, L.M. (1991). Literacy theory. In J. Flood, J. Jensen, D. Flood, & J. Squire (Eds.), *Handbook of research on teaching the English-language arts.* New York: Macmillan.

Ruddell, M.R. (2001). *Teaching content reading and writing,* 4th ed. New York: John Wiley.

Ruiz-de-Velasco, J., & Fix, M. (2000). *Overlooked and underserved: Immigrant students in U.S. secondary schools.* Washington, DC: Urban Institute.

Rumelhart, D.E. (1980). Schemata: The Building Blocks of Cognition. In Rand J. Spiro et al., (Eds.), *Theoretical Issues in Reading Comprehension* (33–58). Hillsdale, NJ: Erlbaum.

Rumelhart, D.E. (1995). Toward an interactive model of reading. In R.B. Ruddell, M.R. Ruddell, & H. Singer (Eds.), *Theoretical models and processes of reading.* Newark, DE: International Reading Association.

Saville-Troike, M. (1984). What really matters in second lanuage learning for academic achievement? *TESOL Quarterly, 18,* 117–131.

Shearer, B.A., Ruddell, M.R., & Vogt, M.E. (2001). Successful middle school intervention: Negotiated strategies and individual choice. In T. Shanahan & F.V. Rodriguez (Eds.), *National Reading Conference Yearbook, 50:* National Reading Conference.

Sheppard, K. (1995). *Content-ESL across the USA* (Volume I, Technical Report). Washington, DC: National Clearinghouse for Bilingual Education.

Short, D. (1991). *How to integrate language and content instruction: A training manual.* Washington, DC: Center for Applied Linguistics.

Short, D. (1994). Expanding middle-school horizons: Integrating language, culture and social studies. *TESOL Quarterly, 28*(3), 581–608.

Short, D. (1999). Integrating language and content for effective sheltered instruction programs. In C. Faltis & P. Wolfe (Eds.), *So much to say: Adolescents, bilingualism, and ESL in the secondary school* (pp. 105–137). New York: Teachers College Press.

Short, D.J. (2002). Language learning in sheltered social studies classes. *TESOL Journal 11* (1), 18–24.

Short, D.J., & Echevarria, J. (1999). *The sheltered instruction observation protocol: Teacher-researcher collaboration and professional development.* Educational Practice Report No. 3. Santa Cruz, CA and Washington, DC: Center for Research on Education, Diversity & Excellence.

Short, D., Hudec, J., & Echevarria, J. (2002). *Using the SIOP Model: Professional development manual for sheltered instruction.* Washington, DC: Center for Applied Linguistics.

Sirotnik, K. (1983). What you see is what you get: Consistency, persistency, and mediocrity in classrooms. *Harvard Educational Review, 53,* 16–31.

Slater, W.H., & Horstman, F.R. (2002). Teaching reading and writing to struggling middle school and high school students: The case for reciprocal teaching. *Preventing school failure (46),* 4, 163–167.

Smith, D. (2001). *Introduction to special education: Teaching in an age of opportunity* 4th ed. Boston: Allyn & Bacon.

Stanovich, K.E. (1986). Matthew effects in reading: Some consequences of individual differences in the acquisition of literacy. *Reading Research Quarterly, 21,* 360–406.

Teachers of English to Speakers of Other Languages (TESOL). (1997). *ESL standards for pre-K–12 students.* Alexandria, VA: Author.

Teachers of English to Speakers of Other Languages, Inc. (TESOL) (2000). *Scenarios for ESL-standards based assessment.* Alexandria, VA: Author.

Teachers of English to Speakers of Other Languages, Inc. (TESOL) (2001). *Scenarios for ESL standards-based assessment.* Alexandria, VA: Author.

Tharp, R., & Gallimore, R. (1988). *Rousing minds to life.* Cambridge: Cambridge University Press.

Thomas, W.P., & Collier, V.P. (2002). A national study of school effectiveness for language minority students' long-term academic achievement. Santa Cruz and Washington, DC: Center on Research, Diversity & Excellence.

Tierney, R., & Pearson, P.D. (1994). Learning to learn from text: A framework for improving classroom practice. In R. Ruddell, M. Ruddell, & H. Singer (Eds.), *Theoretical models and processes of reading.* Fourth Edition. Newark, DE: International Reading Association.

Tolchinsky, L., & Teberosky, A. (1998). The development of word segmentation and writing in two scripts. *Cognitive Development 13,* 1–24.

Tompkins, G.E. (2001). *Literacy for the 21st century: A balanced approach.* Upper Saddle River, NJ: Merrill-Prentice-Hall.

Tucker, M., & Codding, J., (1998). Standards in our schools. San Francisco: Jossey-Boss.

Vacca, R.T. (2000). Taking the mystery out of content area literacy. In M. McLaughlin & M.E. Vogt (Eds.), *Creativity and innovation in content area teaching.* Norwood, MA: Christopher Gordon.

Vacca, R.T. (2002). From efficient decoders to strategic readers. *Educational Leadership 60* (3), 6–11.

Vacca, R., & Vacca, J.A. (2001). *Content area reading: Literacy and learning across the curriculum* (7th ed.). New York: Longman.

Vogt, M.E. (1992). Strategies for leading readers into text: The pre-reading phase of a content lesson. In C. Hedley & D. Feldman (Eds.), *Literacy across the curriculum.* New York: Ablex.

Vogt, M.E. (1995). *Jumpstarting: Providing support in advance rather than remediation.* Paper presented at the Annual Conference of the International Reading Association, Anaheim, CA.

Vogt, M.E. (2000). Content learning for students needing modifications: An issue of access. In M. McLaughlin and M.E. Vogt (Eds.), *Creativity and innovation in content area teaching: A resource for intermediate, middle, and high school teachers.* Norwood, MA: Christopher-Gordon Publishers.

Vogt, M.E. (2002). *SQP2RS: Increasing students' understandings of expository text through cognitive and metacognitive strategy application.* Paper presented at the 52nd Annual Meeting of the National Reading Conference.

Vogt, M.E., & Shearer, B.A. (2003). *Reading specialists in the real world: A sociocultural view.* Boston: Allyn & Bacon.

Vygotsky, L. (1978). *Mind and society: The development of higher psychological processes* (M. Cole, V. John-Steiner, S. Scribner, & E. Souberman, Eds. and trans.). Cambridge, MA: Harvard University Press.

Waggoner, D. (1999). Who are secondary newcomer and linguistically different youth? In C. Faltis & P. Wolfe (Eds.), *So much to say: Adolescents, bilingualism, and ESL in the secondary school* (pp. 13–41). New York: Teachers College Press.

Watson, K., & Young, B. (1986). Discourse for learning in the classroom. *Language Arts, 63*(2), 126–133.

Wiggins, G. (1998). *Educative assessment.* San Francisco: Jossey-Bass.

Wong-Fillmore, L., & Valadez, C. (1986). Teaching bilingual learners. In M.C. Wittrock (Ed.), *Handbook of research on teaching* (pp. 648–685). New York: Macmillan.

Ysseldyke, J., & Marston, D. (1999). Origins of categorical special education services in schools and a rationale for changing them. In D.J. Reshchly, W.D. Tilly, & J.P. Grimes (Eds.), *Special education in transition: Functional assessment and noncategorical programming.* Longmont, CO: Sopris West.

Zeichner, K. (1993). *Educating teachers for cultural diversity* (NCRTL Special Report). East Lansing, MI: Michigan State University, National Center for Research on Teacher Learning.

Index

A

Academic language, 55, 99
Academic learning, 132, 133
Academic literacy, 11
Academic tasks, 68, 76–77, 146
Adapted text, 27–28
Administrators, 17, 170, 179
"All, Some, Few" model, 174
Allen, M.B., 26, 82
Allocated time, 132
Alvermann, D.E., 82, 85
Anderson, R.C., 46, 47, 81
Apple, 51
Arabic language, 167–168, 168
Artiles, A., 170
Assessment, 150, 175 (*see also*
    Evaluation)
    authentic, 149
    definition of, 148
    formal and informal, 148–149, 150
    individual or group, 149, 150
    of language problems, 171–172
    of lesson objectives, 148–151
    multiple, 149, 150–151
    of reading proficiency, 166
    site-based intervention teams,
        172–173
    of student understanding, 161
    subjectivity towards, 172, 181
Au, K., 28, 151, 165, 167
August, D., 12

B

Background experience, 44, 45–47
    (*see also* Schemata)
    and new concepts, 48–49, 62–63
Bahr, M.W., 172
Baker, L., 82
Baldwin R.S., 26
Baren, T., 165, 168
Barnes, C., 172

Barnhardt, S., 81
Bartolome, L.I., 12
Barton, M.L., 85
Baumann, J., 86
Bean, T.W., 26
Bear, D.R., 54, 55, 146, 165, 168
Beck, I.L., 46, 88
Berliner, D.C., 132
Berman, P., 12
Bickel, D.D., 132
Bickel, W.E., 132, 133
Bilingual education, 7–8, 8, 12–13
    late-exit program, 12
    two-way immersion
        program, 12
Birman, B.F., 216
Blachowicz, L.Z., 46, 49
Bloom, B., 88
Bottle Biology, 123
Boyle, O.F., 119, 120
Bransford, J., 48
Brinton, 69
Brown, A.L., 58, 82
Bruner, J., 12
Buehl, D., 26, 53
Burkart, G., 12
Burke, J., 88

C

Calderon, M., 28, 151
Cantoni-Harvey, G., 9
Carrell, P., 45
Center for Research on Education,
    Diversity, & Excellence
    (CREDE), 3, 214
Chamot, A.U., 9, 69, 81, 82, 85
Chiesi, H., 45
Chinese language, 167–168, 168
Christen, W.L., 45, 46
Cloze sentences, 54
Codding, J., 6

Cognitive Academic Language
    Learning Approach (CALLA),
    85
Cognitive strategy, 169
Cognitive theory, 81
Collaborative approach, 18
Collier, V.P., 8
Coltrane, B., 6
Comas, J., 28, 151
Comer, J.P., 170
Comprehensible input, 17, 65, 66,
    70–74, 169
Comprehension strategies, 85
Concept Definition Map, 49, 53
Concepts, 159–160
Consonant sounds, 167
Content, 119–120
    concepts, 69, 147
    and language knowledge, 119–120,
        126–127
    lesson delivery and, 138–139
    objectives of, 29, 131, 184
Content area texts, 46–47
Content-based ESL approach, 8–10
Cooper, J.D., 28, 151
Crandall, J.A., 9, 12
Crawford, L.W., 7, 120
CREDE (*see* National Center for
    Research on Education,
    Diversity, & Excellence)
Cummins, J., 8, 170
Cunningham, P.M., 52–53
Curry, A., 4

D

Darling-Hammond, L., 7, 16, 216
Dermody, M., 82
Deshler, D., 84
Desimone, L., 216
Dialogue journals, 104
Diaz, D., 99

Dictated stories, 165
Dictionary, 51, 52
Dole, J., 45, 82, 85
Duffy, G., 45, 82
Duffy, G.G., 82, 84, 85
Dunn, L., 170

E
Echevarria, Jana, 14, 16, 22, 47, 68, 99,
    103, 170, 173, 175, 197, 214, 215,
    216, 217
Edley, Jr., C., 170
Eighth-grade art/social studies unit,
    151–161
Eleventh-grade unit, 121–128
Elliott, J., 173, 175
Ellis, E., 84
Engaged time, 132
Engelhart, M., 88
English as a second language (ESL),
    7–8, 8
    communicative approach to, 8–9
    content-based, 8–10
    history of, 8
    standards and strategies for, 83–85
    student needs and, 8
English learners (ELs), 2–3, 5, 6–7, 8, 11
    application of content for, 119
    content objectives for, 22
    correcting errors of, 120
    diversity of, 46–47
    grouping of, 105–106
    language comprehension of, 165
    learning gap and, 21
    remedial classes for, 164
    special education for, 163, 164, 171
    subjectivity towards disabilities
        and, 172
    teaching cycles for, 145
Erickson, F., 11
ESL Standards for Pre-K–12 Students
    (TESOL), 6, 10, 83
Evaluation (*see also* Assessment)
    definition of, 148

F
Feedback, 147–148, 152, 160–161
First-grade unit, 107–114
Fisher, D., 82, 84, 85
Fisher, P., 46, 49
Fix, M., 4
Flood, J., 105
Flood, S., 105
Forbes, S., 16, 197, 215, 217
Ford, D., 170
Fourth-grade unit, 13–14, 23, 30–42,
    134–141
Frey, N., 82, 84, 85
Fuchs, D., 172
Fuchs, L.S., 172
Furst, E., 88

G
Gall, M., 88
Garcia, G.E., 46
Garcia, G.G., 165, 167
Gardner, H., 14
Garet, M.S., 216
Genesee, F., 12, 170
German language, 168
Goals 2000: Educate America Act, 6
Goldenberg, C., 99, 103, 165, 167
González, J.M., 7
Goodlad, J., 99
Graphic organizers, 26, 46, 49, 85
Graves, A., 14, 22, 170, 173
Gray, W.S., 21
Greene, G., 99
Group response, 149, 150
Guarino, A.J., 16, 197, 215, 217
Guided practice, 118
Gunderson, L., 23
Guthrie, J.T., 99

H
Hakuta, K., 12
Hands-on experience, 117–119
Hands-on materials, 126
Harry, B., 174
Heidama, C., 85
Helman, L.A., 165, 168
Hiebert, E.H., 105
Highlighted text, 27
Hill, P., 7
Hill, W., 88
Hispanics, 4
Hmong language, 167–168
Horstman, F.R., 82
Hudec, J., 16, 216
Huey, Edmund, 45
Hunter, Madeline, 118–119

I
IGAP, 215
IMAGE (Illinois Measure of Annual
    Growth in English), 215, 217
Immersion programs, 12
Immigrants, 5–6
    demographics of, 3–4
    diversity of, 46–47
Informal reading inventory (IRI), 166,
    167
Instructional setting, 173–174
Interaction, 98, 99–102
    electronic, 104
    grouping configurations, 113–114
    mainstream lesson, 99–100, 103
    opportunities for, 102–104, 113
    sheltered instruction lesson,
        100–102, 103–104
    written, 104
International Reading Association,
    169

Intervention and disabilities, 173–175
    pyramid model of, 174
Invernizzi, M., 54, 55, 146
Italian language, 168

J
Jamieson, A., 4
Jigsaw reading, 28–29
Jimenez, R.T., 46
Johnson, C., 82
Johnson, D., 12
Johnston, F., 54, 55, 146
Jones, L., 86
Jordan, D., 85

K
Kauffman, D., 12, 51, 82
Kaye, C., 88
Kea, C., 173
Keene, E.O., 85
Kennedy, A., 149
Key concepts (*see* Concepts)
    clarification of, 114
Khmer language, 167–168
Krashen, S., 45, 66, 165
Krathworl, D., 88
Kukic, S.J., 174
Kurita, J.A, 82

L
Language development, 29, 45
Language differences, 171–172
Language diversity, 170
Language knowledge, 119–120,
    126–127
Language objectives, 131–132
    lesson delivery and, 139
Language skills, 127–128
    integration of, 120–121
Lapp, D., 105
Learning disabilities, 171–172
    intervention for, 173–174
Learning experiences, 119
Learning strategies, 80–83, 94–95
    cognitive, 82
    Cognitive Academic Language
        Learning Approach (CALLA),
        85
    comprehension, 85
    for English learners, 83–85
    GIST, 85
    graphic organizers, 85
    metacognitive, 82
    mnemonics, 84
    PENS, 84
    questioning, 88–89
    rehearsal, 85
    social/affective strategies, 82
    SQP2RS, 84, 92, 94–95, 96
    and teaching learning process,
        82–83

Leary, B.E., 21
Leinhardt, G., 133
Lemke, J., 11
Lenz, B.K., 84
Lesson delivery, 130, 131
    content objectives and, 138–139
    language objectives and, 139
    and pacing, 141
Lesson objectives
    assessment of, 148–151
    student understanding of, 161
Lesson planning, 21, 39, 45, 179,
        211–213
    and content concepts, 23
Lesson plans, 211–213
Lessons
    eighth grade, 151–161
    eleventh grade, 121–128
    first grade, 107–114
    fourth grade, 30–42, 134–141
    ninth grade, 69–78, 89–96
    seventh grade, 89–96
    sixth grade, 55–63, 183–186
    student strategies, 94–95
Limited English proficient (LEP)
        students, immigrants as, 4
Lipson, M., 28, 84, 151
Listening, 120
List-Group-Label activity, 54
Literacy development, 164–169, 169
Literacy skills, 165–166
Losen, D., 170

M
MacMillan, D., 172
Manipulatives for practice, 117–119,
        126
Marginal notes, 29
Marshall, J., 99
Marston, D., 172
Martinez, G., 4
Master, 69
Mastropieri, M.A., 132
McDonnell, L.M., 7
McGoldrick, J.A., 82
McKeown, M.G., 46, 88
McLaughlin, B., 12
McLaughlin, M., 26, 69, 82, 148, 149
McLaughlin, M.W., 7
McNeil, John, 45
Meaningful activities, 29–30, 169
Menken, K., 6
Mercer, G., 172
Metacognitive strategy, 169
Middle class values, 170
Mims, S., 28, 151
Minicucci, C., 12
Minority students, 170
    and learning disabilities, 174–175
    sheltered instruction and, 214
Mnemonics, 84

Mohan, B.A., 9
Moss, M., 4
Multiple meaning words, 55
Murphy, T.J., 45, 46
Muth, K.D., 82, 85

N
Nagel, G., 86, 88, 105
National Center for Education
        Statistics, 7
National Center for Research on
        Education, Diversity &
        Excellence (CREDE), 16
National Clearinghouse for English
        Language Acquisition, 3
National Commission on Teaching and
        America's Future, 7
National Council of Teachers of
        Mathematics, 6
National Governors Association, 6
Native language, 168–169
Native language (L1), 106–107
Native language texts, 29
Nelson, B., 12
Ninth-grade unit, 69–78
No Child Left Behind Act, 5, 6–7
Normal curve equivalent (NCE)
        points, 8
Number wheels, 149–150

O
O'Malley, J.J., 9, 69, 81, 82, 85
O'Malley, J.M., 148
Oral directions, 68
Oral language, 120
Orfield, G., 170
Outcome sentences, 147
Outlines, 26–27
Ozgungor, S., 99

P
Pacing, 134, 141, 169
Page, S., 28, 151
Palinscar, A.C., 58
Pallay, A., 133
Paris, S., 82
Pasta, D., 99
Patton, J., 170
Pearson, P.D., 45, 46, 49, 82, 85
PENS, 84
Peregoy, S.F., 119, 120
Perfetti, C., 46
Peyton, J., 12
Phonemes, 168
Phonemic awareness, 167
pictures, 25
Pierce, L.V., 148
Pikulski, J.J., 28, 151
Porter, A.C., 216
Powers, K., 170, 172, 173, 175
Practice/Application, 116, 117

Pressley, M., 82, 84
Professional development, 184
Puma, M., 4

Q
QAR (Question-Answer-Relationship),
        88
QtA (Questioning the Author), 88–89
Questioning, 88–89
Question types, 96

R
Rain forest unit, 89–96
Ramey, D., 99
Ramirez, J., 99
Raphael, T.E., 88
Readance, J., 26
Reading comprehension, 22, 120
    consonant sounds and, 167
Reading development, 164–169
    instructional context and, 169
    Language Experience Approach,
        165
    and special education, 163, 164
Reeves, Nicholas, 28
Rehearsal strategies, 85
Repetition, 175
Reschly, D., 172
Research, 179, 214–219
Response boards, 150
Review/Assessment, 143, 144
Roehler, L., 45, 82, 85
Rosenblatt, L.M., 25
Ruddell, M.R., 21, 26, 49, 52, 82, 88, 94,
        146
Rueda, R., 16, 197, 215, 217
Ruiz-de-Velasco, J., 4
Rumelhart, D.E., 49
Russian language, 167–168

S
Saville-Troike, M., 49
Scaffolding, 12, 45, 86–87, 169, 175
    content concepts and, 147
    instructional, 87
    procedural, 86
    techniques of, 95
    verbal, 86
    and Zone of Proximal Development
        (ZPD), 86
*Scenarios for ESL Standards-Based
        Assessment* (TESOL), 144
Schemata, 45, 47, 81 (*see also*
        Background experience)
Schick, J.E., 16, 197, 215, 217
School-based intervention, 174
School language, 55, 99
Schools and ELs, 4
School staffing, 7
"School talk," 146
Science lesson, 23, 70–78, 183–186

Scoring and interpretation
  calculation of, 182–183
  subjectivity and, 181
  uses of, 186–197
Scruggs, T.E., 132
SDAIE (Specially Designed Academic
    Instruction in English).
    See Sheltered Instruction
Seifert-Kessell, N., 86
Seventh-grade unit, 89–96
Shakespeare, T., 172
Shearer, B.A., 52, 82, 170
Sheltered content classes
    interaction, 99
Sheltered Instruction Observation
    Protocol (SIOP), 3, 16–18, 21,
    184, 187–193, 199–208
  abbreviated form of, 208–210
  and academic tasks, 76–77
  adaptation of content and, 26–29,
    40–41
  and background knowledge, 17,
    44, 48
  building background and, 57,
    60, 61
  collaborative approach, 18
  comprehensible input and, 17, 66
  content concepts and, 23–24,
    40, 69
  content objectives and, 21–22, 36
  facilitator's guide, 16
  field-testing of, 215
  heading of, 180
  interaction and, 17, 93, 102–104,
    107–114
  language objectives and,
    22–23, 38
  learning strategies and, 90, 91
  lesson delivery and, 17, 135–137,
    138
  lesson plans and, 211–213
  meaningful activities and, 29–30,
    41–42
  and nonsheltered instruction, 66
  Not Applicable (NA) category,
    181–182
  practice/application and, 17, 122,
    124, 125
  preparation indicators, 21,
    33–34
  questions and, 96
  ratings and, 30
  reading development and, 169
  reliability and validity of, 197
  research on, 179, 214–219
  research results on, 216–217
  review/assessment and, 17, 154,
    155–156
  scaffolding techniques, 95
  scoring and interpretation of,
    178–197

  strategies, 17
  supplementary materials and,
    24–25, 40
  Teacher Rating Form, 184
  and teacher's speech, 75–76
  teaching techniques for, 69,
    77–78
  uses of, 15, 179, 216–217
Sheltered instruction (SI), 2–3, 10–13
  and minority students, 214
  model for, 13–16
  in native language, 106–107
  pedagogical resources for, 13
  research on, 214–219
  supplementary materials for, 15
  university courses in, 179
  uses of, 12–13
  variability of, 12–13
  vocabulary and, 46
Sheppard, K., 12
Short, Deborah J., 9, 11, 12, 14, 16,
    22, 69, 173, 197, 214, 215,
    216, 217
Shultz, J., 11
Site-based intervention teams,
    172–173
Sixth-grade lesson, 56–63, 183–186
Slater, W.H., 82
Smith, D., 170
Sociocultural awareness, 12
Spanish language, 167–168
Speaker, R., 82
Speaking, 120
Special education, 163, 164, 170–175
  earlier intervention, 173
  referral, assessment, and placement,
    171–175
Specially Designed Academic
    Instruction in English (SDAIE).
    See Sheltered Instruction
Special needs students, 175
Spilich, G., 45
SQP2RS, 84
Standards-based reform, 6–7
Stanovich, K.E., 21
Strategies, 80–81 (*see* Learning
    strategies)
Students, 8
  background of, 48, 170
  engagement (attention) of, 14,
    132–134, 140–141
  frustration levels of, 175
  and home language, 5
  learning goals for, 83
  learning strategies for, 94–95
  learning styles of, 14
  and lesson objectives, 161
  past learning and new concepts,
    48–49, 62–63
  reading level of, 165–166
  socialization of, 11–12

Study guides, 27
Supervisors, 17, 18
Supplementary materials, 25
  adapted text, 25–26
  for content concepts, 25–26
  demonstrations, 25
  hands-on manipulative, 25
  multimedia, 25
  realia, 25
  related literature, 25
  visuals, 25
Symons, S., 82

T
Taped text, 27
Task analysis, 24
Teachers, 14–15, 45 (*see also* Teaching)
  appropriate speech for, 75–76
  and background experience, 46
  effective, 45, 102–103, 104, 145
  and English learners, 46, 66–67,
    75–76, 83–84
  and interaction with students,
    99–102
  oral directions to students, 68
  professional development for,
    7, 16
  qualifications of, 7
  and reading development, 169
  self-assessment, 179
  and Sheltered Instruction
    Observation Protocol (SIOP),
    179
  shortage of, 7
  speech rate of, 67, 75–76
  training in special education,
    174–175
Teachers of English to Speakers of
    Other Languages (TESOL), 6, 10,
    15, 83, 84, 120, 144
Teaching (*see also* Teachers)
  SIOP model of, 15–16
  strategies of, 84–85
  techniques of, 69, 77–78, 84–85, 147
Teaching scenarios, 56–63, 70–78,
    121–128
  building background, 57, 60, 61
  and comprehensible input, 70–71,
    73, 74
  concepts linked to background, 62
  interaction, 107–114
  learning strategies and, 90,
    91, 93
  lesson delivery, 134–141
  lesson planning, 31–42
  past learning and new concepts,
    48–49, 62–63
  practice/application and, 121–128,
    169
  review/assessment, 151–161
Teberosky, A., 168

Templeton, S., 54, 55, 146, 165, 168
TESOL (*see* Teachers of English to Speakers of Other Languages)
Thesaurus, 59
Thinking skills, 23, 82, 96
Thomas, W.P., 8
Thumbs up/thumbs down, 149
Tierney, R., 49
Time allowances, 175
Tolchinsky, L., 168
Tompkins, G.E., 105
Townsend, B., 170
Tucker, M., 6

U
United States
   history of, 5
   immigrants in, 3–4, 5
Urban schools, 170
Utley, C., 173

V
Vacca, J.A., 26, 54
Vacca, R.T., 12, 26, 54, 86
Valadez, C., 45, 99
Valencia, S., 28, 151
Videotaping, 46, 179, 186
Vietnamese language, 167–168

Visual stimuli, 175
Vocabulary, 22, 67
   analogy and, 145
   cloze sentences, 54
   Concept Definition Map, 53
   content language and, 50–55
   contextualizing, 52
   games for, 55
   key words, 52, 63, 145–146, 157–158
   List-Group-Label activity, 54
   multiple exposures to, 145–146
   personal dictionaries, 52
   preteaching of, 46
   teaching of, 46
   Word generation, 54
   Word Sort, 54
   Word Study Book, 55, 146
   Word Wall, 52–53, 152, 153, 175
Vocabulary development, 49–50
Vocabulary Self-Collection Strategy (VSS), 49, 52, 92, 94
Vogt, MaryEllen, 24, 26, 28, 52, 69, 82, 84, 88, 149, 151, 165, 167, 170, 215
Voss, J., 45
Vygotsky, L., 12, 25, 45, 86

W
Waggoner, D., 4
Wait time, 106, 114, 169
Watson, K., 88
Wiggins, G., 148
Williams, D., 82, 84, 85
Wixson, K., 84
Woloshyn, V., 84
Wong-Fillmore, L., 45, 99
Woodworth, K., 12
Word generation, 54
Word Sort, 54
Word Study Book, 55, 146
Word Wall, 52–53, 152, 153, 175
Writing skills, 22, 120
Written language, 120
Written objectives, 131

Y
Yoon, K.S., 216
Young, B., 88
Ysseldyke, J., 172
Yuen, S., 99

Z
Zeichner, K., 7
Zimmerman, S., 85
Zone of Proximal Development (ZPD), 86

THE GARDENER'S CATALOGUE—published by William Morrow & Company, Inc., New York, New York

THIS GARDEN EARTH

It was only a few years ago that we were able to step back far enough to see our Earth spin against the velvet backdrop of space for the first time.

For many, the image conjured a vision of Space Ship Earth. But, we saw a garden and conjured the image of THIS GARDEN EARTH.

We saw sunlight filter through the atmosphere and thought of a giant terrarium. We saw life-giving vapors rise from blue seas and form swirling ever-changing clouds contained in the spherical bottle of gravity that keeps our atmosphere from floating away.

We saw the clouds pass over fertile green continents, crossed by many rivers. They released the moisture of the seas as rain. And, we watched as the rivers returned the rain to the sea.

THIS GARDEN EARTH is a closed system, very much like a terrarium. Perhaps, that is why some people like to think of it as a space ship. But they miss the point. We cannot hope to change the course of our vessel as it spirals through the universe. We must always cultivate our garden.

There is something very special in all human beings that draws them to cultivate THIS GARDEN EARTH. Whether they plant a manicured estate, a raucous bloom-filled dooryard, a mayonnaise-jar terrarium or just a city window-box, gardeners share a common spirit. Participation in the annual ritual of propagation and cultivation yields up a harvest of well-being that comes from sharing in the act of giving life.

Awake or asleep, at work or at rest, every creature that shares the bounty of this fruitful planet is a gardener. Life and death, the very act of breathing in and out, is part of the total process that makes the harvest possible.

Those who till the soil for the sheer joy of it, and those, like bacteria, that work without ever knowing why, are all gardeners who hold Eden in trust for their children, and their children's children. If we fail, our once-fertile globe will spin through space without us.

THE GARDENER'S CATALOGUE PEOPLE

THE GARDENER'S CATALOGUE was ~~produced~~ by Harvey Rottenberg.

It was conceived and written by To■■■■■■■■■■ ■■ttenberg, and owes its organization to Tom, whose ■■■■■■■■■■■■■■■■orti-culture, floriculture, and the fine arts—■■■■■■

The Catalogue was designed by Tom ■■■■■■■■■ art director and retrieval specialist.

We owe special thanks to Tamara Safford, ou■■■■■■ who doubled as our editorial and production assistant; ■■■■ Brian Murray, our board men; Karl W. Bruning, our photog■■■■ wizard; Barbara Remington, who did our back cover, sweetened ■■■ and contributed many original illustrations; Lars Skattebol, author ■■ several areas, who gave us both editorial and technical help; D■■■■ Spindell, who helped us through the presentation and or■■■■■ Murray for numerical calligraphy; Jenni Dean Ell■■■■■■■■■ Thomson Krausz, who kept the studio strai■■■■■■■■■■■■■ masha, Wisconsin, who did our printing; Northwes■■■■■■■■■ ulso of Men-asha, who did our colorwork; and all our ■■■■■■■■ s who helped make THE GARDENER'S CATALOGUE.

Page 10, "Some Words About Seeds" by Maurice Franz; reprinted from ORGANIC GARDENING AND FARMING. Copyright 1974 by Rodale Press, Inc.

Page 14, "Plant Labels" by Bill Davidson; reprinted from FLOWER AND GARDEN MAGAZINE. Copyright 1974 by Mid-America Publishing Corp.

Page 48, "Happy House Plants" by Henry M. Cathey; reprinted from PLANTS ALIVE. Copyright 1973 by Plants, Inc.

Pages 66-67, illustrations of cactus grafting reprinted from CACTI AND THEIR CULTIVATION by Margaret J. Martin, P. R. Chapman, H. A. Auger; published by Winchester Press. Copyright © 1971 by P. R. Chapman, Margaret J. Martin and H. A. Auger.

Page 76, excerpts reprinted from A HANDBOOK OF COLD CLIMATE CACTI AND SUCCULENTS by Ben M. Haines. Copyright 1972 by Ben M. Haines.

Pages 86-87, "The Development of Horticulture in America" by John M. Fogg, Jr.; reprinted from MORRIS ARBORETUM BULLETIN. Copyright © 1974 by Morris Arboretum.

Page 118, "Six Ideas to Make Ornamentals More Useful" by M. C. Goldman; reprinted from THE BEST GARDENING IDEAS I KNOW by Robert Rodale. Copyright 1974 by Rodale Press, Inc.

Pages 192-193, "Organic Roses," first published under the title "Roses Are Strictly for Growing," by M. C. Goldman; reprinted from ORGANIC GARDENING AND FARMING. Copyright 1974 by Rodale Press, Inc.

Page 207, "Some Facts About Bees" by Clarence M. Larson and Ward L. Gossett; reprinted from ORGANIC GARDENING AND FARMING. Copyright 1974 by Rodale Press, Inc.

Page 210, "Spring Lawn Preparation" by Robert W. Schery; reprinted from RESORT MANAGEMENT. Copyright 1974 by Resort Management, Inc.

Page 260, "Our Composting Program" by Dr. Warner F. and Mrs. Lucile Bowers; reprinted from THE BEST GARDENING IDEAS I KNOW by Robert Rodale. Copyright 1974 by Rodale Press, Inc.

Page 262, "Before Winter Sets In" by Dorothy Schroeder; reprinted from THE BEST GARDENING IDEAS I KNOW by Robert Rodale. Copyright 1974 by Rodale Press, Inc.

Page 263, "Root Cellars Are Great Harvest Holders" by Darlene Kronschnabel; reprinted from THE BEST GARDENING IDEAS I KNOW by Robert Rodale. Copyright 1974 by Rodale Press, Inc.

Pages 264-265, "Organic Food Really Is Better" by John Feltman; reprinted from ORGANIC GARDENING AND FARMING. Copyright 1974 by Rodale Press, Inc.

Page 270, "Have Fun with Herbs" by Mrs. Albert D. Farwell; reprinted from AMERICAN HORTICULTURIST. Copyright © 1974 by The American Horticultural Society.

Pages 314-315, "Green Is the Color of Hope" by Henry M. Cathey; reprinted from AMERICAN HORTICULTURIST. Copyright © 1972 by The American Horticultural Society.

Printed in the United States of America.

1 2 3 4 5 78 77 76 75 74

Library of Congress Catalog Card Number: 74-17429

ISBN 0-688-05327-0 (pbk.)